MW00657991

IMAGES
of America
HARRIMAN

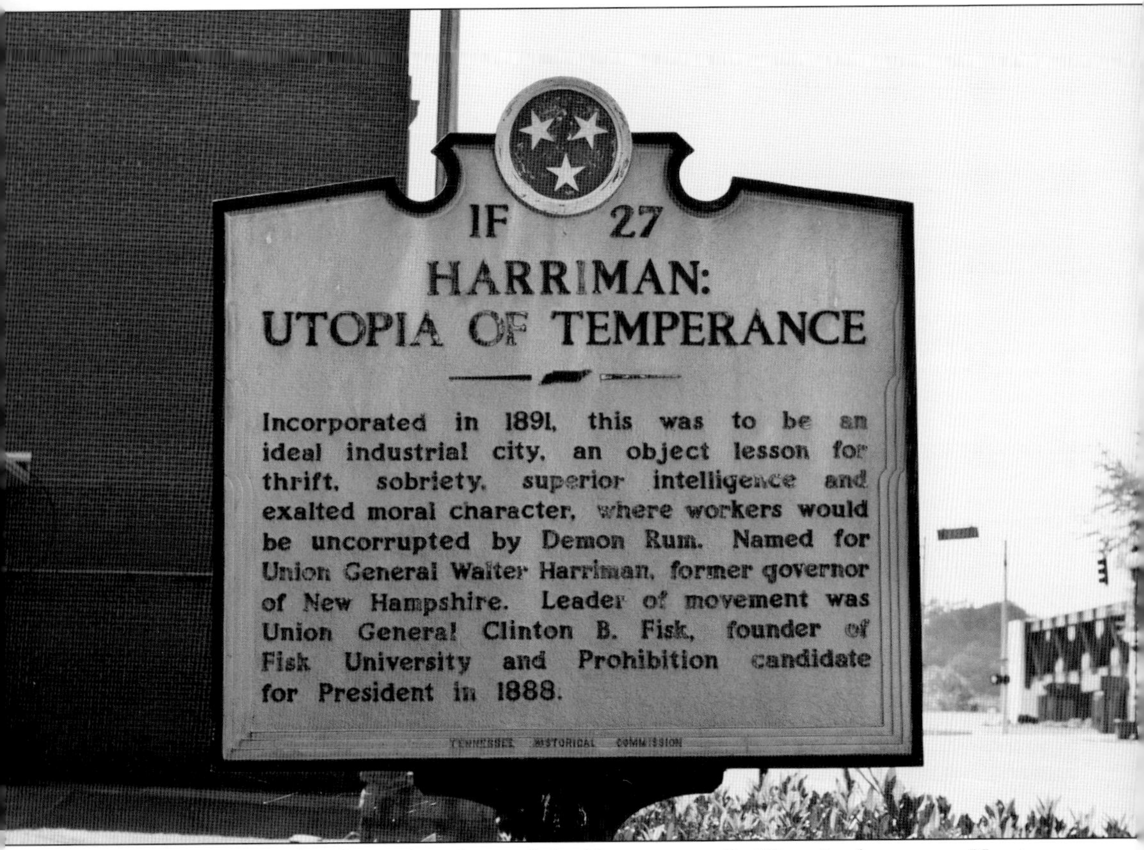

This historical marker, located in front of the Temperance Building in downtown Harriman, gives a brief overview of the city's history. (Author's collection.)

ON THE COVER: Harriman Hosiery Mill celebrates its 25th anniversary in 1937. Founded in 1912 by Tom Tarwater, Harriman Hosiery Mills manufactured seamless cotton hose for ladies and employed mostly women. The mill was purchased by Burlington Industries just after World War II and remained in operation until 1985. When the mill closed, 1,200 workers lost their jobs. (Courtesy of David Webb.)

IMAGES
of America

HARRIMAN

John Norris Brown

ARCADIA
PUBLISHING

ISBN 978-1-4671-1187-4

Published by Arcadia Publishing
Charleston, South Carolina

Printed in the United States of America

Library of Congress Control Number: 2013952059

For all general information, please contact Arcadia Publishing:
Telephone 843-853-2070
Fax 843-853-0044
E-mail sales@arcadiapublishing.com
For customer service and orders:
Toll-Free 1-888-313-2665

Visit us on the Internet at www.arcadiapublishing.com

Contents

ACKNOWLEDGMENTS

Compiling the photographs necessary for this book would not have been possible without the generous help of Michael Demyanovich, director of the Harriman Heritage Museum. Mike spent many hours going through the photographs archived at the museum and generously allowed me to reproduce them here. Unless otherwise noted, all photographs in this work are from the museum's collection.

I am indebted to David Webb, owner of Rocky Top General Store, located at 316 Ruritan Road in Harriman. Part museum, part retail store, Rocky Top General Store is a treasure trove of local history. David allowed me to use several photographs for this book.

Noah Howard, one of Harriman's greatest citizens, also provided invaluable support in writing this book. He loaned me several photos for publication and shared his fascinating personal history with me.

Much thanks to the ladies at the Harriman Public Library, among them my former teacher Mrs. Pat Estes, for their help in researching this book.

My cousin Dr. Julian Ahler, a civic leader for many years in Harriman, was generously willing to look over the photographs with me and help identify people, places, and events.

In addition to personal accounts, the historical information contained in this book is drawn primarily from three sources: Walter Pulliam's *Harriman: The Town That Temperance Built*, a 1976 work that remains the definitive history of the city; The East Tennessee Land Company's 1893 pamphlet *Two Years of Harriman*, which provided information on the city's early history and insight into the founders' vision; and Rudy Abramson and Jean Haskell's *Encyclopedia of Appalachia*, a valuable resource for Appalachian studies.

Arcadia Publishing, and particularly my editor Liz Gurley, has been extremely helpful and patient, guiding me in completing my first book.

I give thanks to my family, particularly my beautiful and understanding wife Maggy for her support in this project, and my parents, George and Patricia Brown, both longtime Harriman residents who have also helped by providing information on the Harriman of their youth and have helped me identify some of the people, places, and events in this book.

Finally, I would like to thank all the people of Harriman, both past and present, for building and maintaining such a fascinating city whose history I continue to learn.

INTRODUCTION

Harriman has a unique history. Incorporated in 1891 as a temperance town in the Appalachians, Harriman was intended to be "an object lesson for thrift, sobriety, intelligence, and exalted moral character, where workers would be uncorrupted by Demon Rum," as the historical marker explains. The city's founders envisioned a model city for the world in which Victorian morality could be commercialized for both the betterment of mankind and for business profit. Harriman's founders believed so strongly in this vision that many of them mortgaged their futures on it.

Harriman's founders had big dreams: a city of 50,000 people that would someday rival Pittsburgh and Birmingham in ore production. The 300,000 acres owned by the East Tennessee Land Company (the company that purchased and sold the land on which Harriman was built) was rich in coal and ore. The great land sale, held in late February 1890, in which lots were sold off to settlers, was a major success, drawing around 3,000 bidders from at least 12 states. Over the next two years, Harriman saw rapid growth as the population swelled to 719 by the fall of 1890 and to 3,672 by December of the following year.

The dreams of the founders would turn into a nightmare for many, however, and the Panic of 1893, coupled with the assumption of major debt and reckless speculation, drove the East Tennessee Land Company into bankruptcy. Their dreams shattered, it appeared Harriman might become a total failure. Many of Harriman's founders returned to their home states disillusioned and broken.

Harriman, like most proposed utopias, failed to fully realize the dreams of its founders. Nevertheless, the city rebounded from the early disasters and experienced growth in the early 20th century. The East Tennessee Land Company's headquarters was converted to the American University, then the Mooney School, and finally city hall (a role it retains), known locally as the Temperance Building.

Unfortunately, in 1929, two other disasters struck: a major flood of the Emory River and the stock market crash. The flood washed away much of Harriman's industry, killed 20 people, and left as many as 200 homeless. Many of the businesses never resumed operation in the city. The economic impact was staggering and was further compounded by the Great Crash of 1929 and the arrival of the Great Depression. The 1930s were lean times for the city, just as they were for the rest of the country.

By the 1940s, the city appeared on the road to recovery. The 1940 Semi-Centennial celebration was a time of renewed optimism. World War II, though certainly a tragedy for the world, brought economic growth to Harriman, as the Manhattan Project in nearby Oak Ridge led to a flood of new people into the city.

From the 1940s to the 1960s, Harriman was doing well. With an economy centered on two hosiery mills and a paper mill—the three of which provided the majority of jobs in the city and employment for generations of residents—the city grew.

Downtown Harriman was the social center of the city, with numerous stores, diners, theaters, and other businesses. Commercial ventures that served generations thrived during this time, among them Edward's, Miller-Brewer, Chase Drugs, and the Princess Theatre.

Harriman's Diamond Jubilee in 1965 seems to have even outdone its Semi Centennial of a quarter century before. Lasting a week, the celebration included a parade, pageant, the return of early settlers, and renewed civic pride. The city had much to celebrate, for it was then that it seems to have reached its peak economically.

The latter decades of the 20th century saw decline for the city, however. By the end of the century, the hosiery mills and paper plant had closed, leaving Harriman with significantly fewer jobs. Partially due to the interstate highway system, many businesses had also moved out of downtown, and some of the buildings fell into disrepair.

In spite of these setbacks, Harriman rightfully remains proud of its heritage, and civic groups continue to work to preserve the city's history. The annual Hooray For Harriman event, held over Labor Day weekend, attracts thousands each year. The Princess Theatre, one of the city's greatest landmarks, which had closed in 1999, was recently restored by the city and reopened, providing concerts, plays, and other cultural activities for the community.

Today, the legacy of Harriman's past remains apparent in the Temperance Building and the Victorian architecture of Cornstalk Heights. With many of the houses built during the time of Harriman's rapid growth (1890–1893), the city is in some ways frozen in that time period, with homes and buildings reflecting the architecture popular at that time.

The temperance philosophy also lasted a long time in the city. Following the repeal of the 18th Amendment (Prohibition) in 1933, Harriman passed Ordinance No. 486, outlawing the sale of beer within the city. Temperance for the city officially ended in the 1990s, when the sale of liquor was legalized, a very controversial and divisive issue even then. Today, many residents still hold strong to the ideals of temperance.

This book is an attempt to bring this history to life through historical photographs of the people, places, events, and institutions that have made Harriman special. It is divided into 10 chapters, each devoted to a certain aspect of the city's colorful history. The images are presented in roughly chronological order by chapter, though at times they have been organized thematically. As with any historical work, mistakes may have seeped in, for which the author apologizes.

As a native of Harriman, it is an honor to work on such an important project, and it is the author's sincere wish that this book will help reignite interest in preserving the history of the "Town that Temperance Built." There is much in the town's past to be proud of, and there is much about its future that looks bright.

One

The Early Years

The city that would be Harriman began as an idea of a New York–born minister and businessman named Frederick Gates. An ardent prohibitionist, he believed the principles of temperance could be commercialized for both moral virtue and economic gain. Toward this end, he recruited a number of prominent prohibitionists of his day—among them A.A. Hopkins, Clinton Fisk, Ferdinand Schumacher, and others—to form the East Tennessee Land Company, with the ultimate goal of creating his idealized city.

The company, chartered in 1889, acquired large tracts of land in what is now Harriman, beginning with 10,000 acres from the widow of Col. Robert King Byrd. In December of that year, surveyors staked out the first lots for what would become the city.

The great land sale was held February 26–28, 1891, with prohibitionists from across the eastern United States showing up to purchase land. The sale was advertised extensively in newspapers throughout New England, New York, New Jersey, Pennsylvania, and Ohio, attracting many bidders from north of the Mason-Dixon line to seek their fortunes and build a model city free of "demon rum."

A horrendous rainstorm could not dampen the enthusiasm as 3,000 men from 18 states bid on land. Bidders came by train, horse, and foot, and by the end of the auction, 573 lots had been sold for a total cost of $604,705.

The settlers' excitement was channeled into extremely hard work. Harriman experienced incredible growth in the early 1890s, growing from only two farms to a city of nearly 4,000 residents. After two years, it appeared the dream was well on its way to fruition.

Unfortunately, the rain may have been a harbinger of things to come, as many dreams would be broken by the Panic of 1893, when the East Tennessee Land Company was forced into bankruptcy. Investors lost their fortunes and their dreams died with the company. Many early settlers returned to their home states disappointed, but others refused to give up the dream, remaining in Harriman to continue working on their beloved city.

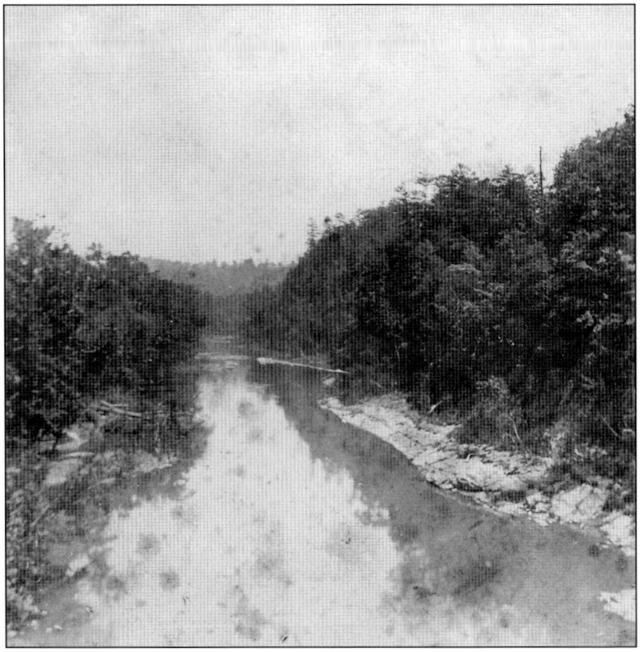

The Emory River is visible here from the "old bridge" (now at the site of the actual "new bridge") near the present-day Lon Mee Bridge on Pansy Hill Road. Advertised extensively in promotional booklets for the East Tennessee Land Company, the beautiful Emory River proved a powerful draw for early settlers, who came predominantly from northern cities.

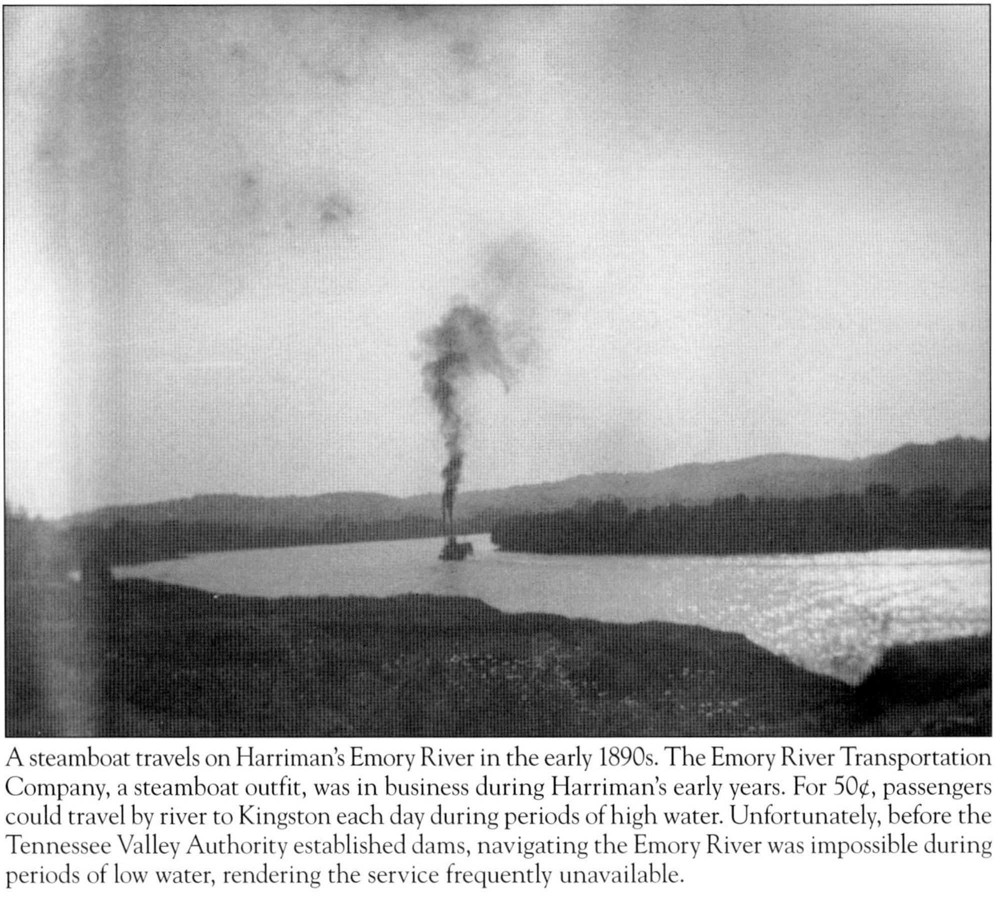

A steamboat travels on Harriman's Emory River in the early 1890s. The Emory River Transportation Company, a steamboat outfit, was in business during Harriman's early years. For 50¢, passengers could travel by river to Kingston each day during periods of high water. Unfortunately, before the Tennessee Valley Authority established dams, navigating the Emory River was impossible during periods of low water, rendering the service frequently unavailable.

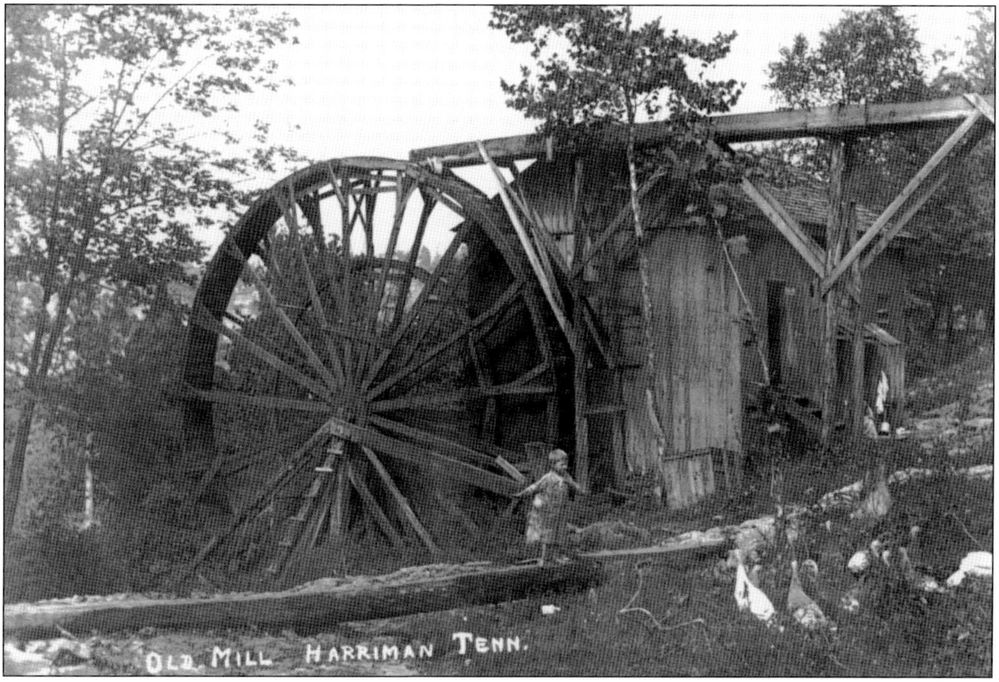

The Baumann gristmill was located near the present-day Pansy Hill Road Bridge, across the Emory River from downtown. Established shortly after the Civil War, the mill was active during Harriman's early years. It was eventually destroyed by the Flood of 1929.

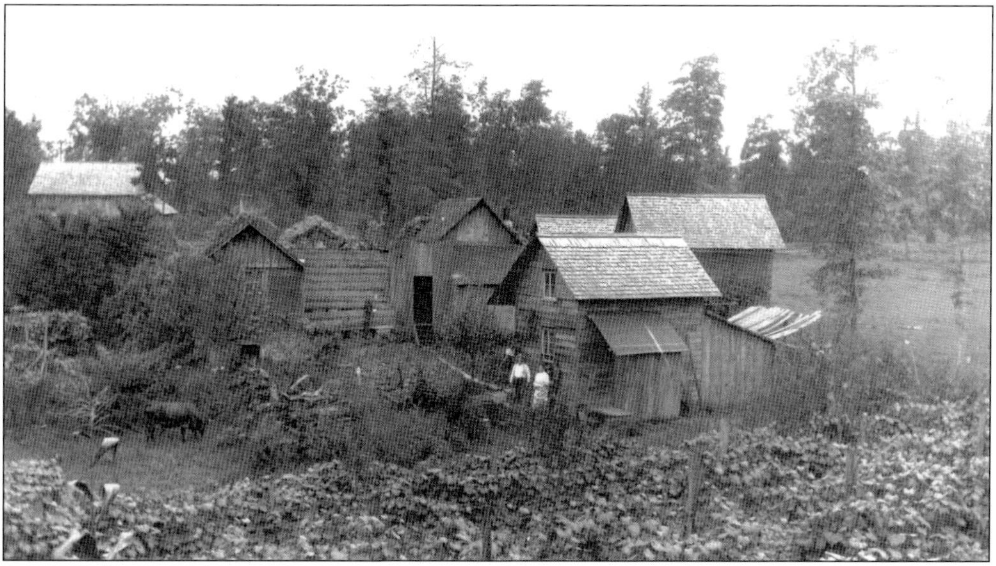

Pansy Hill, pictured around 1898, is just across the Emory River from downtown Harriman. In 1895, E.J. Bridge and his wife moved to the area and began planting pansies. An avid florist, Mrs. Bridge established two greenhouses and planted crocuses in her front lawn to spell out the name "Pansy Hill," thus giving the area its name. Walter Pulliam records an account from the Bridges' daughter of American University students purchasing pansies from Mrs. Bridge to give to their girlfriends. Though initially outside the city, much of the Pansy Hill area would be annexed by Harriman in the 20th century.

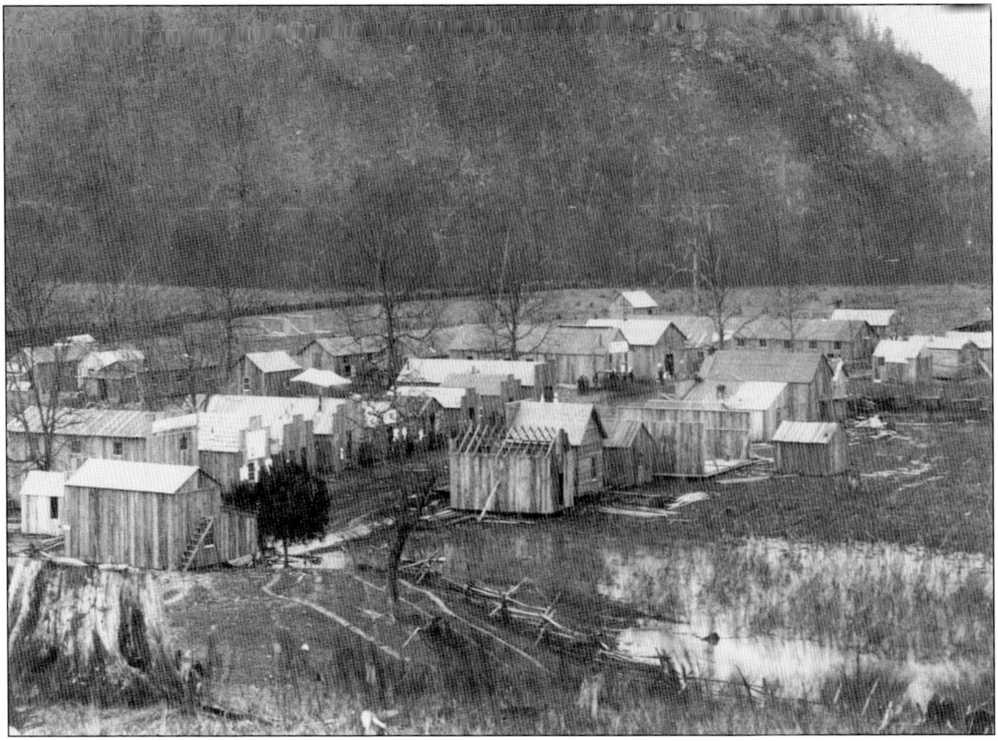

Before there was Harriman, there was the hastily assembled "Shacktown." The first photograph (above), taken just before the great sale of lots on February 26–28, 1890, depicts the lower part of the city where businesses and homes were under construction. Shacks were assembled extremely quickly, sometimes as rapidly as six hours per structure. Due to flooding, this section was abandoned for higher ground in the fall of 1890. The photograph below shows Broadway looking toward the Emory River in Shacktown, and was also taken in 1890.

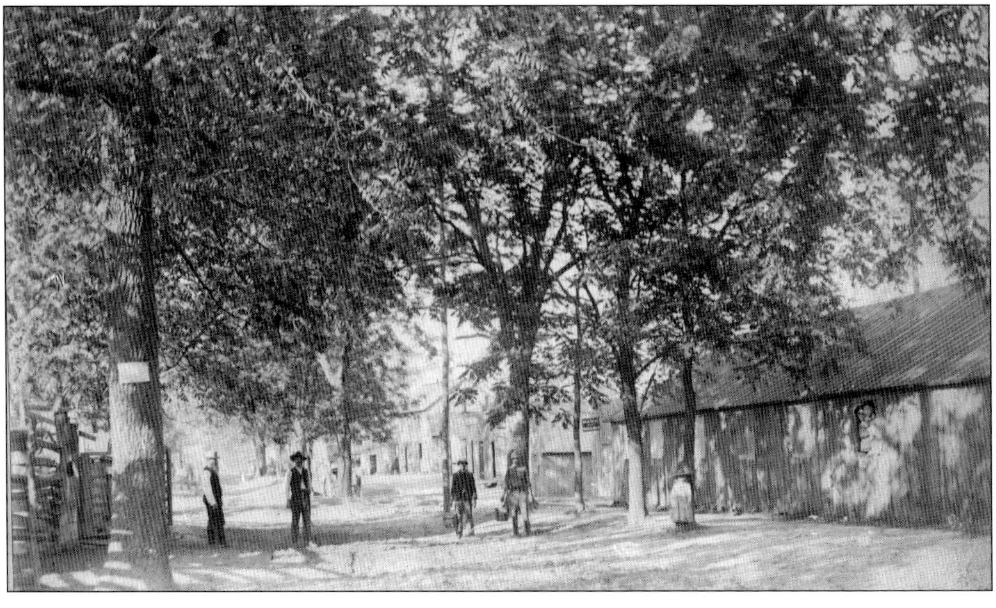

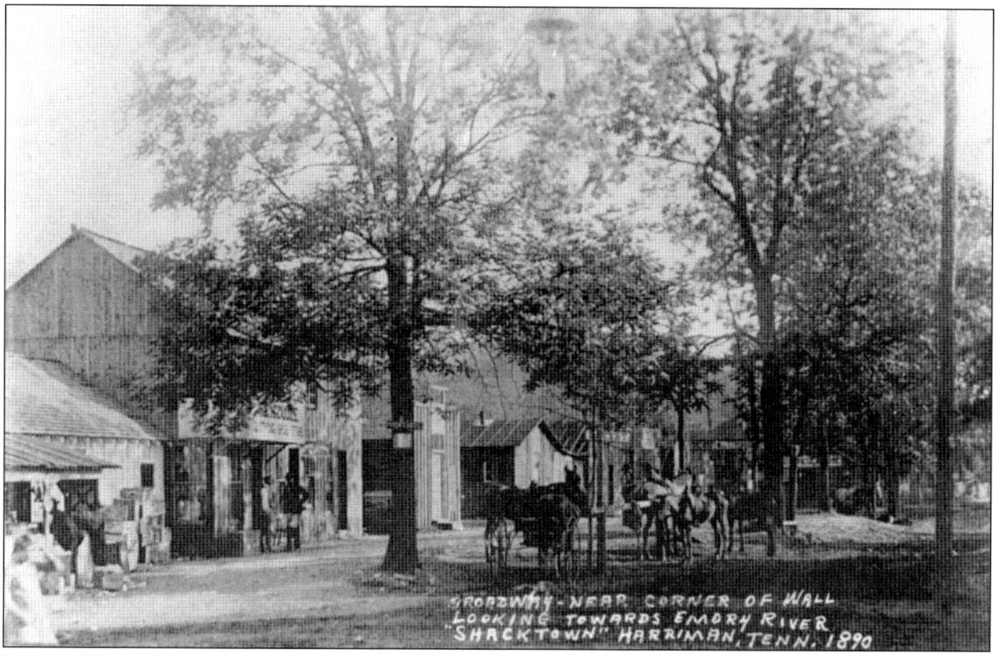

Pictured here is Broadway near the corner of Wall Street looking towards the Emory River. Early arrivals hoping to buy land ironically named the streets in Shacktown after much more famous streets in New York City, perhaps reflecting their high hopes for Harriman.

This 1890 photograph of Shacktown gives the "city" more perspective. Shacktown was a fully functioning—if very primitive—city, complete with a post office, drug stores, a hardware store, and of course, a real estate office. The shack accommodations were Spartan: shacks had as many as 40 to 50 hardboard beds, with each bed shared by three or four men. To make matters worse, the shacks often leaked.

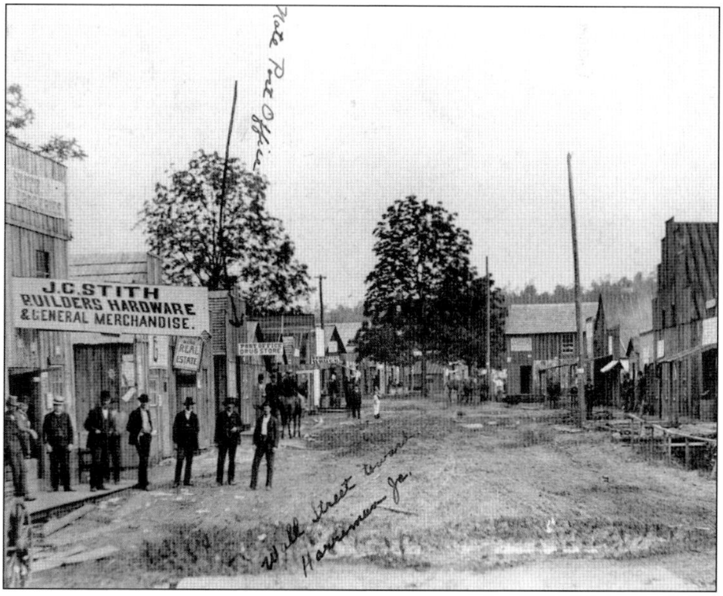

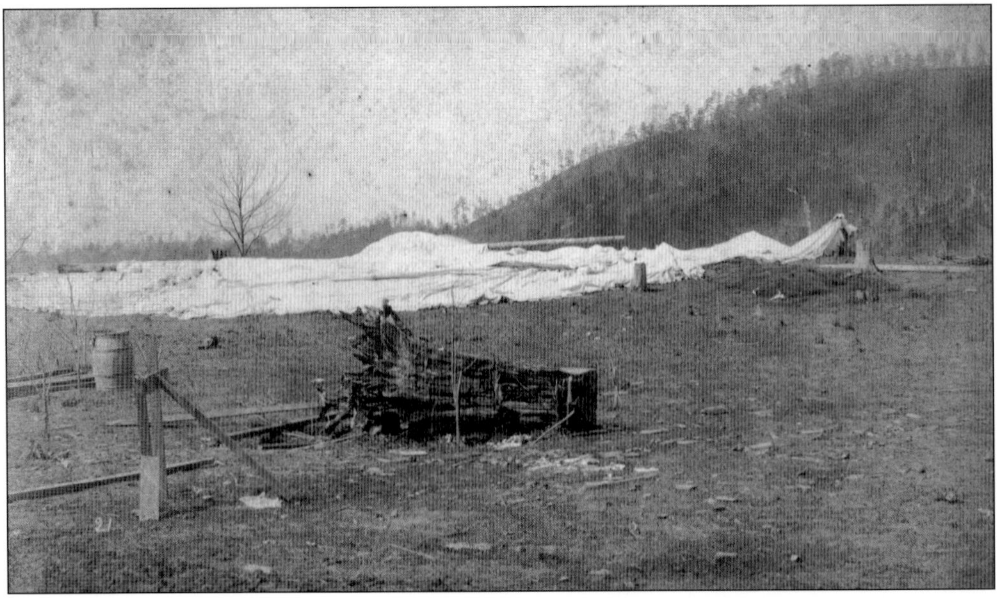

It was under this tent that the first sale of lots was held in 1890 on Devonia Street. The weather was very bad during the land sale, with a major rainstorm causing flooding and turning all solid ground into mud. The tent was blown down during the night before the last day of the auction, necessitating a change in location. The third and final sale day took place at the old Byrd Mansion.

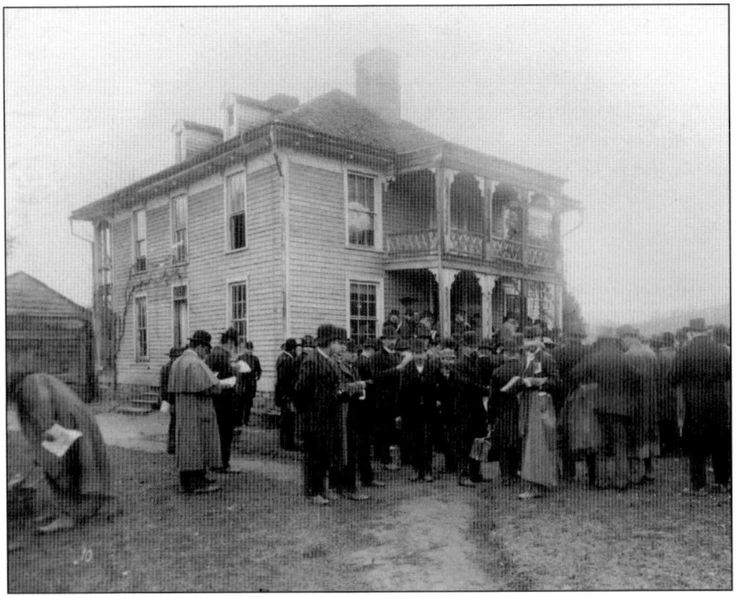

This photograph shows the third and final day of the great land sale, which was held at the old Byrd Mansion on February 28, 1890. On this day, around 3,000 people from at least a dozen states bid to purchase the remaining lots. The final available lots sold were on Walden Street, the last sale being to J.C. Snow of Brockton, Massachusetts. Byrd Mansion would stand until the Flood of 1929.

Harriman's rapid growth has begun. Here, Roane Street is shown looking east in July 1890, with construction of permanent buildings well underway. Note the wooden sidewalks, as well as the pigs—probably abandoned from the former Byrd farm—roaming in the mud of Roane Street.

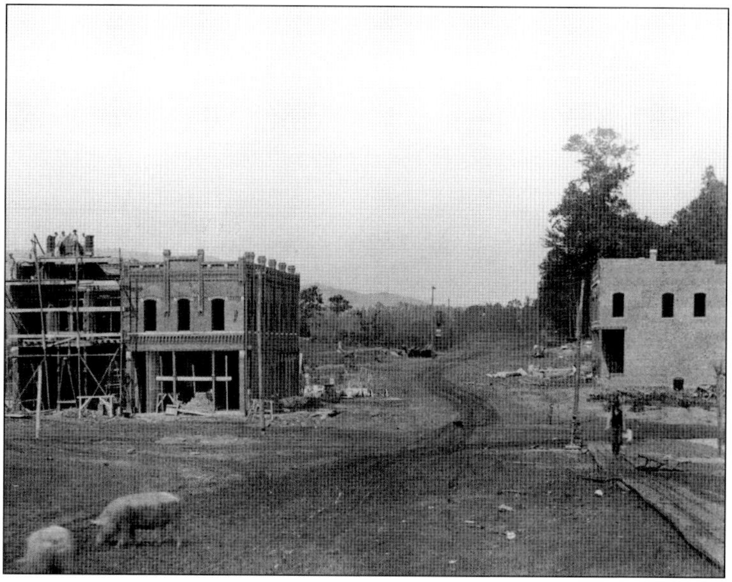

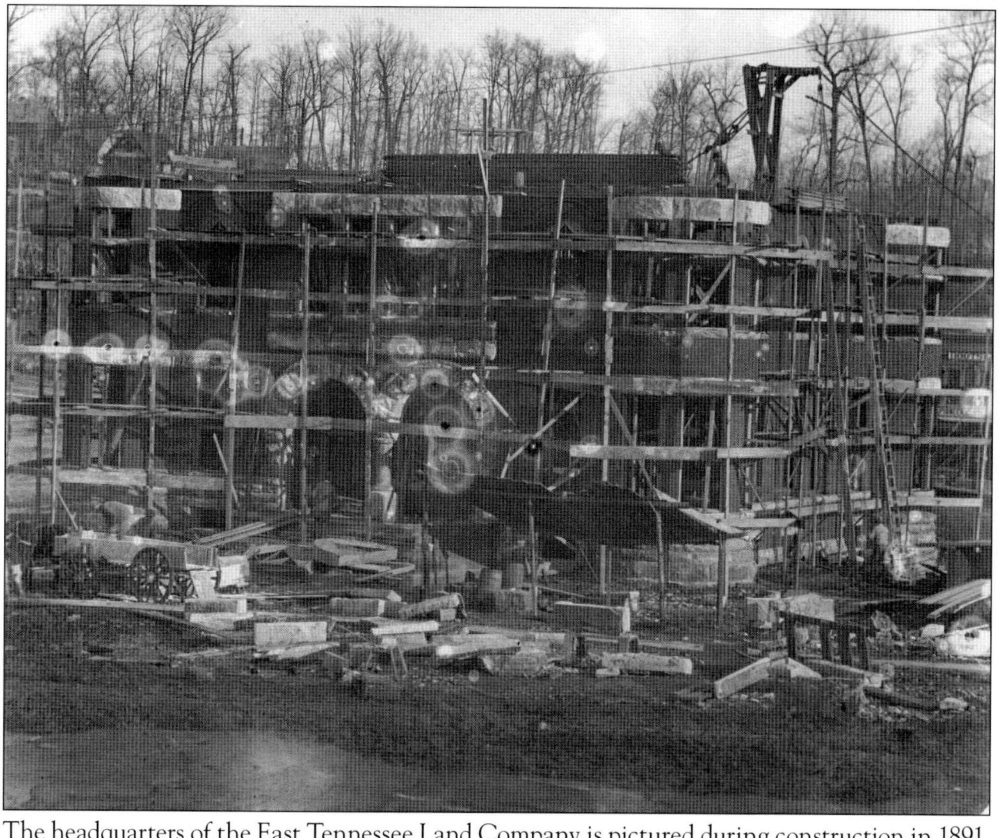

The headquarters of the East Tennessee Land Company is pictured during construction in 1891. This is the only known photograph of what is now known as the Temperance Building while it was under construction. Ironically, the workers may have enjoyed drinking a little too much (which is to say, at all) for the city's sensibilities: the Committee of 100 was formed to enforce "better enforcement of laws in the interest of Prohibition and good morals."

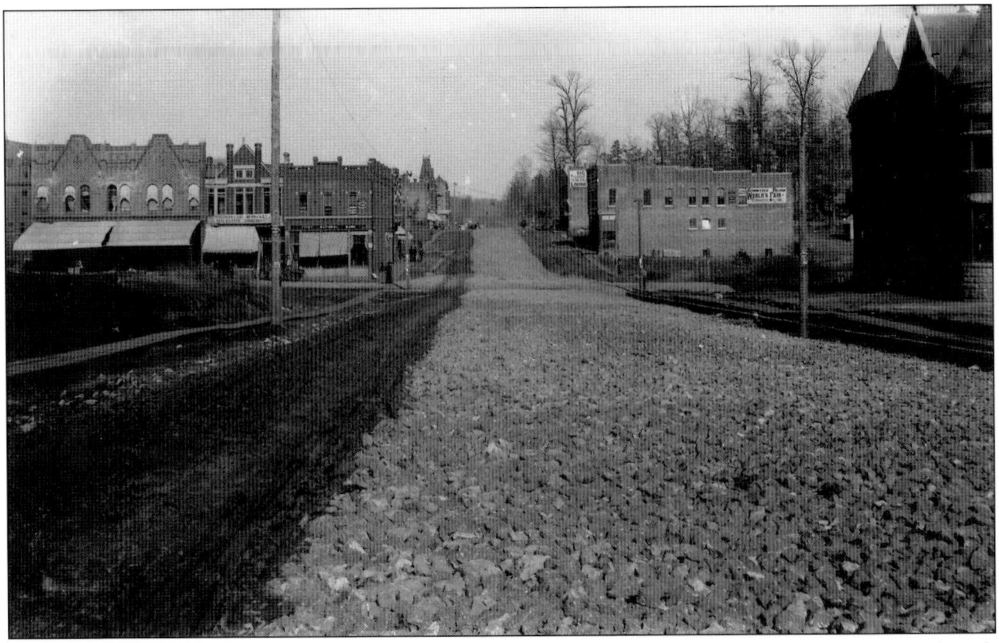

This was the view looking east on Roane Street, probably in 1891. An amazing amount of work had been done since the previous year. The Temperance Building is on the right and the First National Bank is on the left at the corner of Walden Avenue. By 1891, there was not a vacant house in the city.

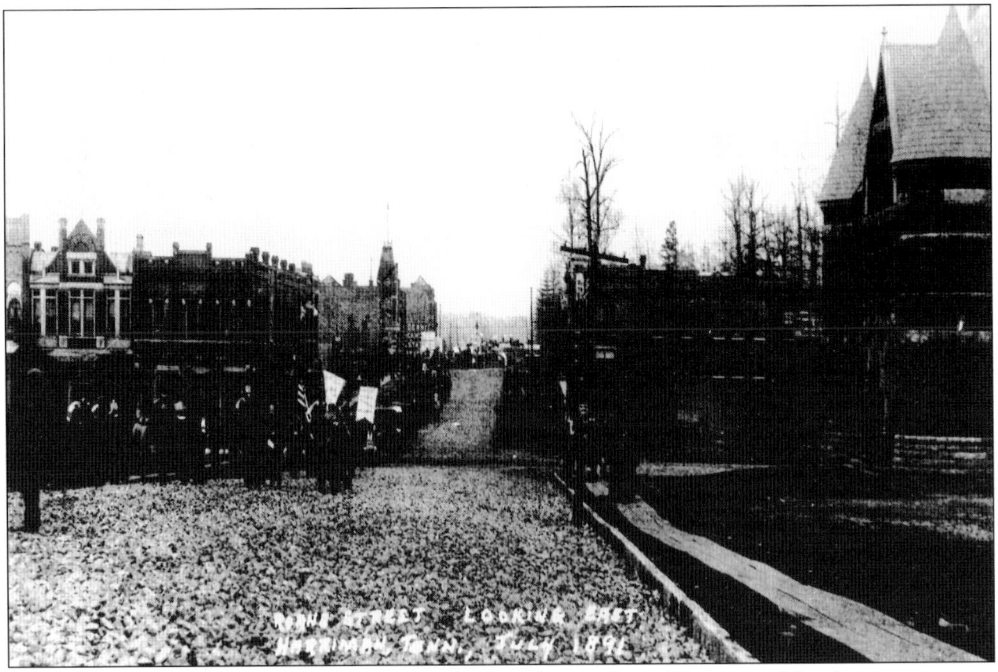

Roane Street is shown here, facing east in July 1891 during the celebration of the first anniversary of Harriman. After one year, the city appeared to be well on the way to fulfilling its vision with a booming economy, expanding industry, and a growing population. Unfortunately, the city would take a major hit with the upcoming Panic of 1893.

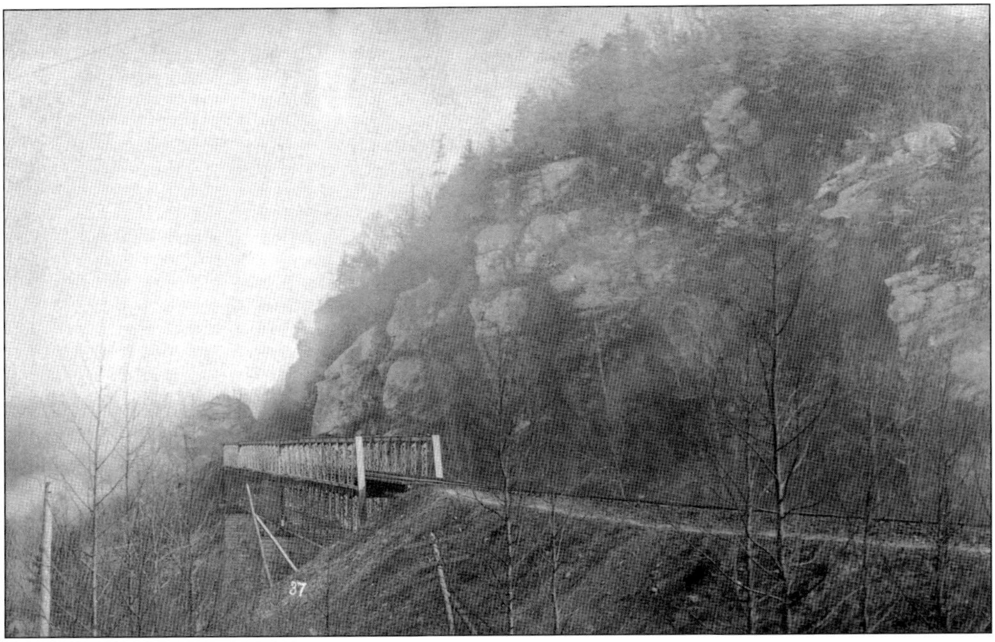

These photographs show what became known as Harriman Junction. Above, the C.S. Bridge is visible at Keathley Junction. The site for Harriman was chosen in large part because of the railroads—the Cincinnati Southern Railroad ran through the gap made by the Emory River through Walden's Ridge and met the Virginia & Georgia line a mile upstream from the site of Harriman. After the city was founded, this rail junction became known as Harriman Junction. Pictured below is the approach to Harriman Junction, formerly known as Keathley Station.

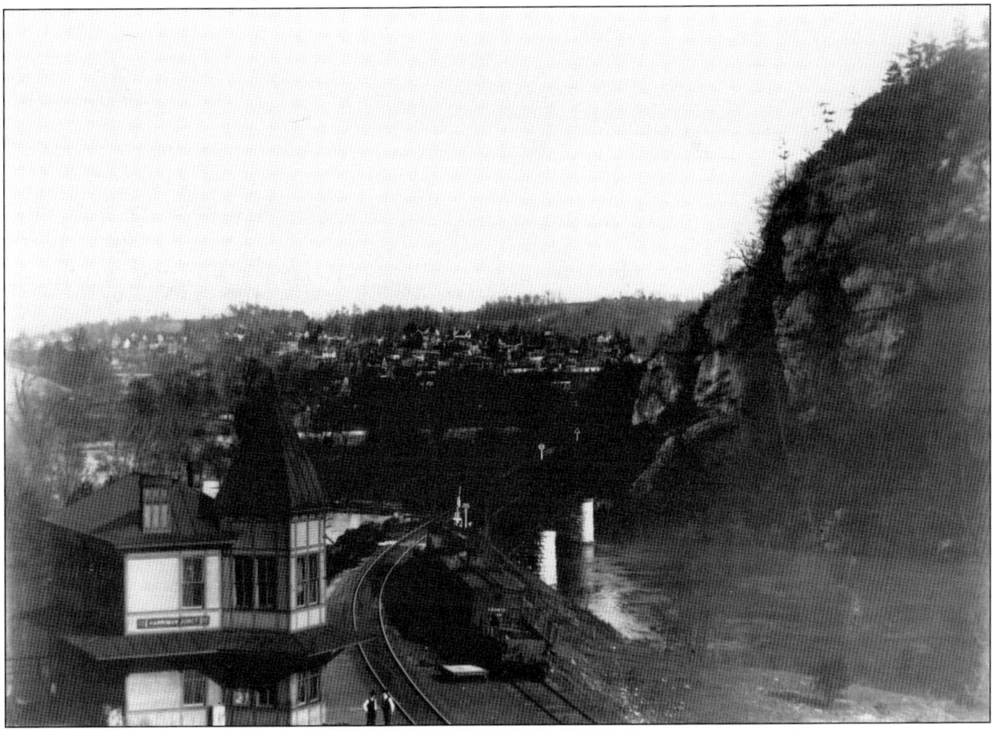

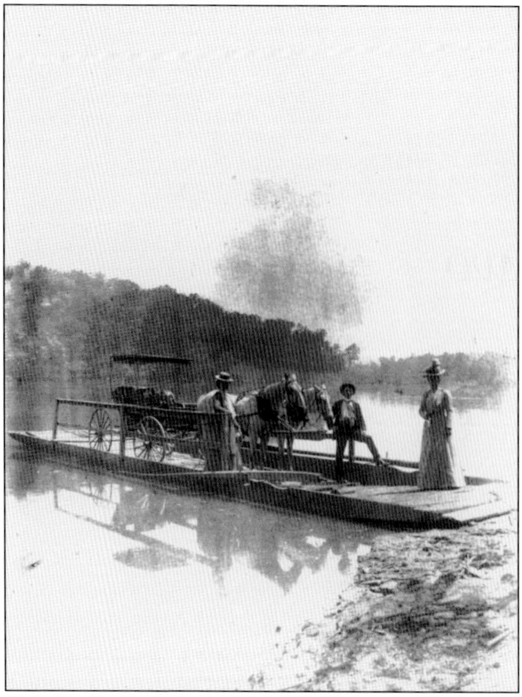

Before there was a bridge, there was Byrd's Ferry. Here the ferry is bringing two ladies and a man across the Emory. This photograph was probably taken around 1890.

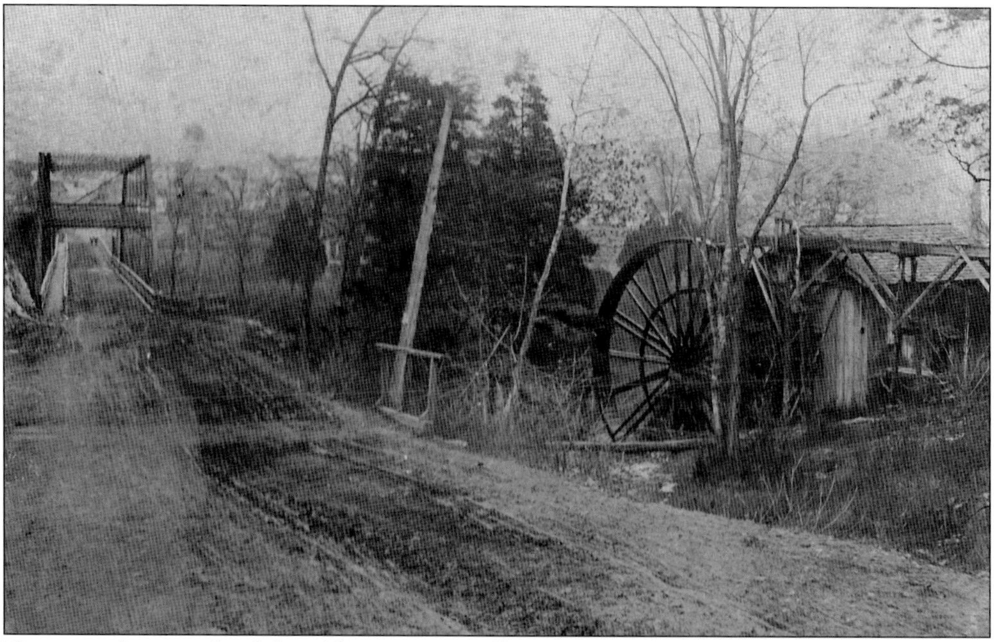

This is a photograph of the old Baumann mill next to the bridge over the Emory River in Harriman before the bridge washed away during a flood in March 1902. The bridge, a steel and wood structure, was the first bridge over the Emory River in Harriman. According to an account at the Harriman Heritage Museum, Charles W. Adkisson Sr., then only a young boy, was standing near the middle of the bridge as it was collapsing but was pulled to safety by a woman standing nearby. Adkisson would go on to become a well-known photographer and, interestingly, would document the Flood of 1929 with his own photographs.

Two

EARLY 20TH CENTURY

After the failure of the East Tennessee Land Company, Harriman's economy slowly improved during the first decades of the 1900s. It did not become as large a city as its planners envisioned, but it developed an industrial base and a vibrant downtown that would remain the center of economic activity in the city until the completion of Interstate 40.

The city experienced its share of setbacks. The influenza epidemic of 1918 hit so hard that the city's two funeral homes could not accept all the bodies. Though official numbers of those killed locally are unknown, the impact was staggering.

The biggest natural disaster for Harriman came in 1929, when a flood on the Emory River washed away much of the city's economic base, wiping out industries along the riverfront, destroying several homes, and killing 20 people. At least five industries were completely destroyed: Enterprise Ice Company, Harriman Junk Company, North Carolina Blanchard Company, the American Fork and Hoe Company, and the Dame Furniture Company.

The recovery was complicated six months later by the stock market crash of 1929, which threw the entire world into the Great Depression and made it impossible for many of the destroyed businesses to rebuild. It is safe to say that 1929 was an especially devastating year for the city.

The news was not all bad, however. In the Temperance Town, there was significant support for women's suffrage. Harriman sent a delegation to the Equal Suffrage League Convention in Nashville in 1919 to encourage ratification of the 19th Amendment, granting women the right to vote. State Representative (and later Roane County resident) Harry Burn would later credit Harriman women with influencing his decisive vote in favor.

In spite of the flood and the Depression, the city rebounded. Highway 27 (known in Harriman as Roane Street) was a major artery and brought travelers through the city. Harriman also boasted three major employers, a paper mill and two hosiery mills. These three companies accounted for a majority of the jobs in Harriman and many families were supported by the paychecks.

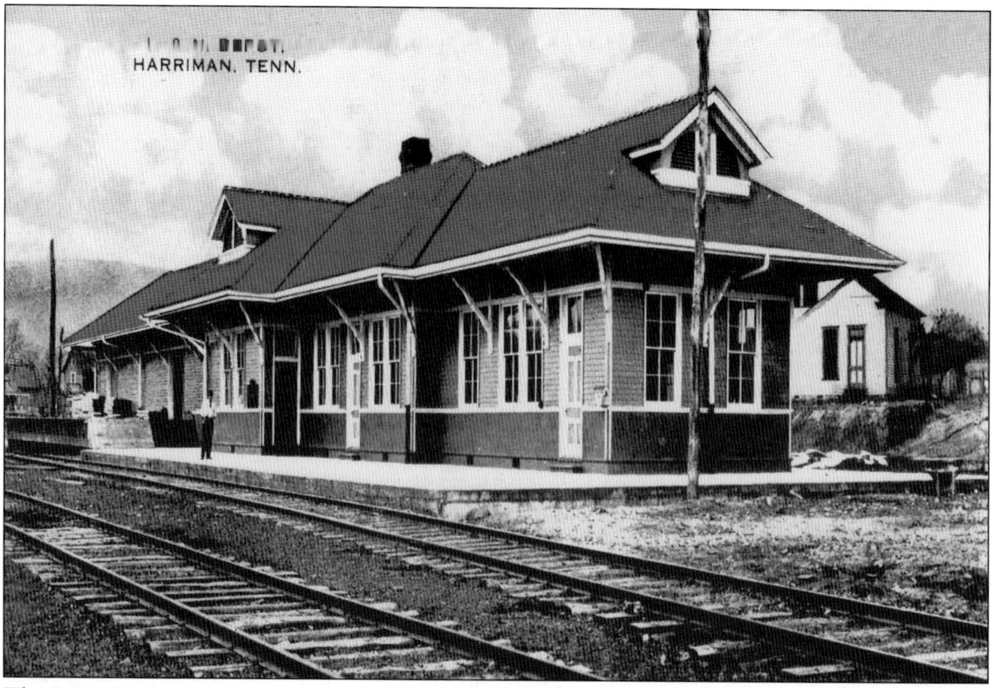

The L&N Depot was located at the end of Morgan Street and is shown in this photograph that was most likely taken in the 1910s. Harriman's founders purposely chose to place the city near railroad tracks to ensure efficient travel and shipping. By the 1920s, Harriman was a major whistle stop with as many as 24 passenger trains stopping each day.

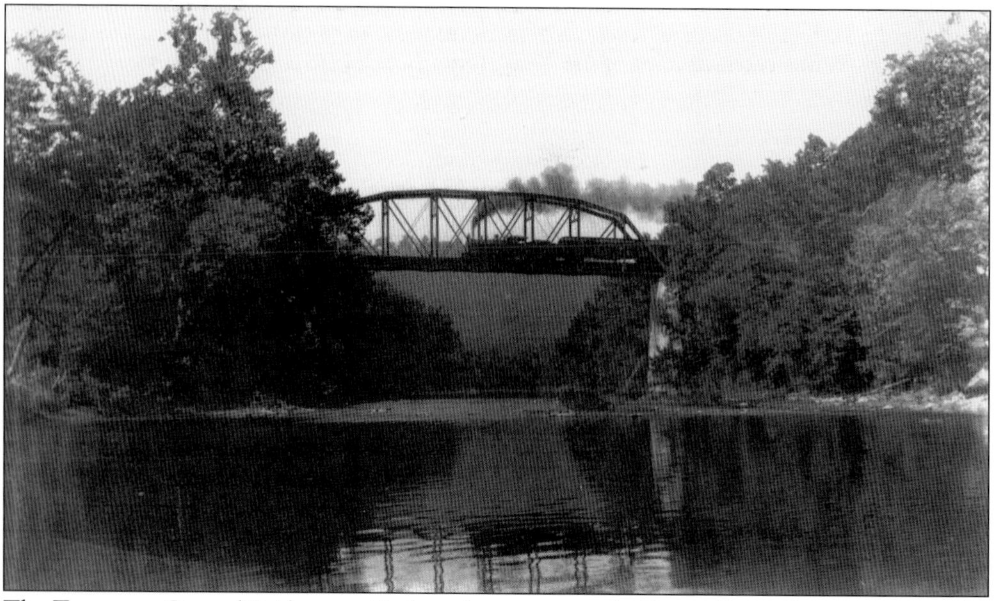

The Tennessee Central Bridge provided a rail crossing on the Emory River. For many years, the Tennessee Central was the only east-west railway providing direct service for passengers between Nashville and Knoxville. A major artery in the Upper Cumberland, it continued to offer passenger service until 1955.

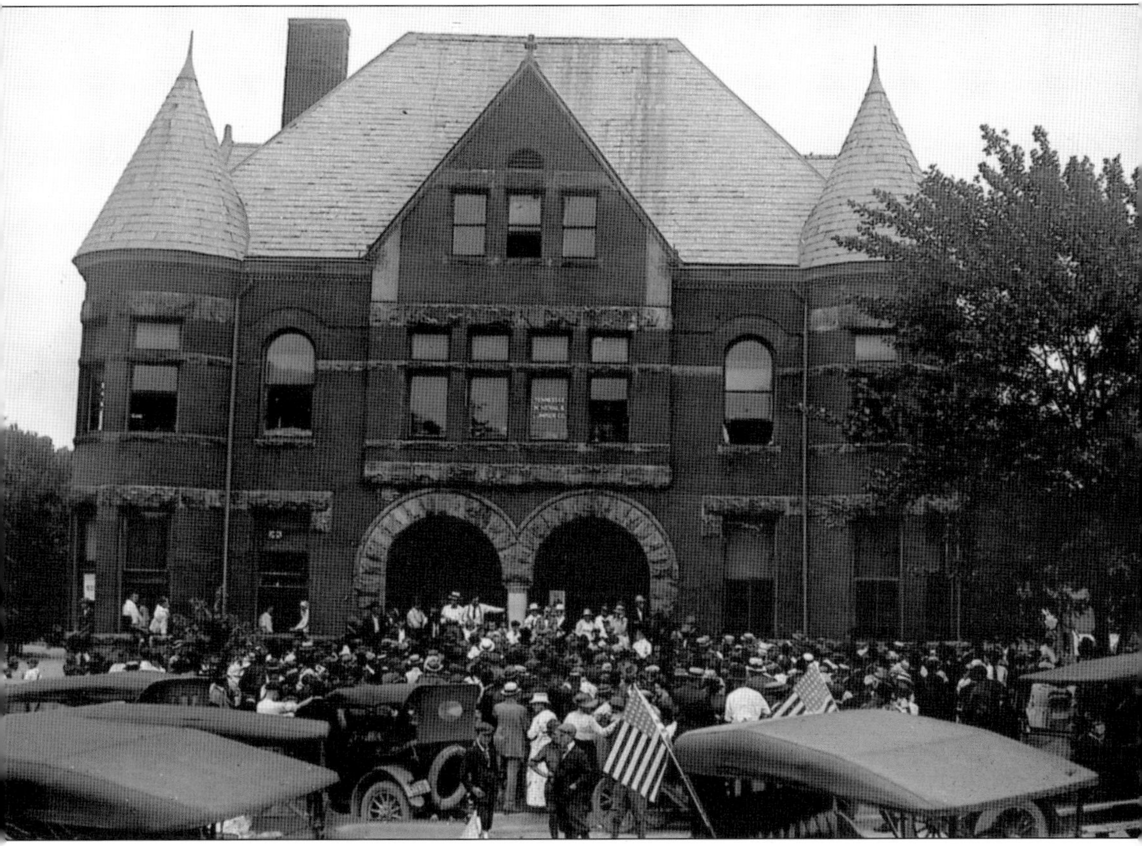

World War I touches Harriman as hundreds of residents turn out to see men off to fight in Europe. This photograph was taken in front of the Temperance Building in September 1918.

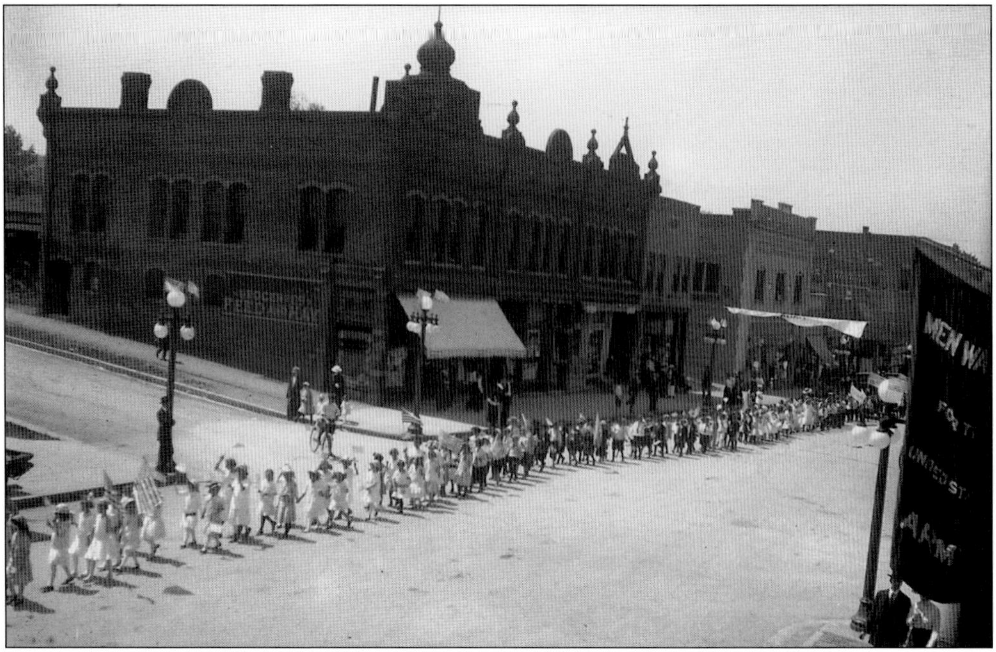

Harriman residents show their patriotic spirit in a parade to see men off to the Great War in 1918. Note the Army recruitment poster at right in the photograph above. The photograph below shows the crowd in front of Kodak's Stationery, directly across Roane Street from the old post office.

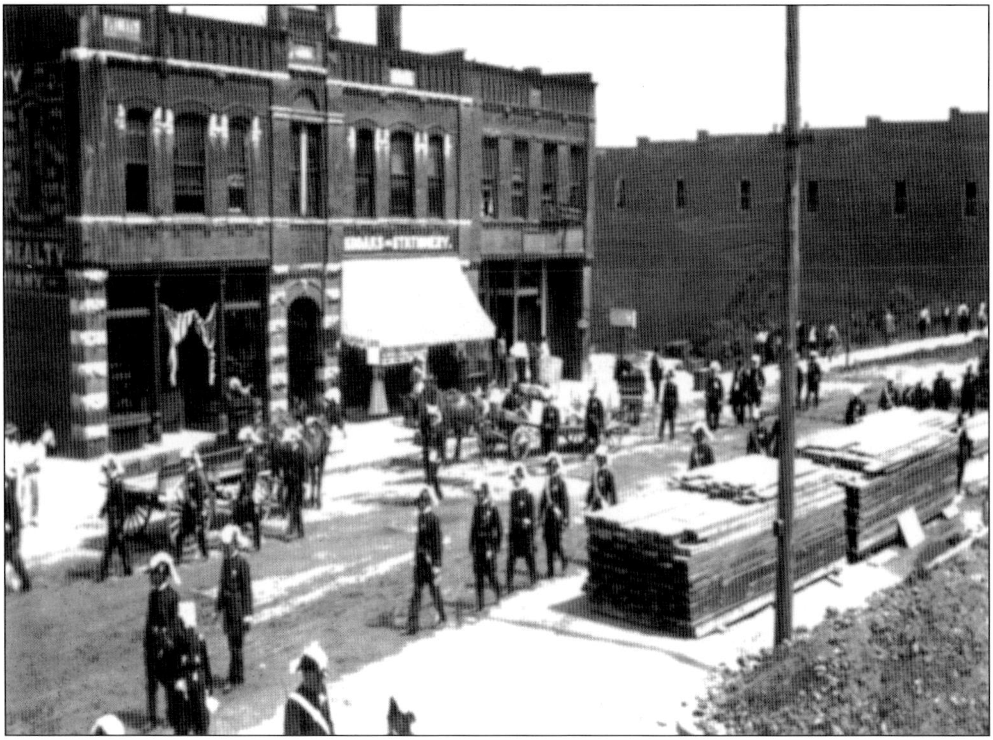

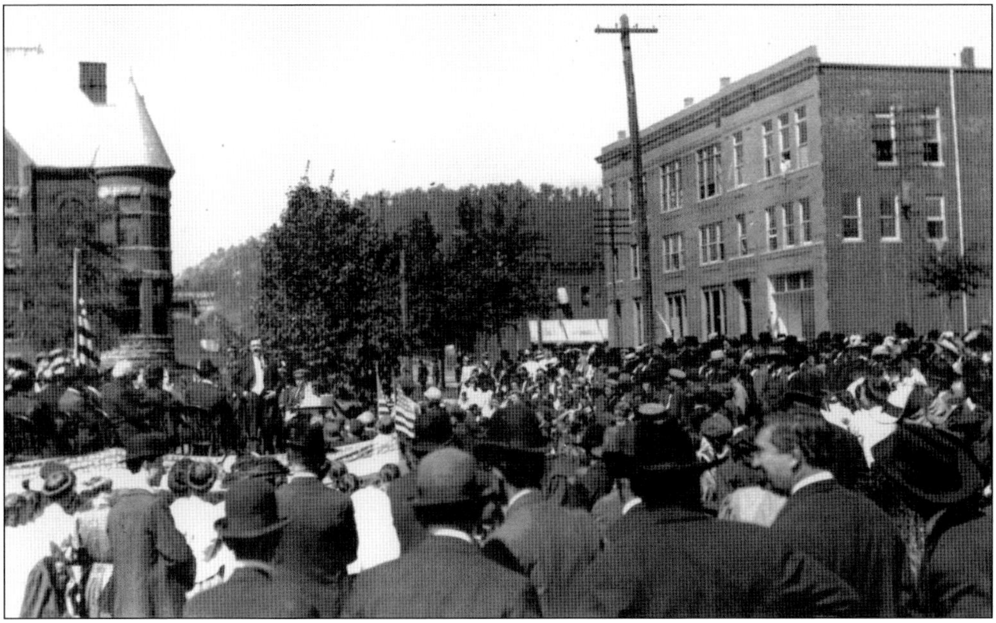

These street scenes show soldiers who left for World War I, on September 10, 1917. The view is looking south from the corner of Roane and Queen Streets. Cumberland Club Coffee and Rudenshiold Tailors are visible on Roane Street.

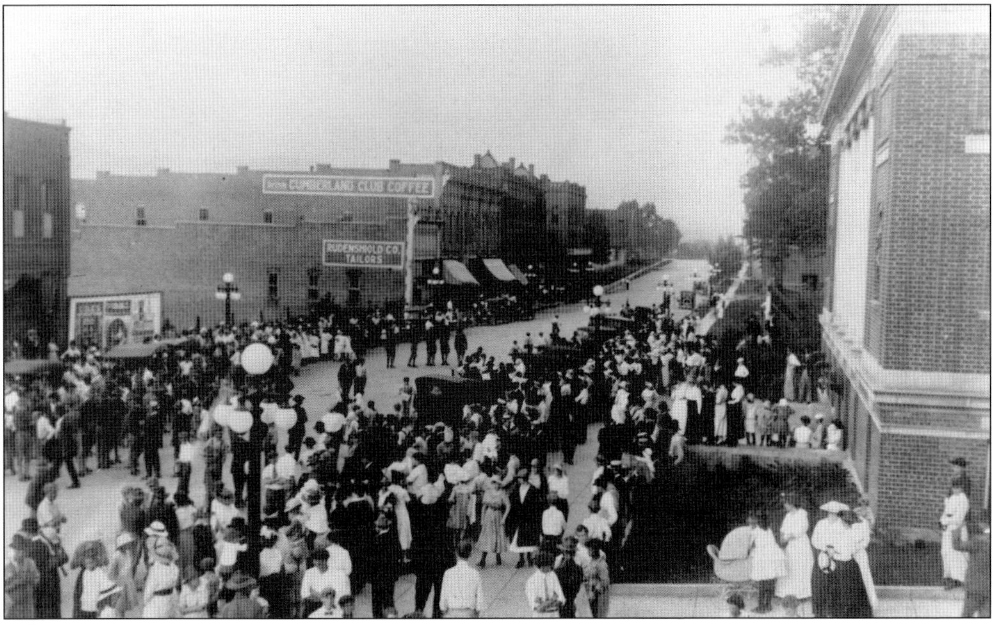

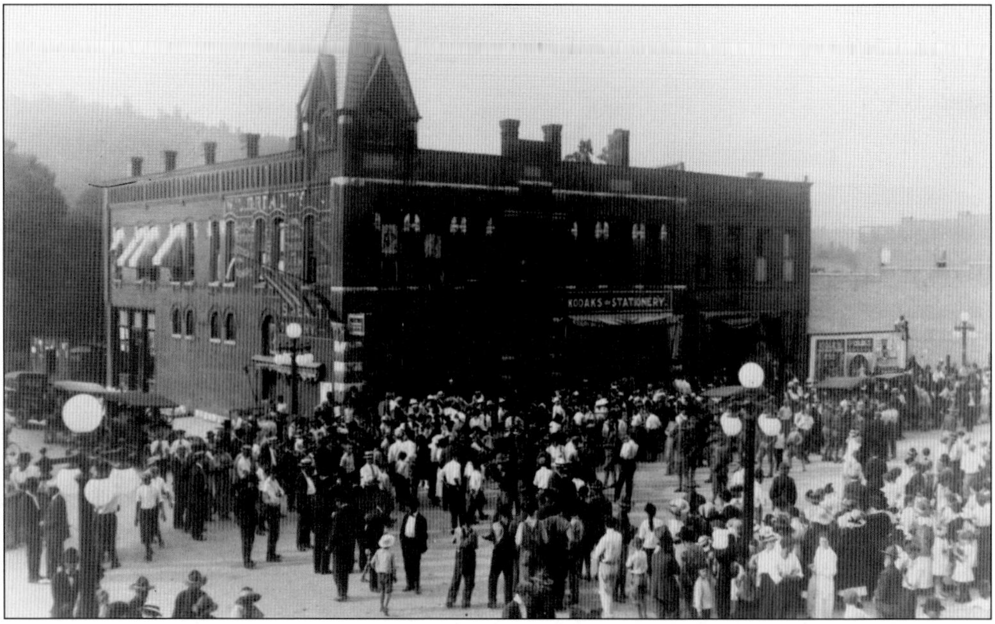

The photograph above was taken in front of Kodak's Stationery, at the corner of Roane and Queen Streets. The image below shows some of the men who served. These were a small number of the many Harriman men who went off to fight in the trenches of Europe.

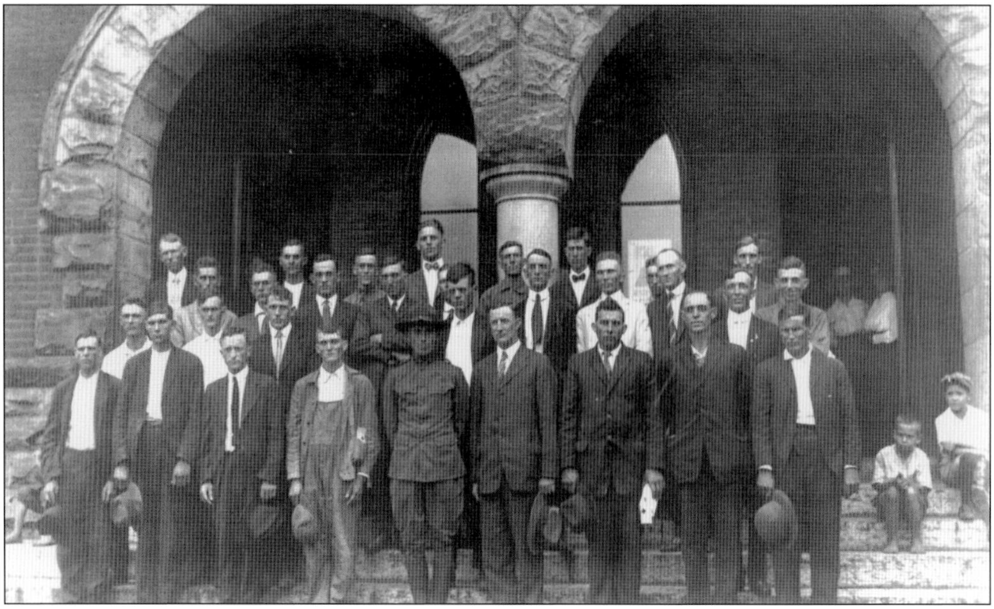

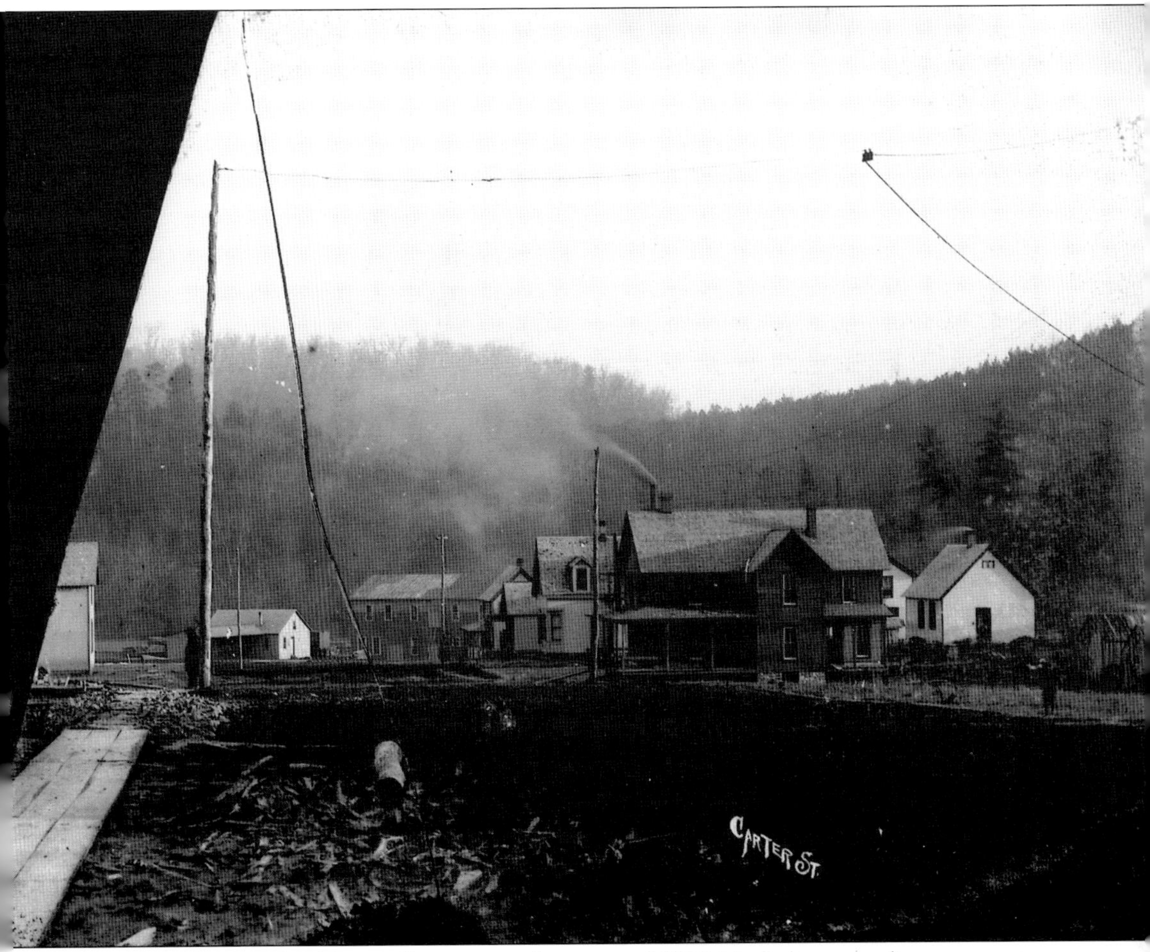

This early photograph of Carter Street was taken around 1920. Note the power lines.

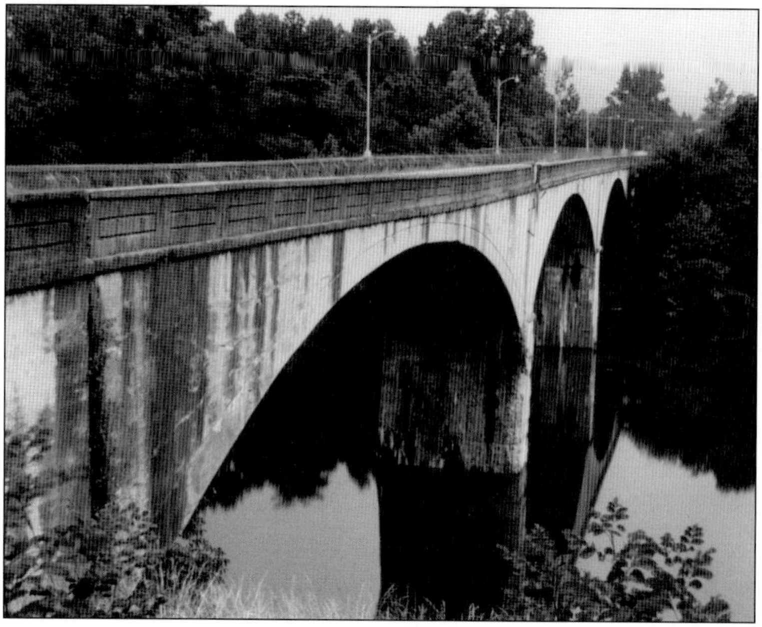

The Emory River Bridge was originally constructed as the primary bridge in Harriman, but it was eventually replaced in this role by the William Hamilton Browder Bridge on Highway 27 (the "new bridge"). The "Old Bridge," as it then became known, continued in operation on Pansy Hill Road until the new Old Bridge replaced it in the early 1990s.

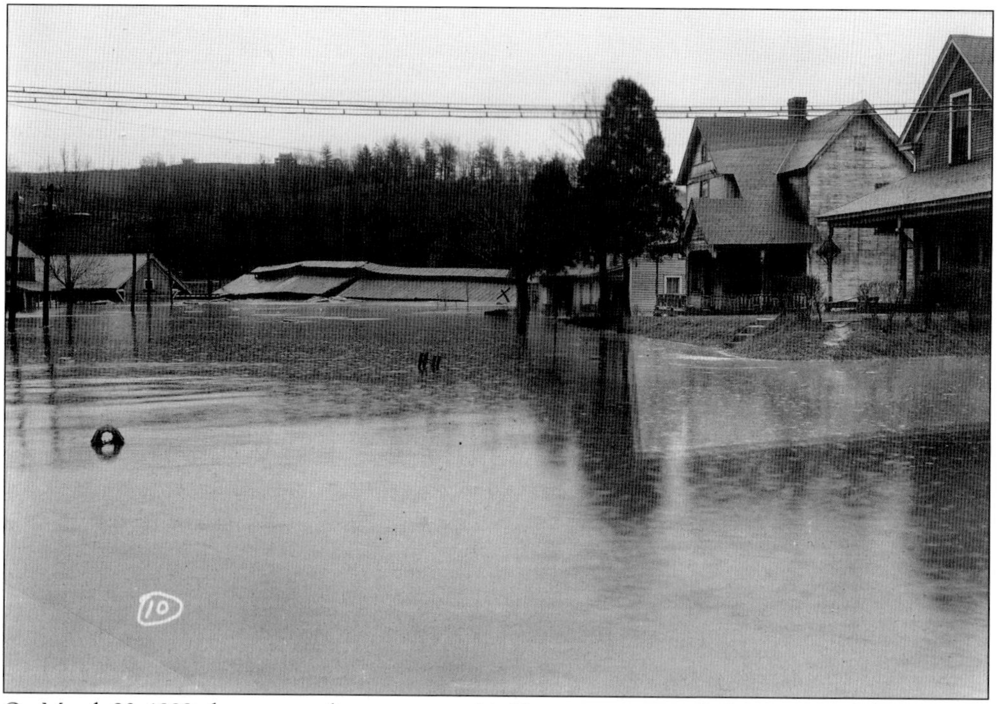

On March 23, 1929, the greatest disaster ever to hit Harriman occurred when extremely heavy rains caused a major flood of the Emory River. The problem was worsened when the bridge upstream in Oakdale collapsed, releasing a surge of water that had been backed up by debris against the bridge. The result was a wall of water surging downstream, which hit so quickly many people did not have time to get out of its path. Here, Morgan Street is visible facing the L&N Depot. Charles W. Adkisson Sr. took all photographs of the Flood of 1929.

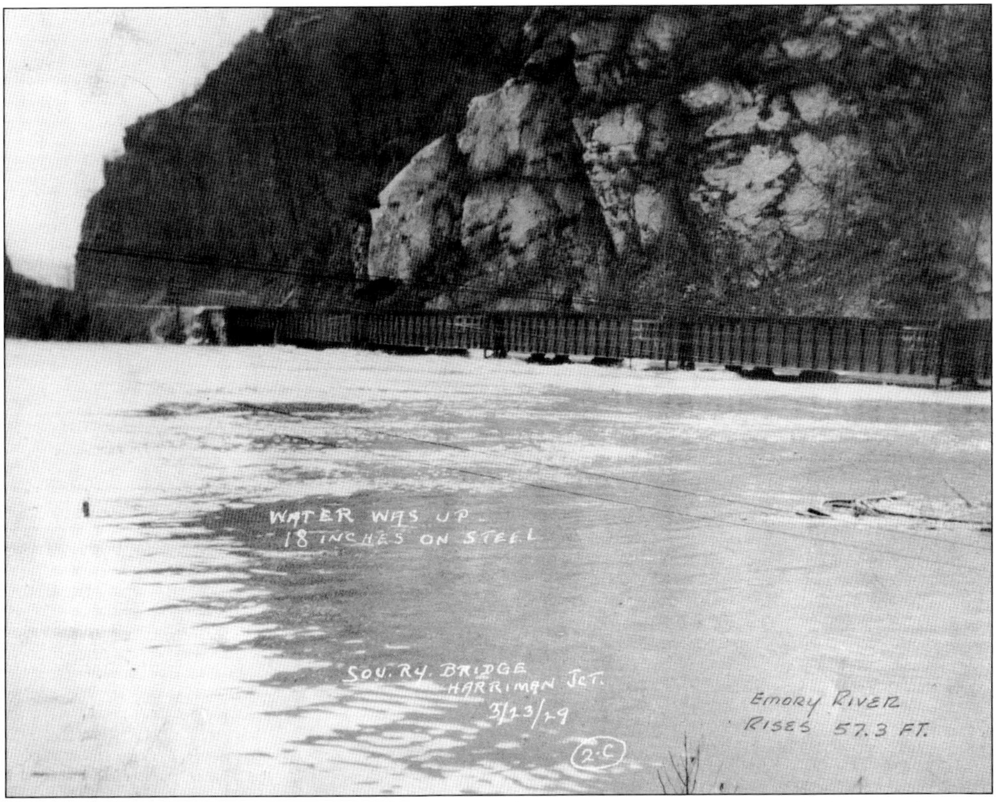

In this photograph, also by Charles Adkisson, the Emory River is rising to over 57 feet, overflowing the bridge at Harriman Junction.

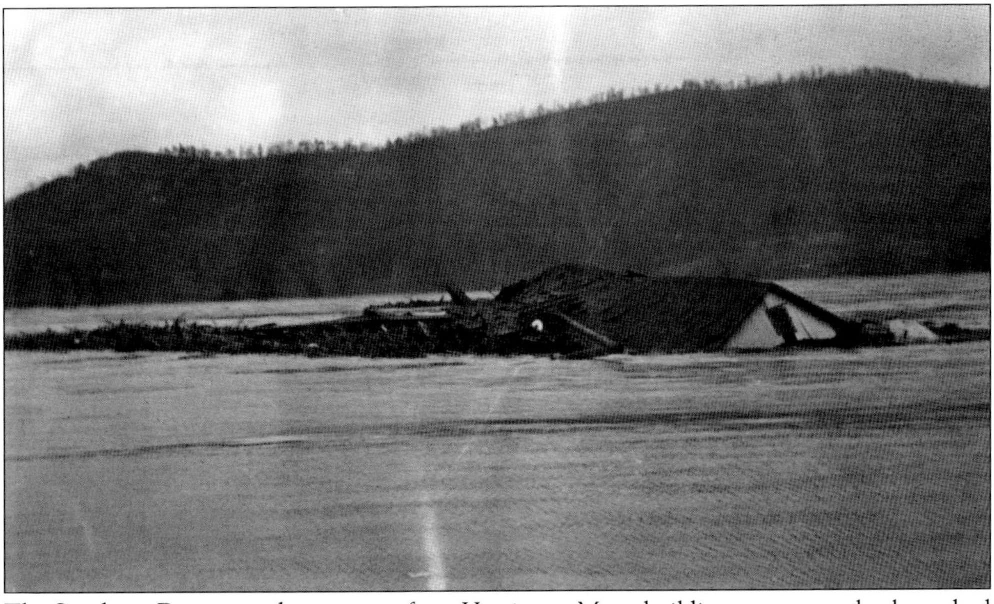

The Southern Depot was downstream from Harriman. Many buildings were completely washed away by this devastating flood. A 1958 study by the Tennessee Valley Authority determined the flood hit at a velocity of 195,000 square cubic feet per second.

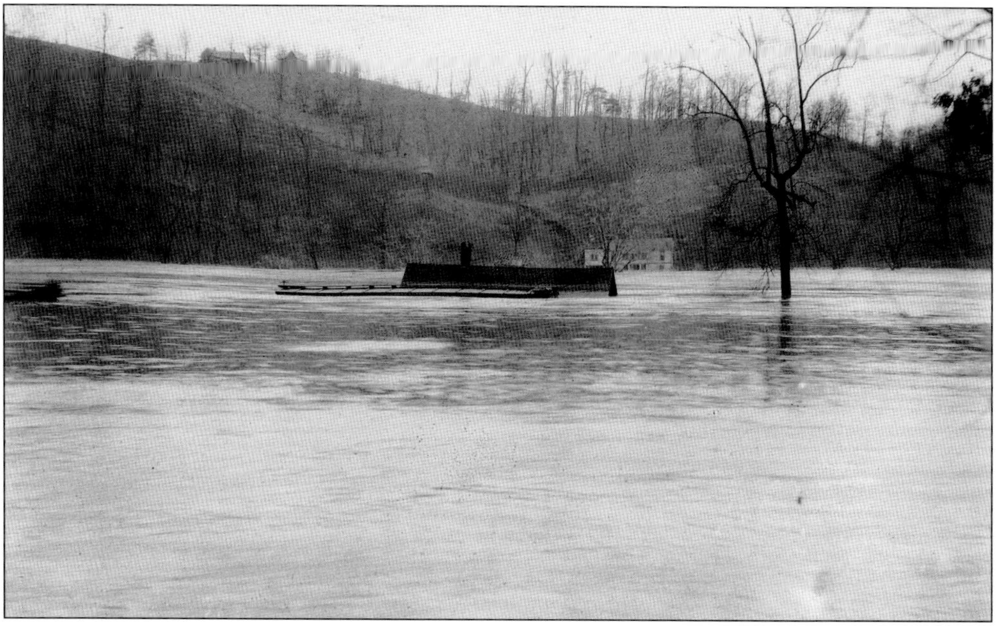

This was the view from Trenton Street, across the Emory River. The river crested at an incredible 61.1 feet at 10:30 a.m. on March 23, 1929. The flood killed 11 adults and 9 children. About half of the bodies were never recovered.

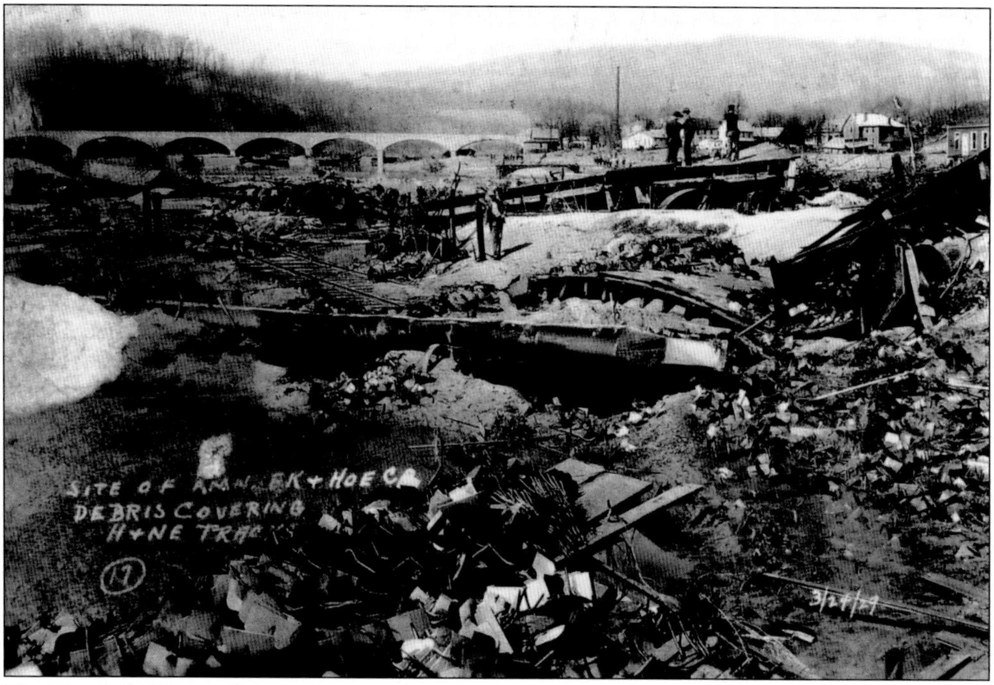

The Flood of 1929 was the worst natural disaster ever to hit Harriman, killing 20 people, leaving over 200 homeless, and washing away industries along the Emory River—several of which never resumed operation in the city. This photograph from March 24, 1929, taken the day after the flood, captures only a small part of the devastation. The property damage was estimated to be over $3 million. One wonders how Harriman's history might have been different had the flood not occurred.

Three

Mid-20th Century

The 1930s were a difficult time for nearly everyone, and Harriman was no exception. Movies were very popular, and patrons flocked to the Princess, Prince, and Webbo Theatres (and others) to escape the harsh realities of the Depression.

In 1940, Harriman celebrated its 50th year with festivities. It must have been a time of optimism in the city. A year later, the country would plunge into World War II, a war many residents would take part in both on the battlefields and through the Manhattan Project in nearby Oak Ridge. As there would not be enough housing in the Secret City to support all the jobs there, many Oak Ridge workers lived in Harriman, along with former residents who had been displaced by the project.

During the 1950s and 1960s, downtown Harriman was a bustling place with stores familiar to generations of residents. Among them were Miller-Brewer, Chase Drug Store, Edward's, and Norris Creamery.

The 1950s saw the establishment of Kingston Power Plant, bringing in another influx of workers. In 1961 the city annexed new territory, much of it in South Harriman, Pine Hills, Bazeltown, and Emory Gap. In the first post-annexation election, Mayor A.B. "Salty" Foster, who had overseen the annexation, was defeated by South Harriman's Elmer Eblen, reflecting the dissatisfaction of those annexed. The new territory doubled Harriman's population, and over the coming years, many businesses would relocate to South Harriman.

In August 1965, the city celebrated its 75th anniversary with a Diamond Jubilee celebration that lasted for a week. Pioneers Day saw many early residents return to the city. Women's Day was a pageant featuring clothing styles popular in Harriman's early years. It was during the 1960s that the city reached its peak.

Sadly, Harriman, like many small towns, was hit hard by the shifts in the economy during the last decades of the 20th century. Unable to compete with foreign labor, both hosiery mills closed. Additionally, Interstate 40, while bringing growth to the region and connecting the city with Knoxville, also played a role in businesses leaving downtown.

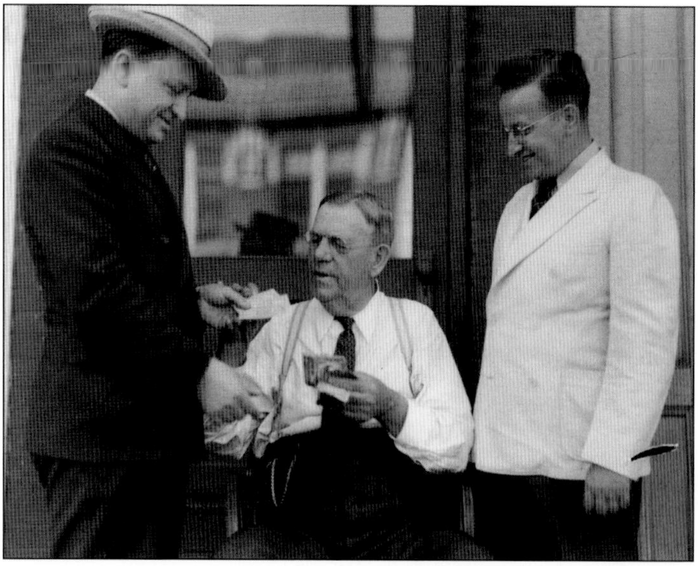

Harriman mayor H.M. Carr (seated) buys the first set of wooden nickels from L.W. Bevel, chairman of the Semi-Centennial celebration. The wooden nickels served as the first official souvenirs of the celebration, were backed 100 percent by collateral in US currency, and were legal tender in the city. Looking on at right is Bob Colton of Rogers Producing of Ohio, who served as pageant director.

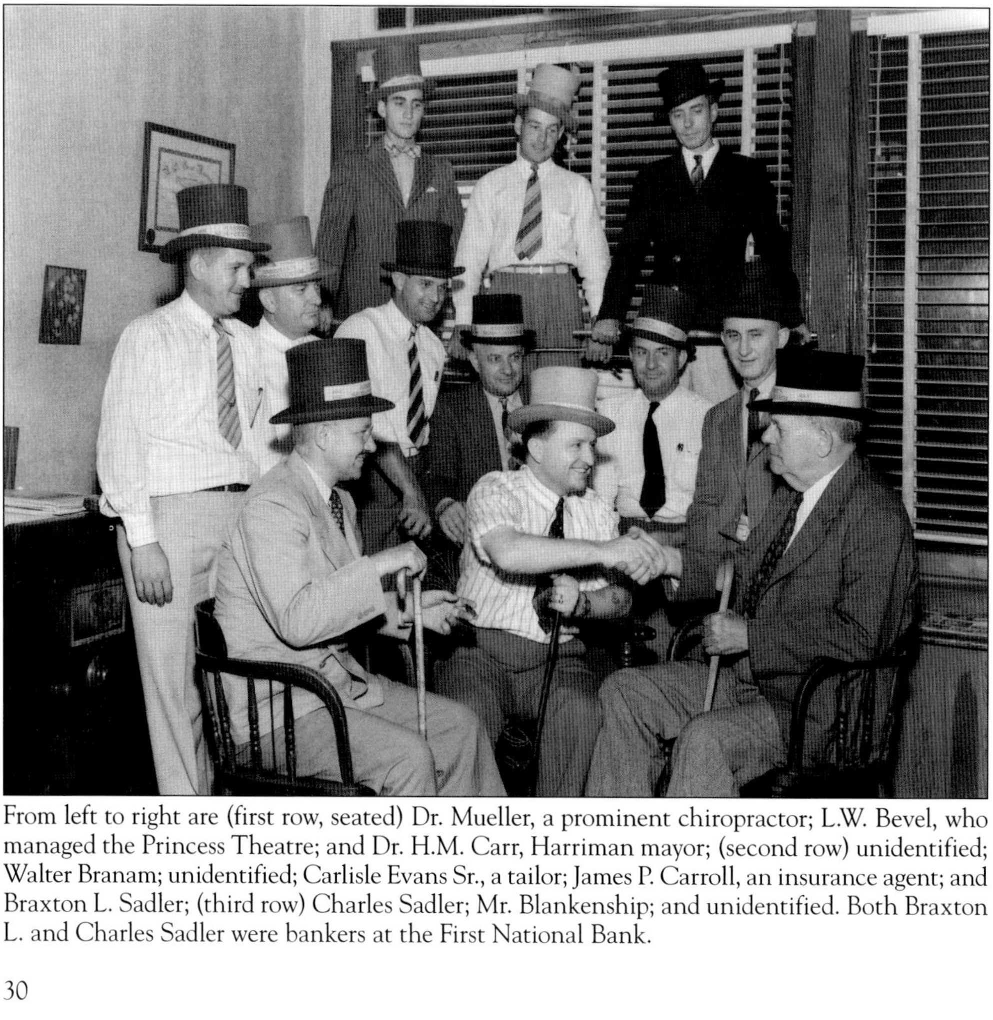

From left to right are (first row, seated) Dr. Mueller, a prominent chiropractor; L.W. Bevel, who managed the Princess Theatre; and Dr. H.M. Carr, Harriman mayor; (second row) unidentified; Walter Branam; unidentified; Carlisle Evans Sr., a tailor; James P. Carroll, an insurance agent; and Braxton L. Sadler; (third row) Charles Sadler; Mr. Blankenship; and unidentified. Both Braxton L. and Charles Sadler were bankers at the First National Bank.

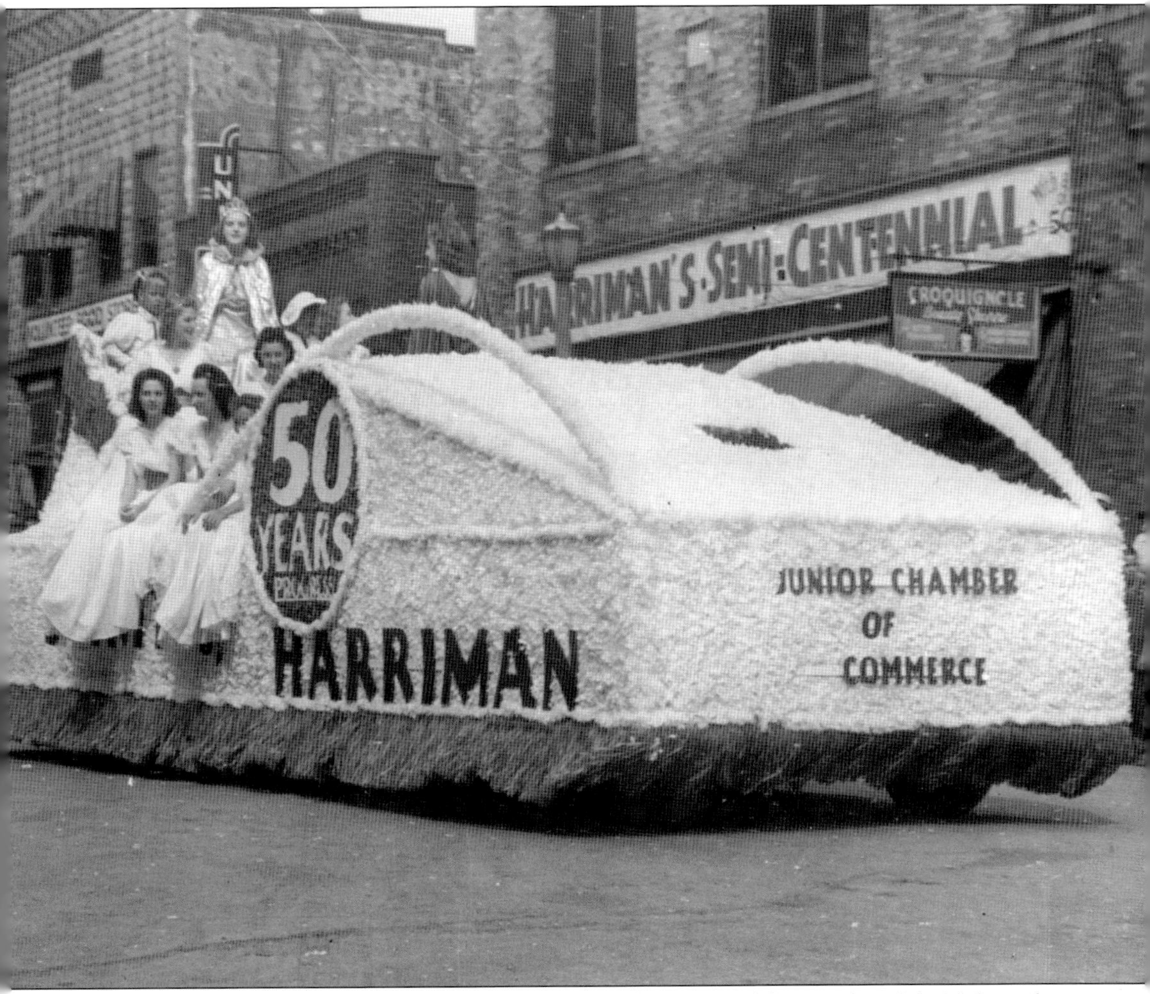

Harriman's 50th anniversary was observed in July 1940 with a major celebration from July 24 through 27. Among the events was a four-night performance of *Harriman on Parade*, a play featuring over 300 residents reenacting the city's most important events. This photograph shows the "mammoth float parade," as described by Walter T. Pulliam, on the afternoon of July 25 on Roane Street. Viewed by over 8,000 spectators, the parade featured 80 units and was over a mile long.

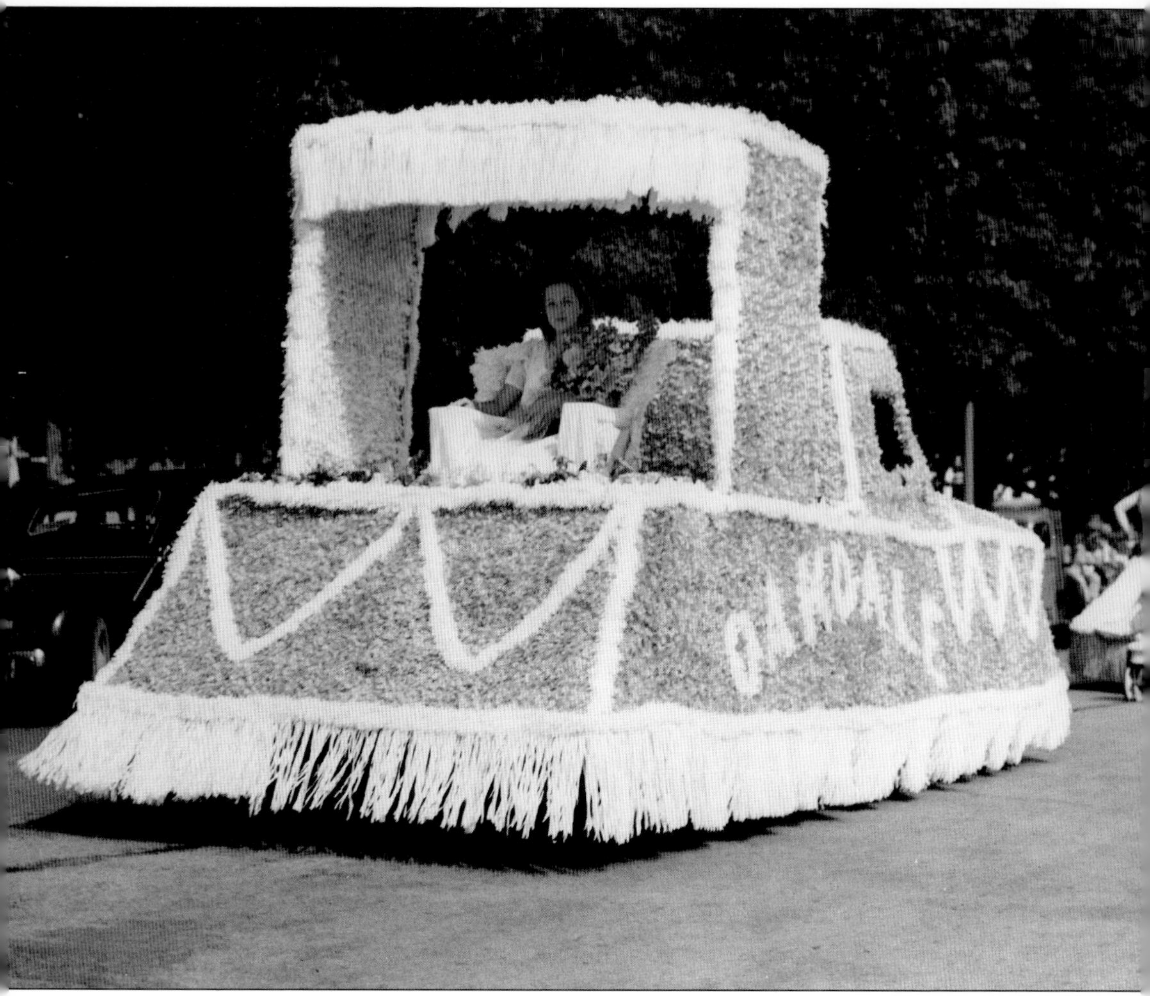

Several neighboring towns took part in the festivities. In this photograph, Oakdale High School's contribution is visible.

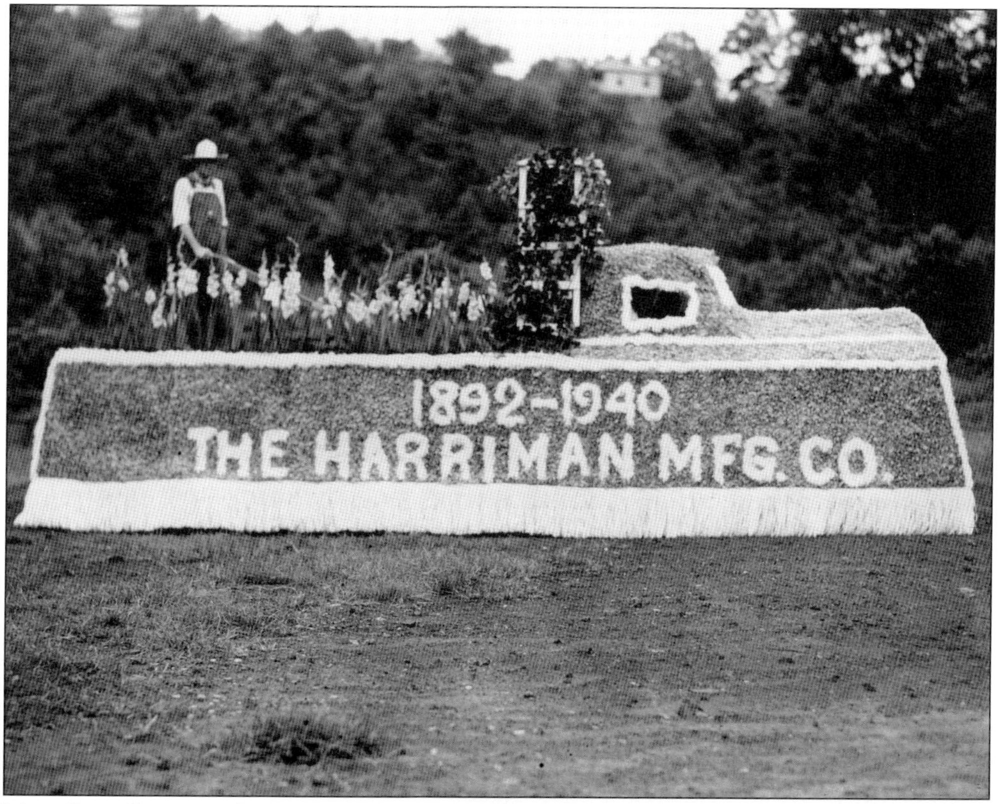

More Semi-Centennial excitement came in the form of Harriman Manufacturing Company's float. It was awarded an honorable mention in the float competition. The Harriman Manufacturing Company had been in the city since the 1890s, beginning as a subsidiary of the East Tennessee Land Company.

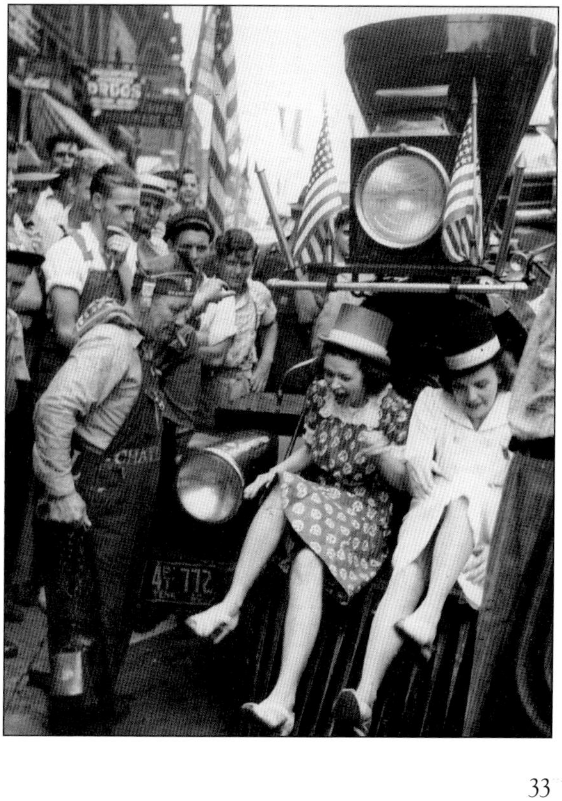

The Semi-Centennial was a time of jubilation in Harriman. This 1940 photograph captures a small part of the excitement, as Ann Harriman (left) and Margie Bowman (right) celebrate on the pilot of a train engine on Roane Street. Mayor H.M. Carr looks on.

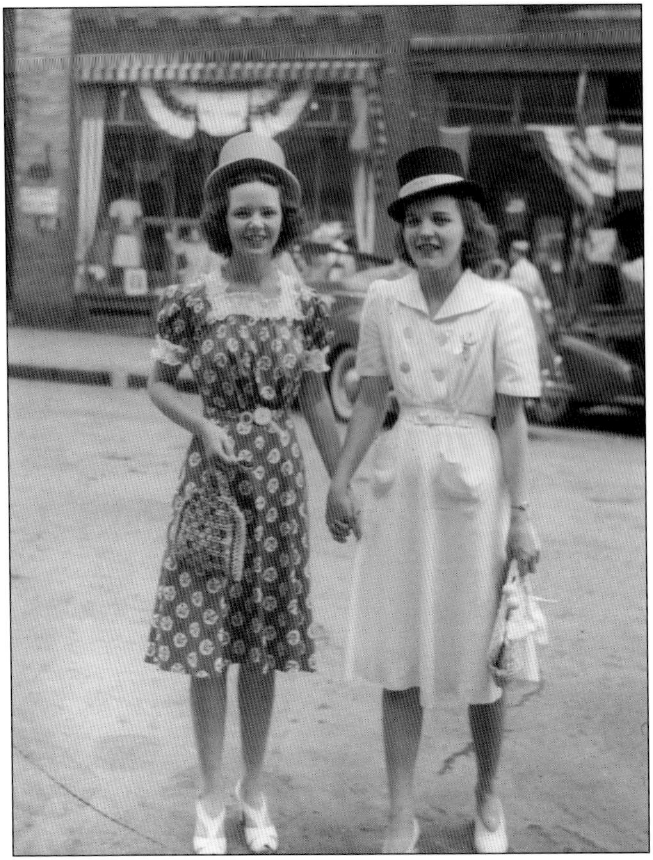

Ann Harriman (left) and Margie Bowman (right) are pictured at the Harriman Semi-Centennial celebration. Bowman, a 1938 graduate of Harriman High, was crowned Semi-Centennial Queen at the opening ceremony by W. Hartwell Harriman of Hartford, Connecticut, the grandson of Gen. Walter Harriman.

Roane Street was a busy place during the 1940s. In this photograph, several popular businesses are visible, including McKinney Hardware, Rexall Drugs, and Patton's Jewelry.

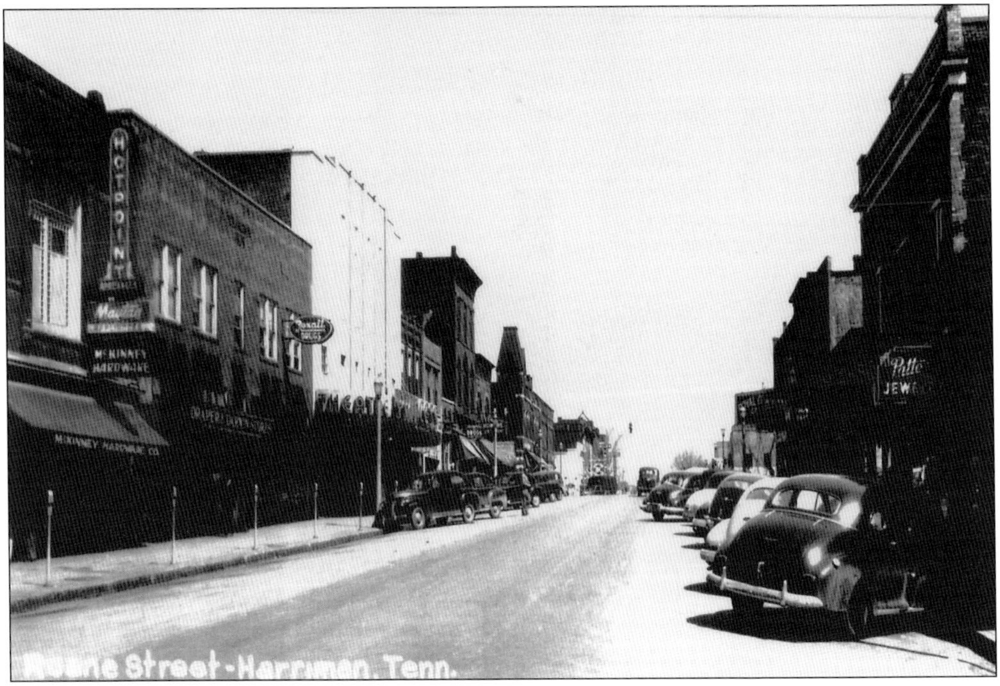

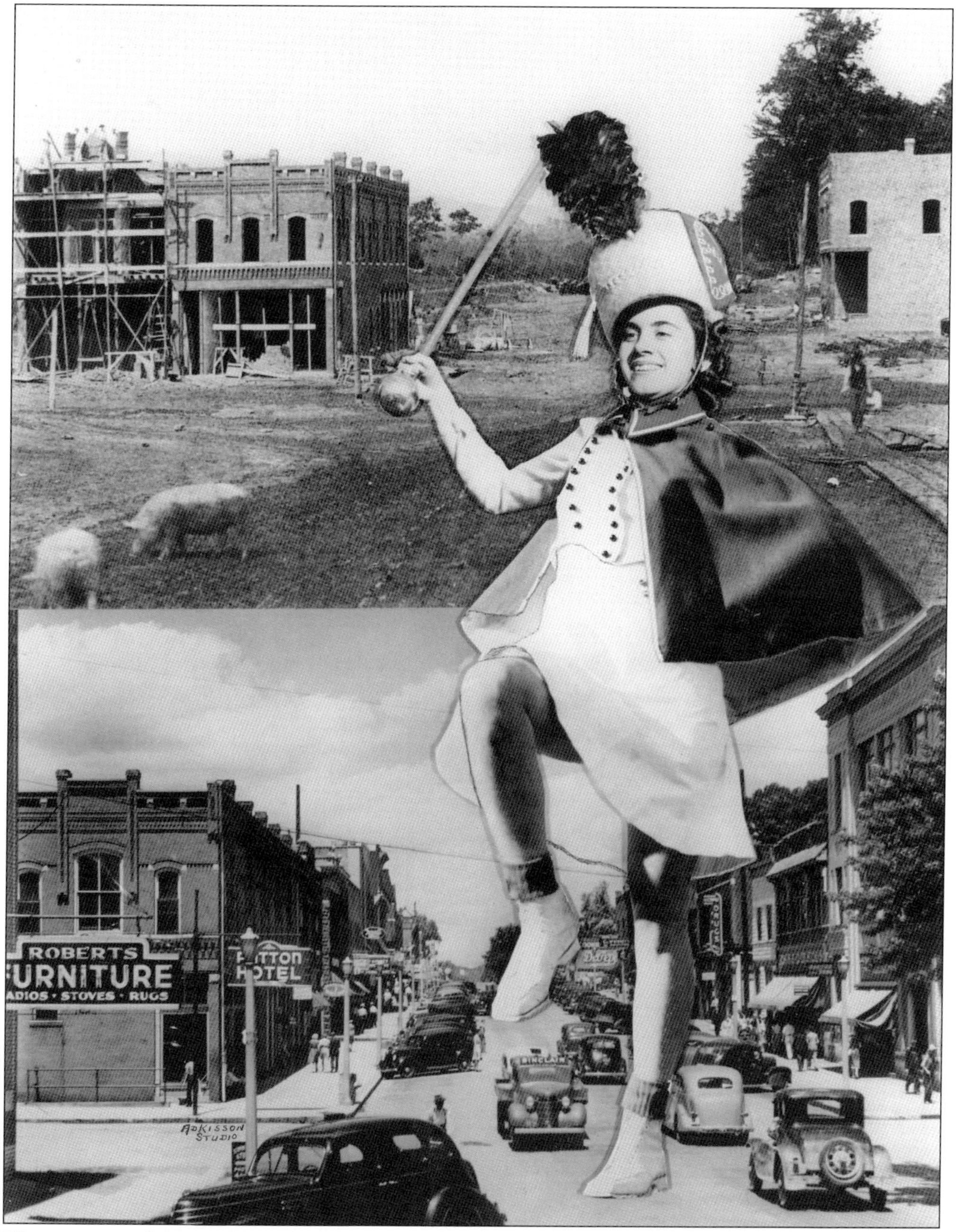

This poster celebrates Harriman's Semi-Centennial. In the top half, Roane Street is depicted looking from the east in July 1890. The bottom half shows the same scene in July 1940. The drum majorette is Stacia Gardner of the Harriman High School band. C.W. Adkisson designed this poster. On the final day of celebration, Gov. Prentice Cooper spoke to a crowd of about 3,000.

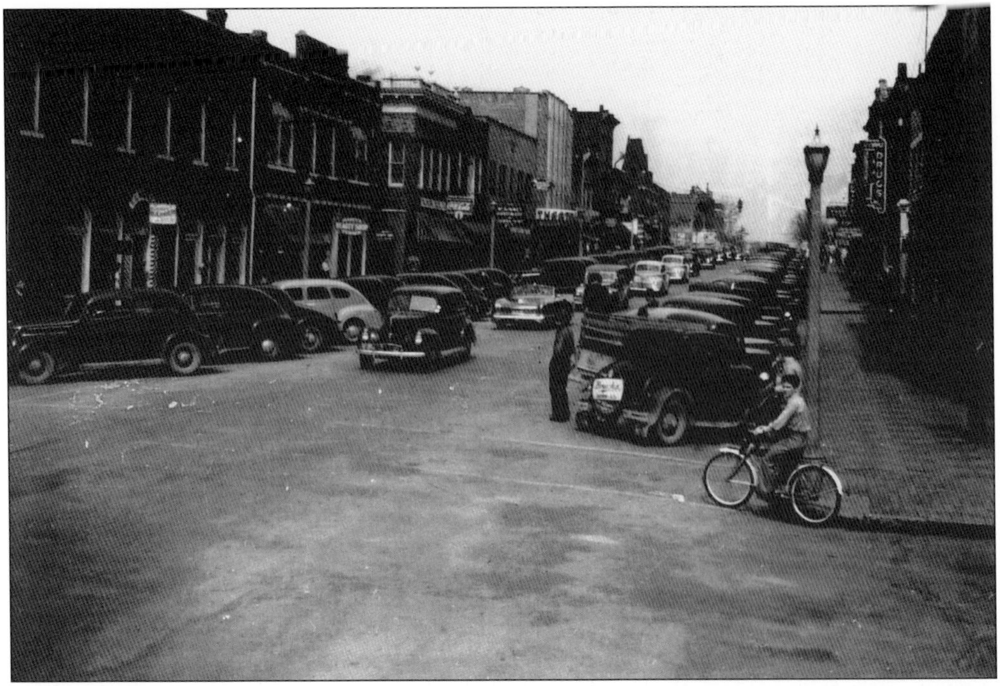

This photograph of Roane Street was probably taken around the time of Harriman's 50th anniversary in 1940 and shows a busy downtown area. At this time, Roane Street was a two-lane road. It would be widened to four lanes in 1957.

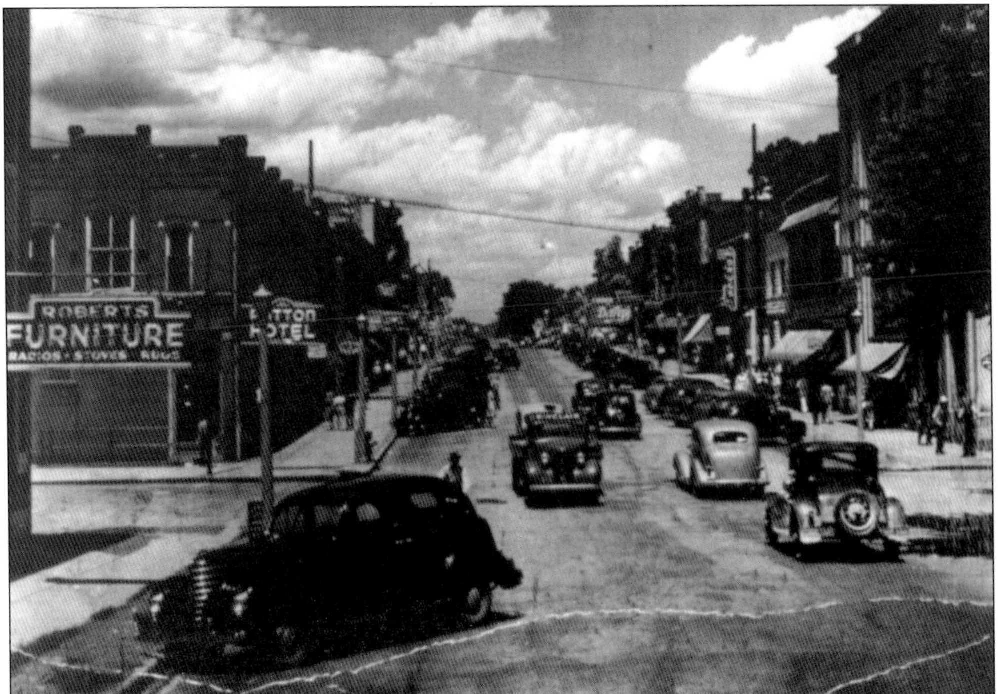

This photograph, taken at the corner of Queen and Roane Streets in 1940, captures some well-known landmarks of downtown Harriman, namely Roberts Furniture and the Patton Hotel.

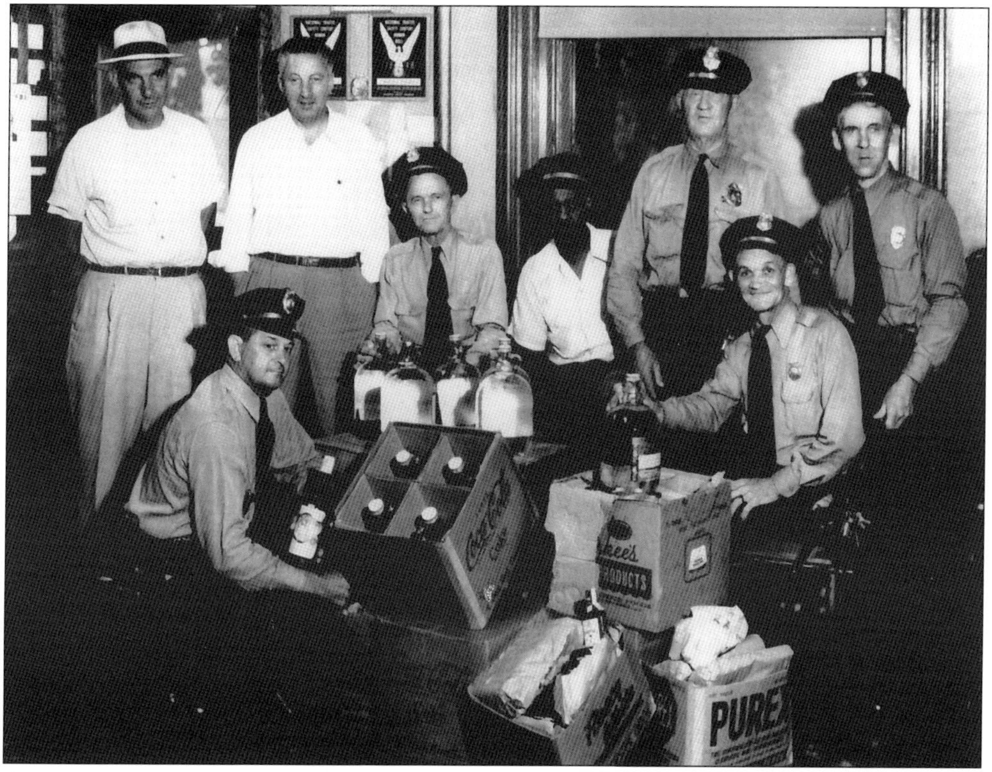

As a temperance town, alcohol was strictly prohibited in Harriman. This photograph shows the enforcement of this prohibition during the early 1950s. In the back row on the far left is Mayor Harold Williams. To the right of him is Marvin Stinecipher.

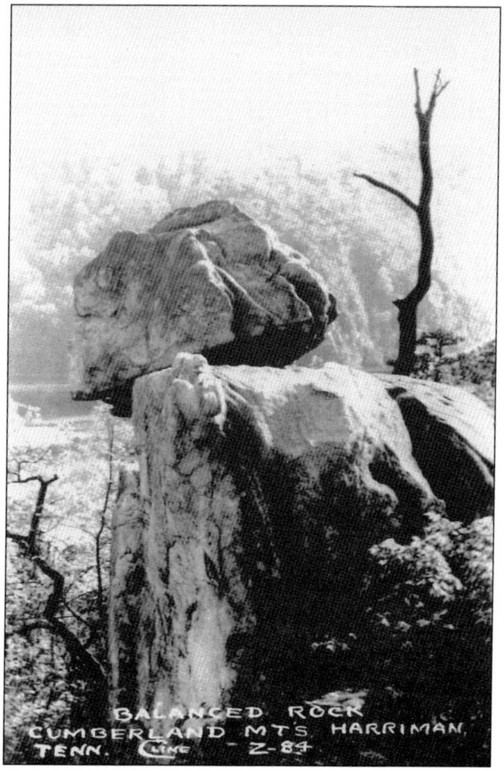

Balancing Rock, also known as Balanced Rock, became a local landmark overlooking Harriman from Walden's Ridge. Generations of residents have hiked to the rock, and more than a few have carved their names on it.

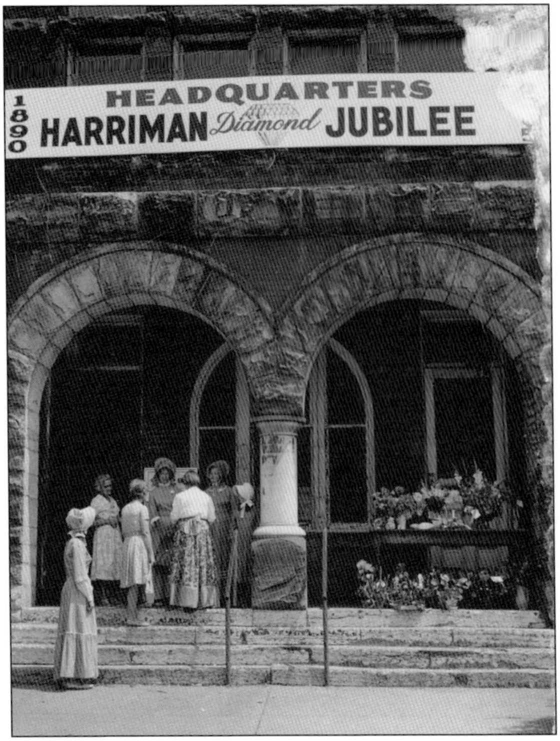

This photograph of Harriman's Diamond Jubilee in August 1965 was taken by Bob Ivory Studios, located in the Miller-Brewer Building at the time. Harriman's 75th anniversary celebration lasted from August 7 to 14, 1965, and featured a parade, a speech from Gov. Frank Clement, and the burying of a time capsule to be opened in 2065.

Harriman's Diamond Jubilee was partially patterned after its Semi-Centennial 25 years before. Every night during the celebration, *Harriman-O-Rama*, a pageant produced by the John B. Rogers Company (which had also produced a pageant in 1940) was held. One feature of the celebration was that men were supposed to grow beards—those who shaved during the festivities were subject to fines. Here we see some men sporting facial hair due to this rule.

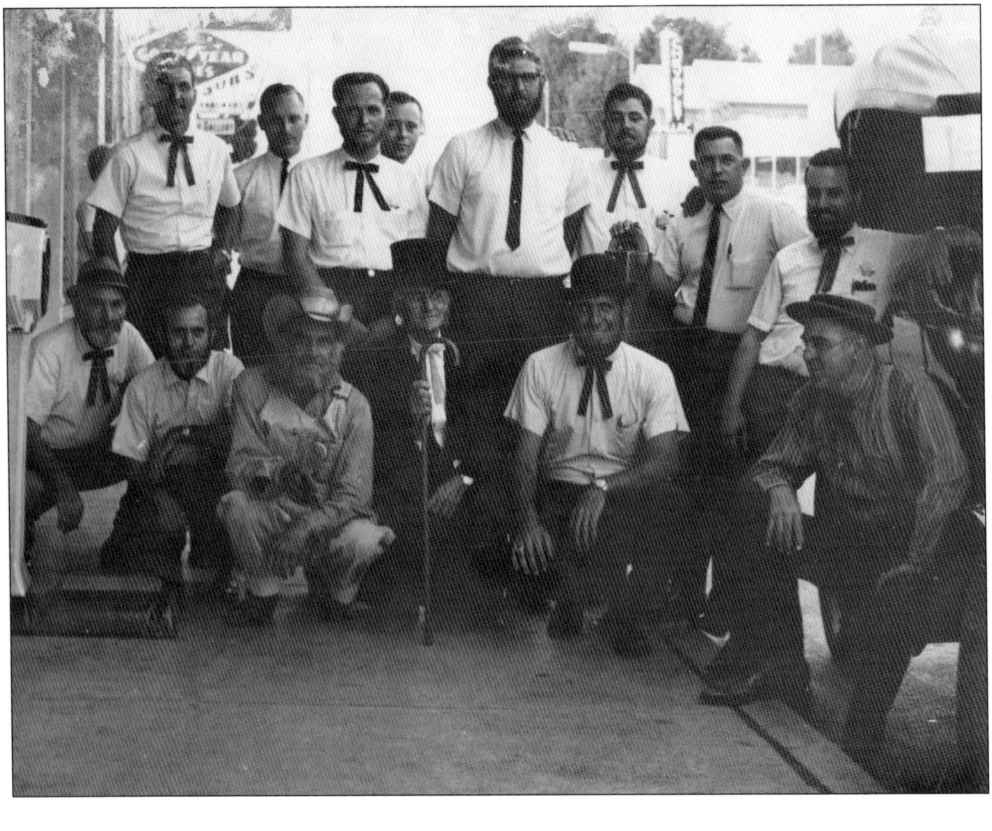

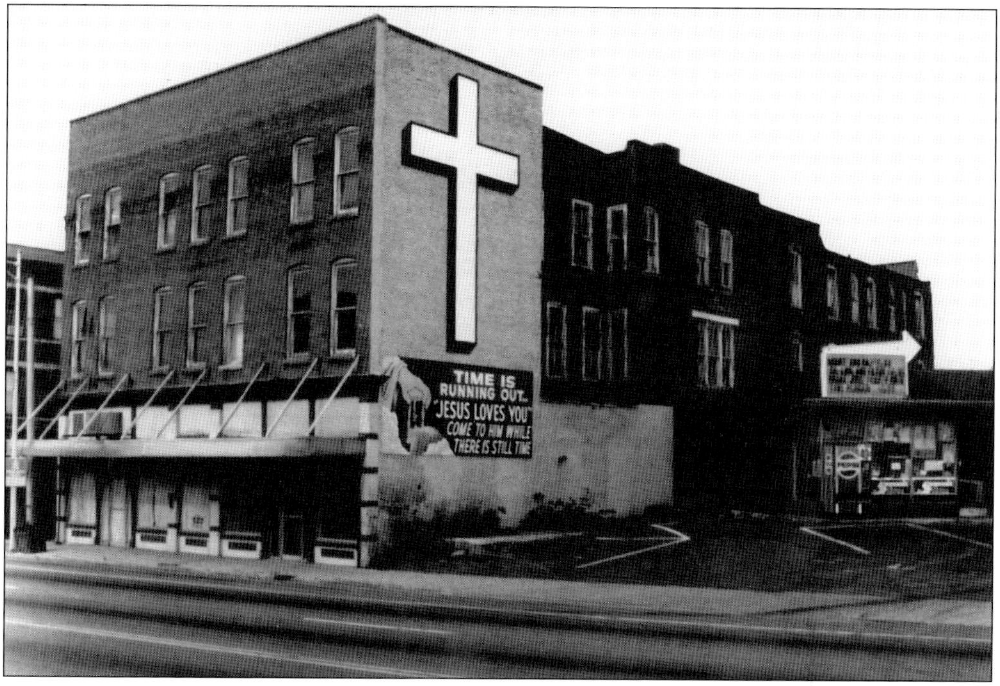

Roane Street is pictured here, probably in the 1980s. The photograph above shows the building just north of the Queen Street intersection. Below is the street looking south from the Queen Street intersection. Note the Princess Theatre on the right.

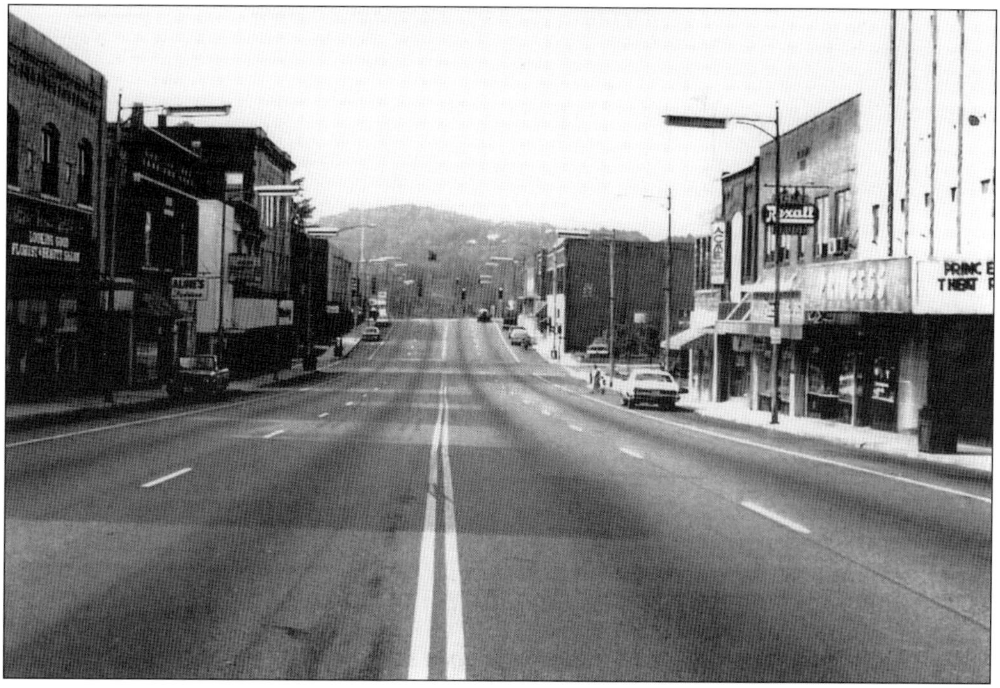

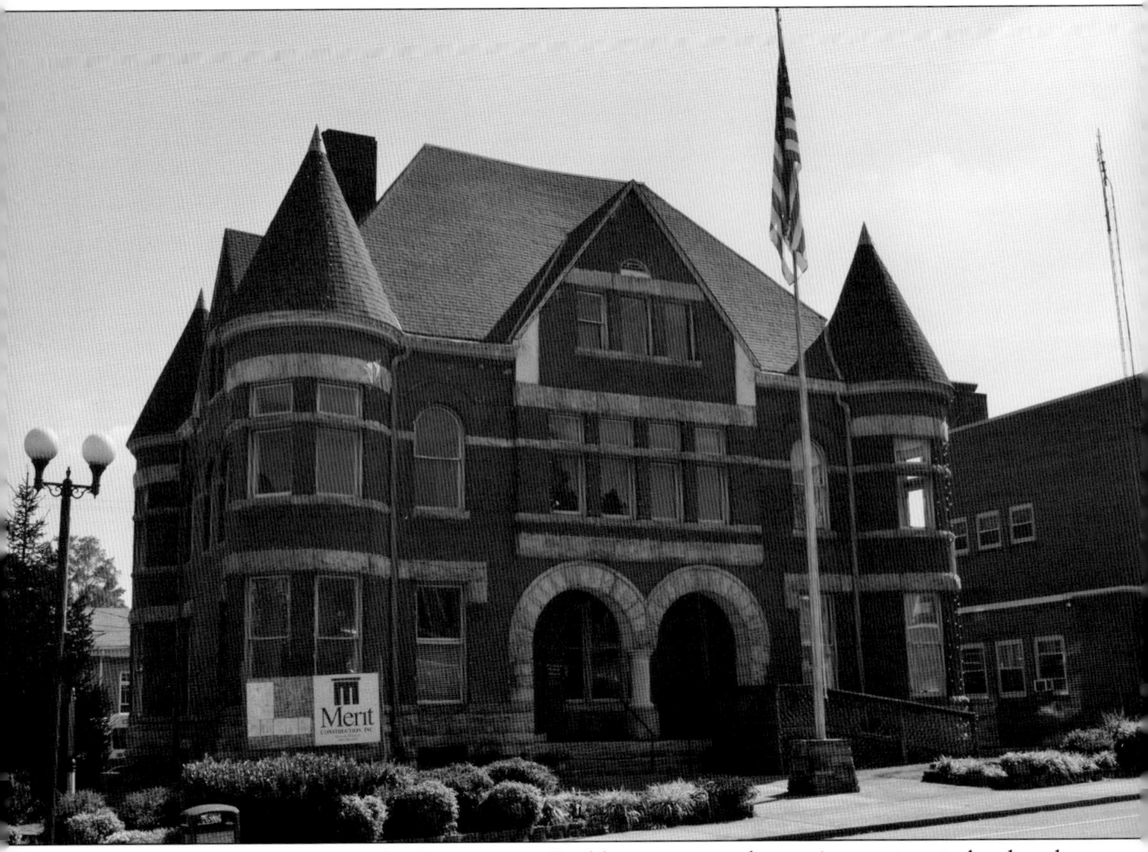

After more than 120 years, the Temperance Building remains the city's most iconic landmark. (Author's collection.)

Four

Education

One of the primary concerns of Harriman's founders was providing a quality education for its citizens. Toward this end, Harriman's first school was paid for and constructed by the East Tennessee Land Company, opening its doors in the fall of 1890. The first graduating class, with fewer than 10 members, was the class of 1891.

The first public school in Harriman was located between Clinton and Trenton Streets on Crescent Street, the present site of the First Presbyterian Church. Known interchangeably as Central School and Harriman, the high school moved to its present site in 1917.

Around this time, the school adopted the nickname of Blue Devils. The reasons for this are unclear, though legend says an early teacher or administrator was a Duke graduate and suggested using the university's nickname and colors.

The school saw an increase in enrollment during the 1930s, and a new high school was built by 1938 because of overcrowding. Though planned to serve the community for decades, the school burned in 1945 and was replaced with a new building, which also burned in 1969.

From its beginning through the 20th century, Harriman had its own school system. This was a point of contention in the city, and several votes were held concerning whether to turn the schools over to the county. In 2002, voters chose to do so. Harriman's schools are currently administered by the Roane County School System.

In addition to public schools, Harriman has also been home to colleges and universities. The American Temperance University, later simply called American University, operated from 1893 to 1908 before folding following an academic scandal and declining enrollment.

Other early schools include the Mossop School for Girls, the East Tennessee Normal and Industrial Institute (an African American school modeled after the Tuskeegee Institute), and Harriman College, a short-lived business school.

In 1971, Roane State Community College was opened in Harriman, holding its first classes that fall at the former Fairmont School before moving to its current Patton Lane location just south of the city. In 2011, the college celebrated 40 years of serving the community.

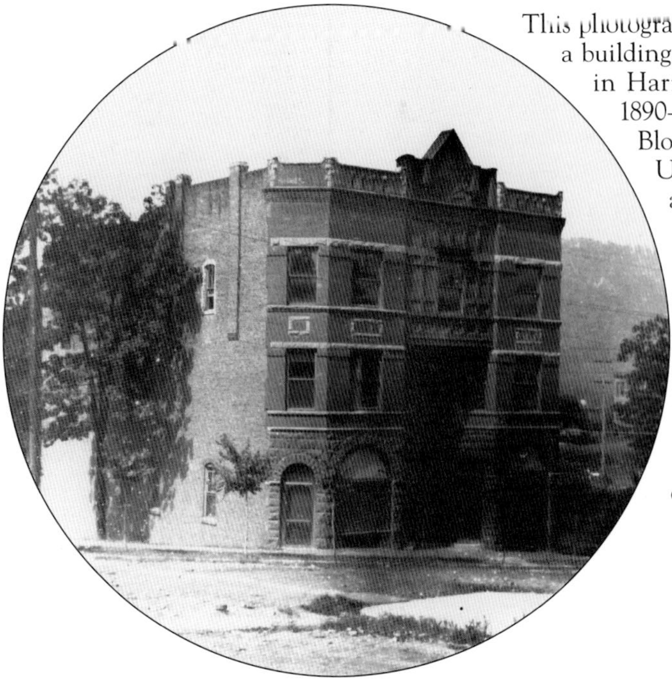

This photograph, taken around 1900, shows a building that would play a major role in Harriman's early years. Built in 1890–1891, it was first known as Fales Block and was part of American University. It was later known as Munyon Hall in honor of James Monroe Munyon, who purchased and donated it to the university. Later, it was acquired by the Holston Methodist Conference and became the Hiwassee Apartments. Located at 503 Walden Street at the corner of Clinton Street, it was demolished in 1971.

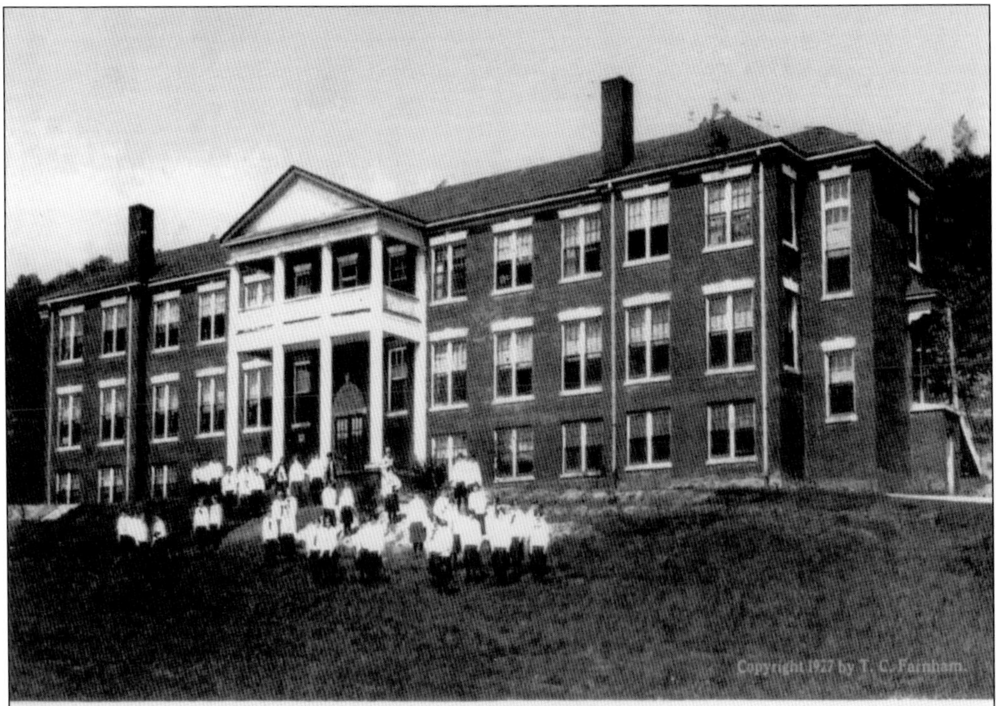

Mossop School for Girls is shown on this 1927 postcard. Mossop, sponsored by the Presbyterian Church, operated in Harriman from 1922 to 1942. A mission school for mountain girls, Mossop was located on Walden's Ridge overlooking the city, and provided instruction in history, reading, math, home economics, and the Bible.

The Mossop School for Girls maypole dance is shown here. Mossop continued to operate until 1942, surviving the Great Depression. It was closed because the Presbyterian Church viewed it as antiquated in light of the development of local public schools in Harriman.

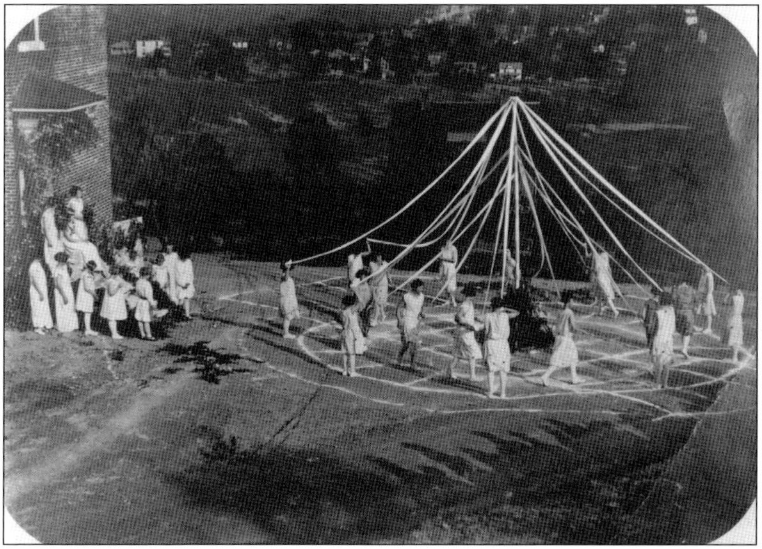

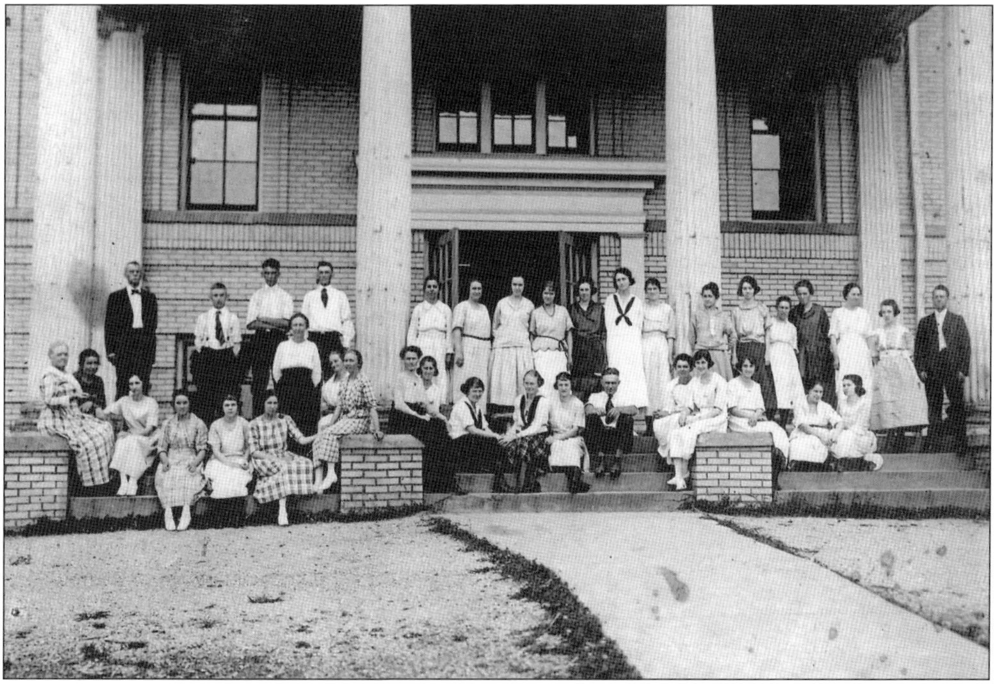

South Harriman High School is seen here—perhaps in the 1930s. This photograph shows the old school building, which is the current headquarters of the Harriman Police Department. South Harriman had its own schools, and the Harriman–South Harriman rivalry was one of the greatest in the county. After being annexed by Harriman, South Harriman's schools fell under the administration of the Harriman City School System. South Harriman High was closed in the early 1960s, and its students were sent to Harriman High, along with African American students who had previously been segregated, creating a single high school for the entire city.

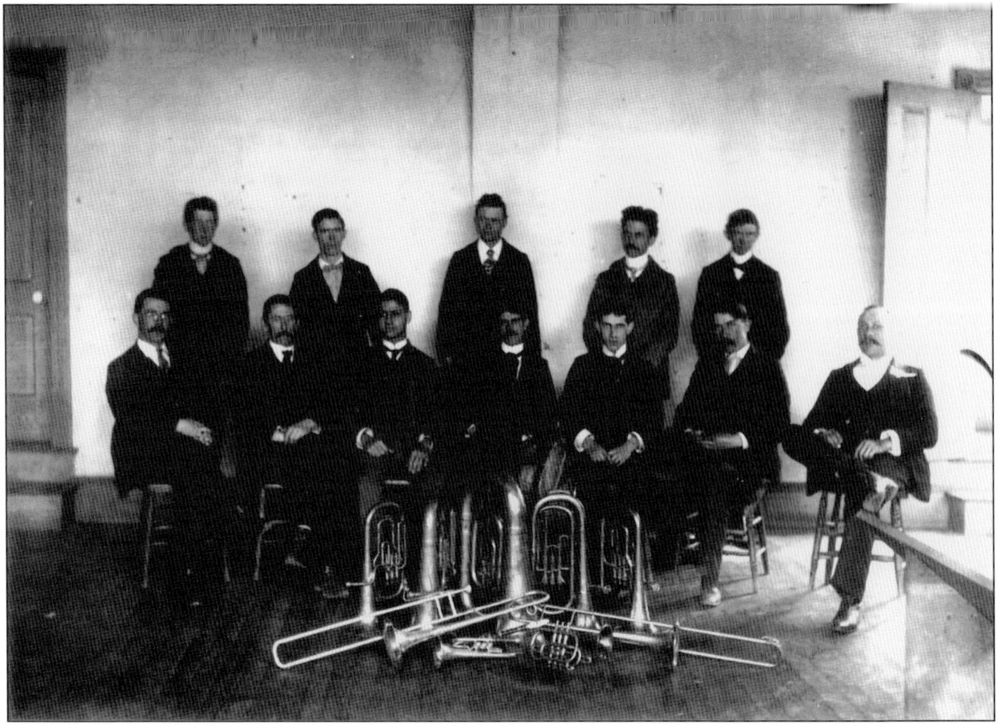

The American University Band is pictured here around 1905. American University, also known as American Temperance University, opened in 1893 and was for a time a respected institution, but by 1905 was derided as a "sham." It closed in 1908 and was replaced by Mooney School, which itself folded four years later. In the final years of the university, administrators combed the surrounding communities in search of potential students.

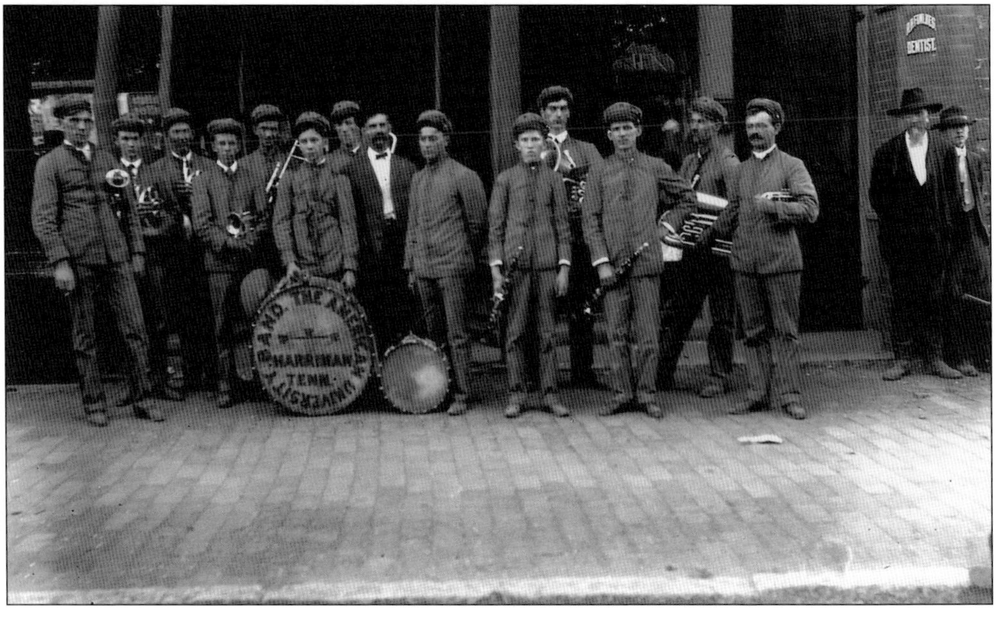

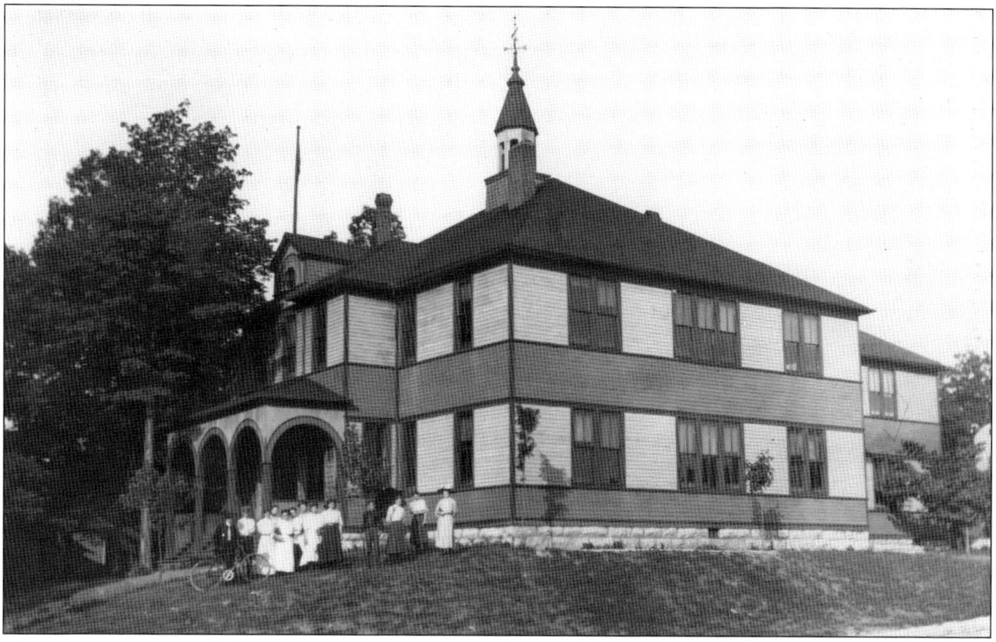

This photograph of Harriman Public School was taken around 1908. The school opened its doors in the fall of 1890, having been paid for and built by the East Tennessee Land Company. At that time, the city was not yet incorporated and thus had no tax revenue to fund schools, so the school received funding from the company for its first two years. It graduated its first class in 1891. The school was located between Clinton and Trenton Streets on Crescent Street. First Presbyterian Church stands there at present, but faces Clinton Street.

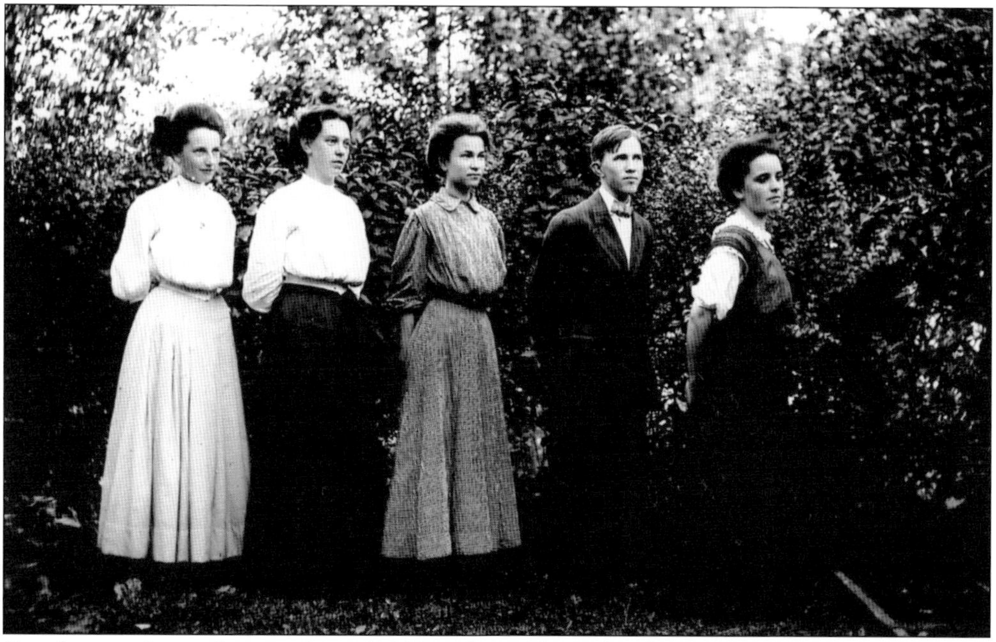

Seen here is the graduating class of 1908 at the public high school in Harriman. The graduates were (not in order) Myrtle Cooper, Elmer Deatherage, Frances Harsh, Margaret Henninger, and Maude Treadwell. The school's original colors were blue and orange.

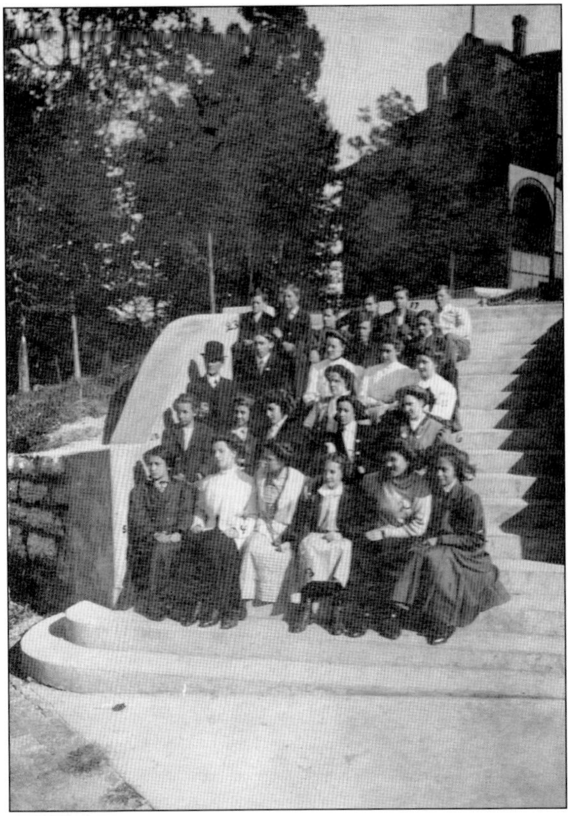

Harriman's eighth grade class was photographed in front of the Harriman school on November 1, 1909. The steps are now located on Trenton Street, behind the First Presbyterian Church.

Second and third grade students at the first Harriman School are posing on the corner of Clinton and Crescent Streets. Lucille Treadwell Newman donated this picture to the Harriman Heritage Museum. She is in the second row, fourth from the right.

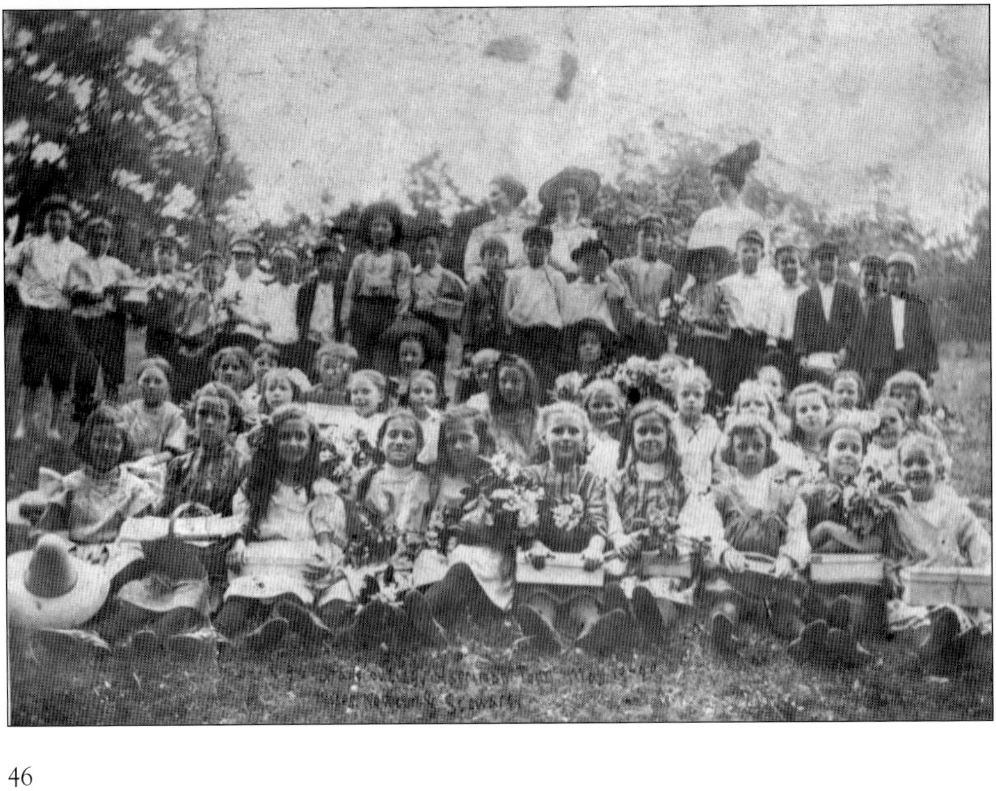

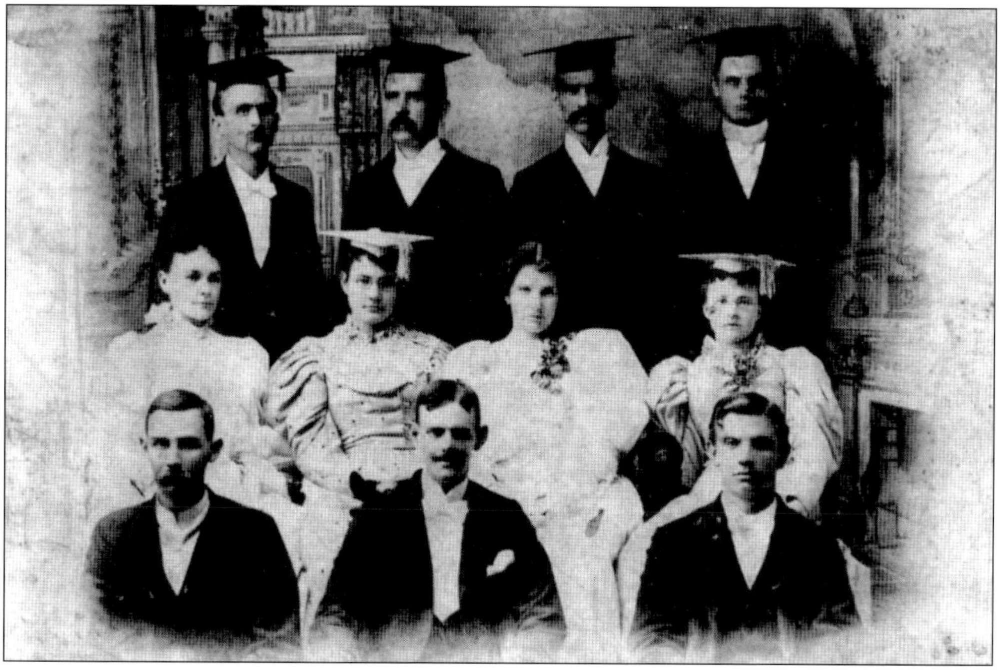

This turn-of-the-century photography most likely depicts a graduating class from American University. The university enrolled as many as 345 students at its peak, and had over 200 students at the time it folded in 1908.

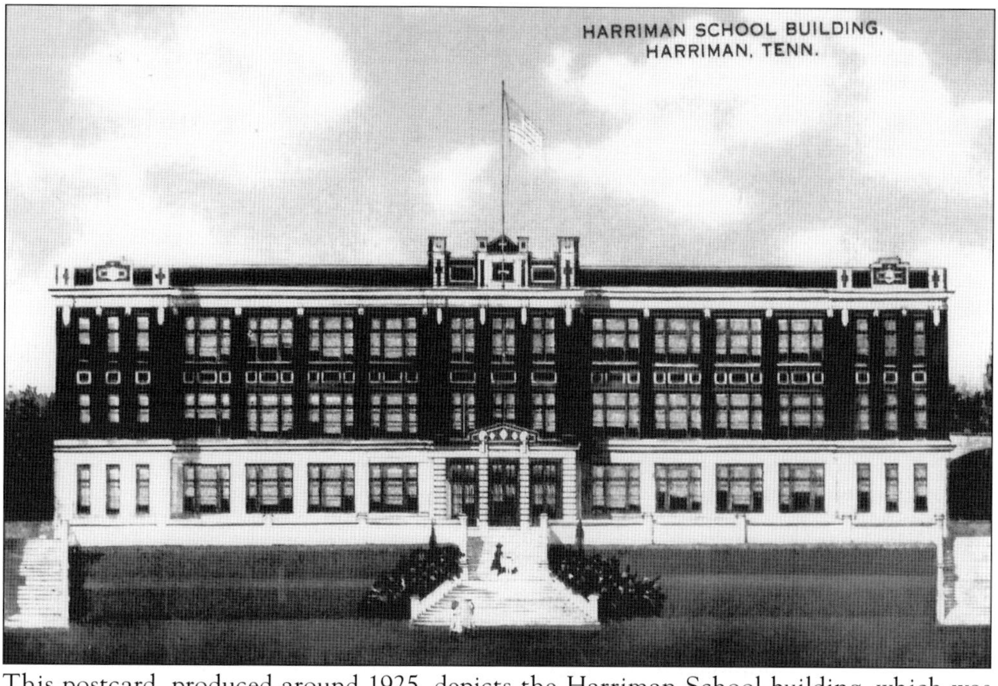

This postcard, produced around 1925, depicts the Harriman School building, which was constructed in 1917. The school was located at the corner of Roane and Georgia Streets on the north end of the city. It would serve students until 1938, when it was replaced with a new building due to overcrowding.

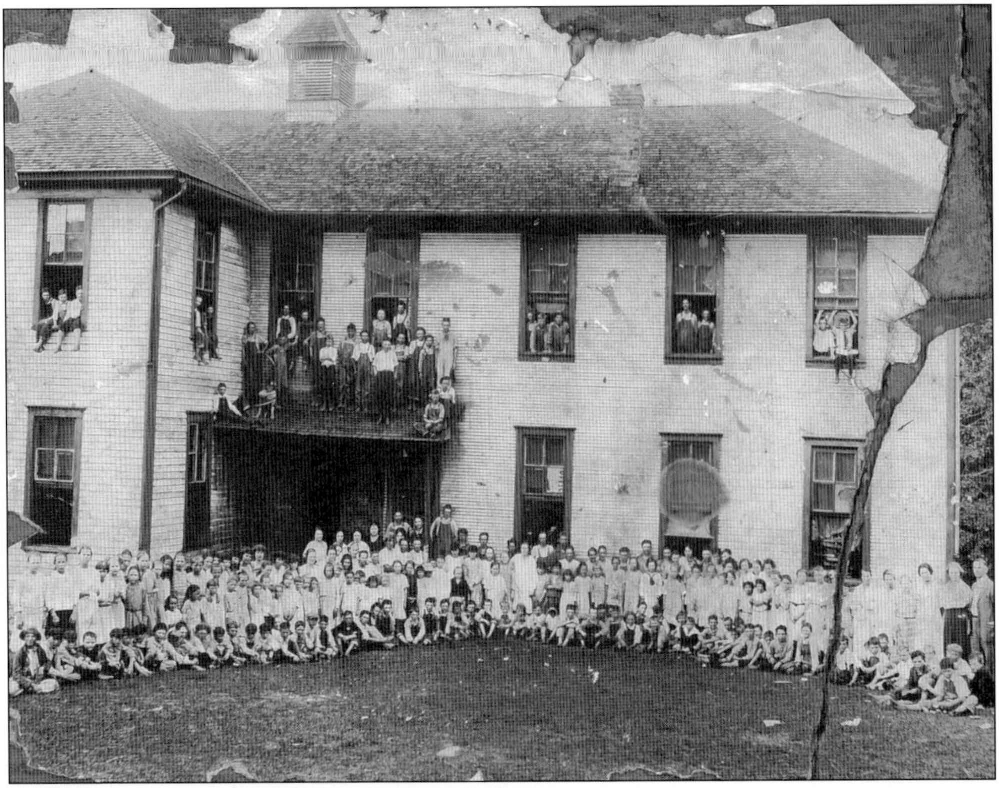

South Harriman High School is shown here in 1914. As this photograph demonstrates, overcrowding was a problem for the school. It was located on School Street in South Harriman. South Harriman would continue to have its own high school until the 1960s, when it was merged with Harriman High.

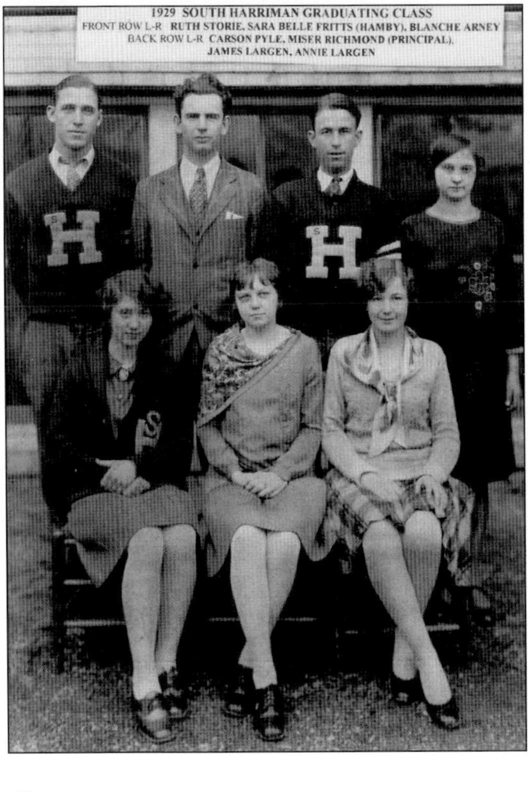

The South Harriman High graduating class of 1929 was entering adulthood at a difficult time. They had already survived the flood, and the Great Depression was just on the horizon. Pictured are, from left to right, (first row) Ruth Storie, Sara Belle Fritts (Hamby), and Blanche Arney; (second row) Carson Pyle, Principal Richmond, James Largen, and Annie Largen.

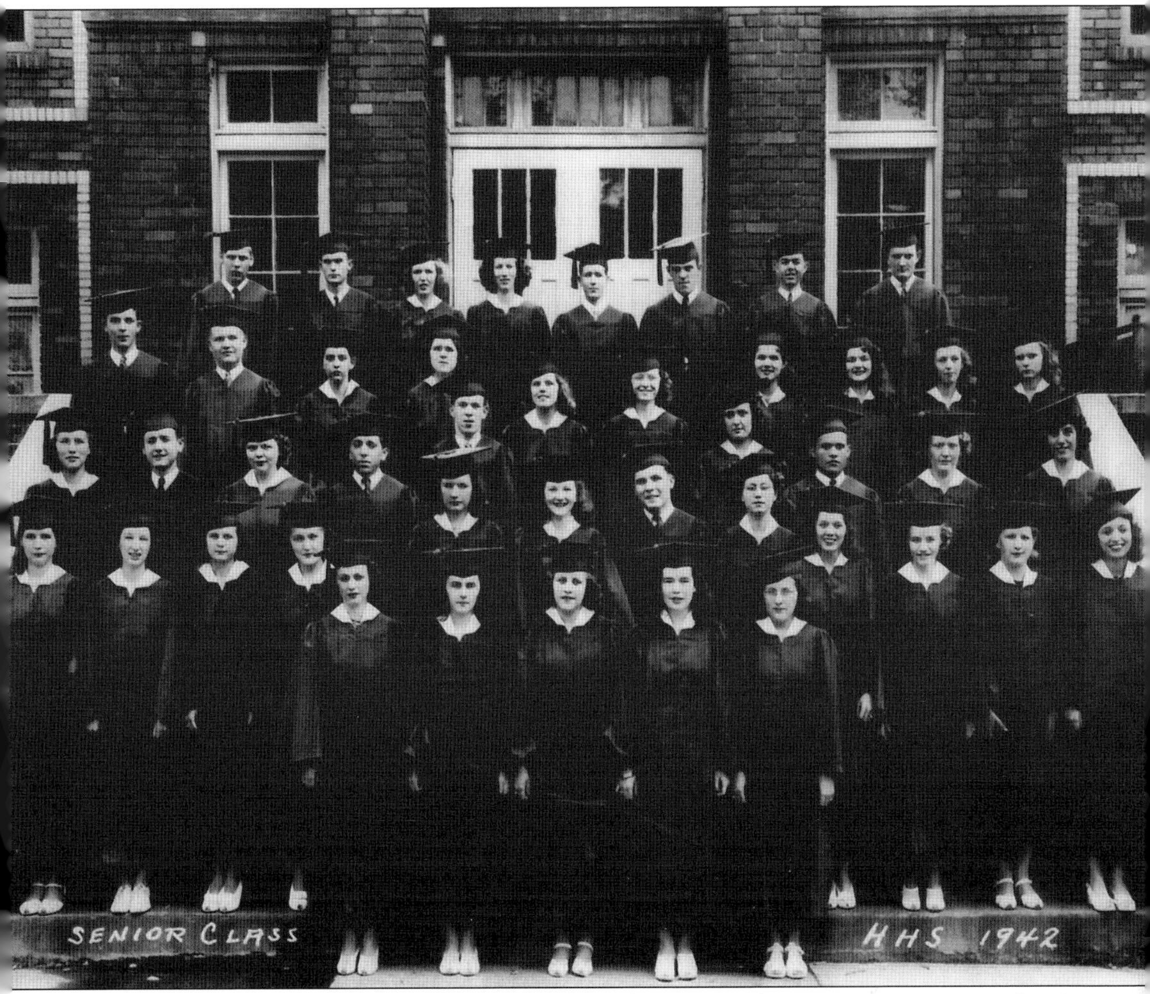

This is the Harriman High School graduating class of 1942. Another generation coming of age in a difficult time, as World War II ravaged much of the globe. Many of the students would soon find themselves on foreign battlefields.

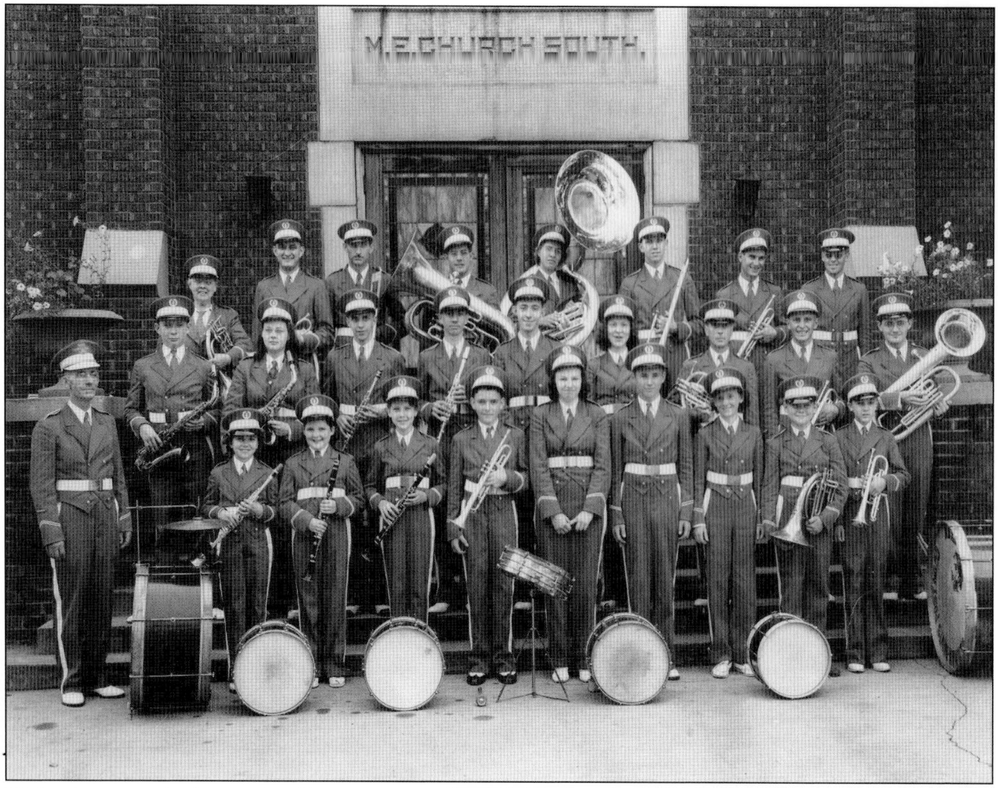

This photograph shows the Harriman band in 1942, the first year they had uniforms, posing in front of the Harriman Methodist Church. Pictured from left to right are (first row) Prof. Ingmar Skatrod, Mary Gusta Hamilton, unidentified, Betty Jo Loggins, John Shannon, Marguerite Miller, Jimmy Carroll, Myra Harding, John Palmer, and Bobby Rutherford; (second row) unidentified, Betty Suddath, Richard Gallaher, Ernest Foster, Howard Marsh, Martha Jean Robinson, Ralph Patton, Alois Palso, and Max Johnson; (third row) Mrs. Skatrod, Carlisle Evans Jr., Rev. John Paxter Howes, Jack Allen, Mildred Ooegaard, Milton Marney, James Palko, and Louis Goddard.

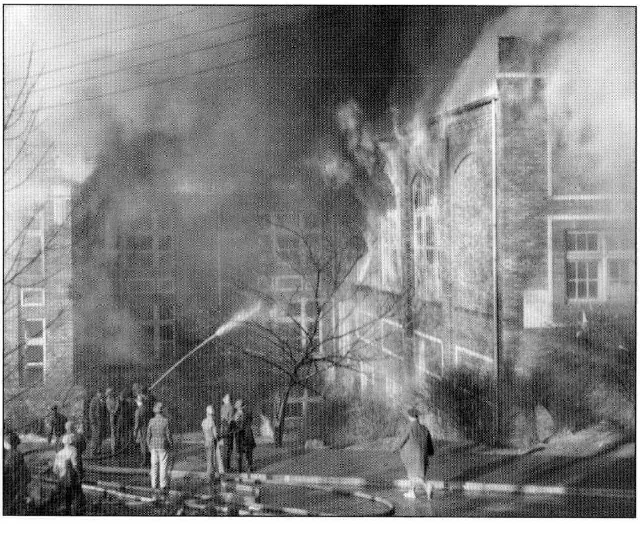

Harriman High School burned on January 31, 1945. The fire broke out during a band concert, and the band continued to play as students were orderly evacuated, band members being the last to exit. The band's calm reaction received notice and praise by many in the community. The cause of the fire was accidental, originating under the auditorium stage.

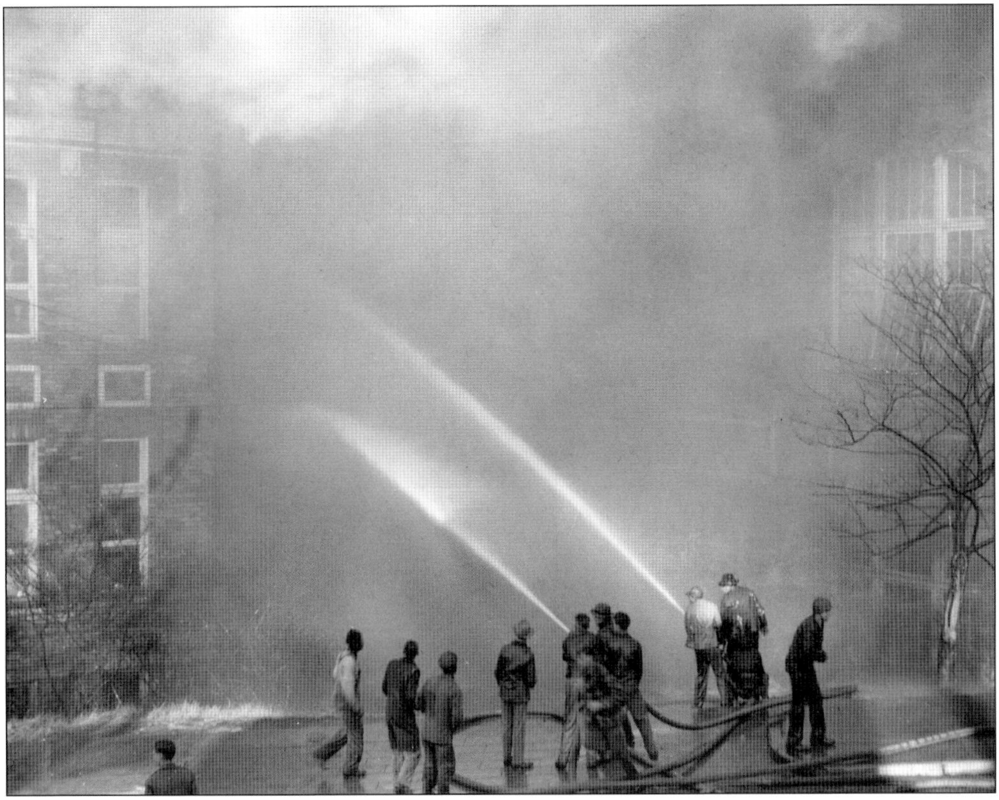

Firefighters fought to put out the blaze, but the fire consumed most of the school. The overworked firefighters had already responded to two other fires that day, one that morning at Howard's Café on Carter Street and another in the early afternoon that destroyed Lon Mee's barn. Firefighters responded from Harriman, Rockwood, Oak Ridge, and Lenoir City.

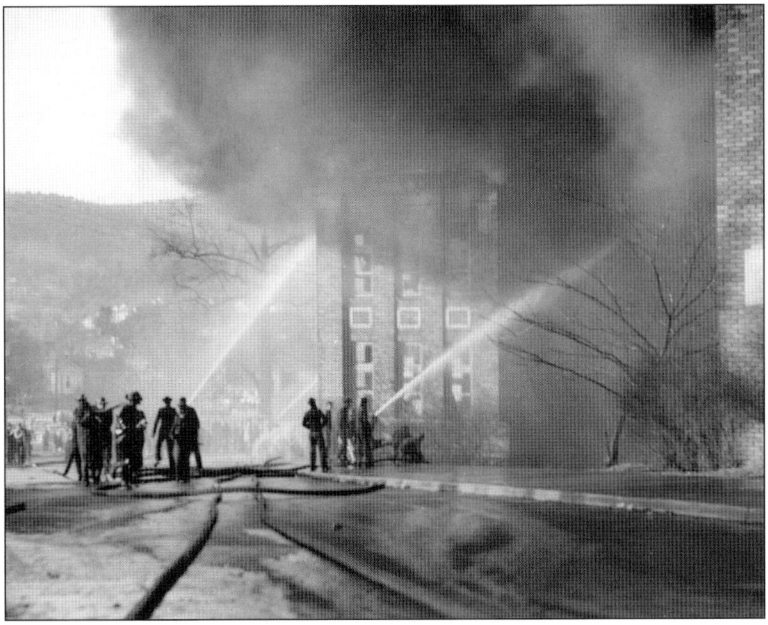

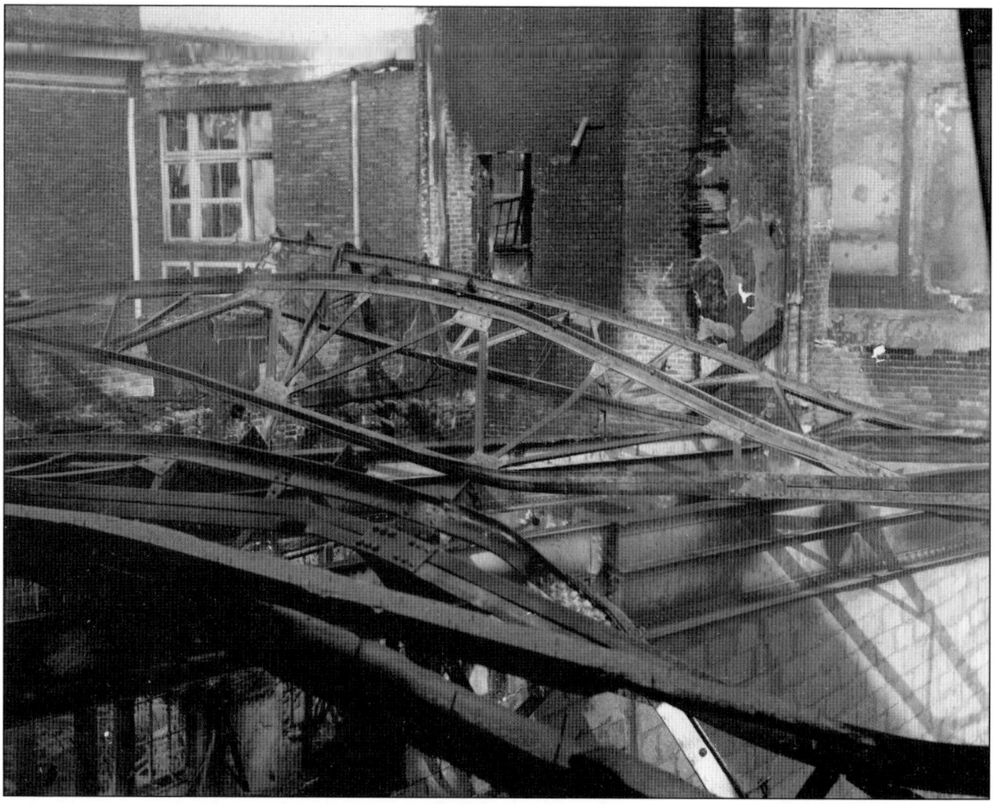

School records were saved, but the fire destroyed almost everything else. Damages were estimated at nearly $100,000, quite a sizable sum in 1945.

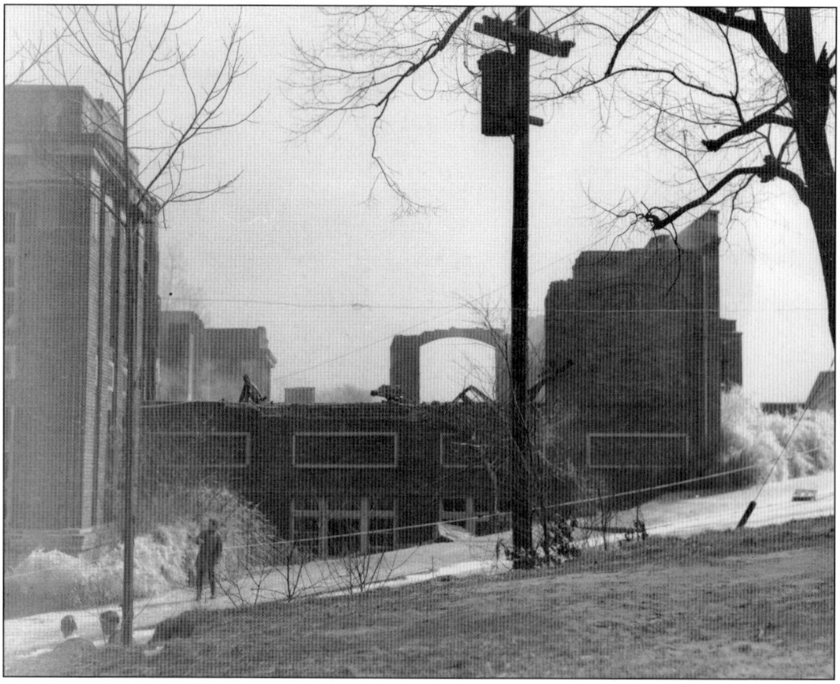

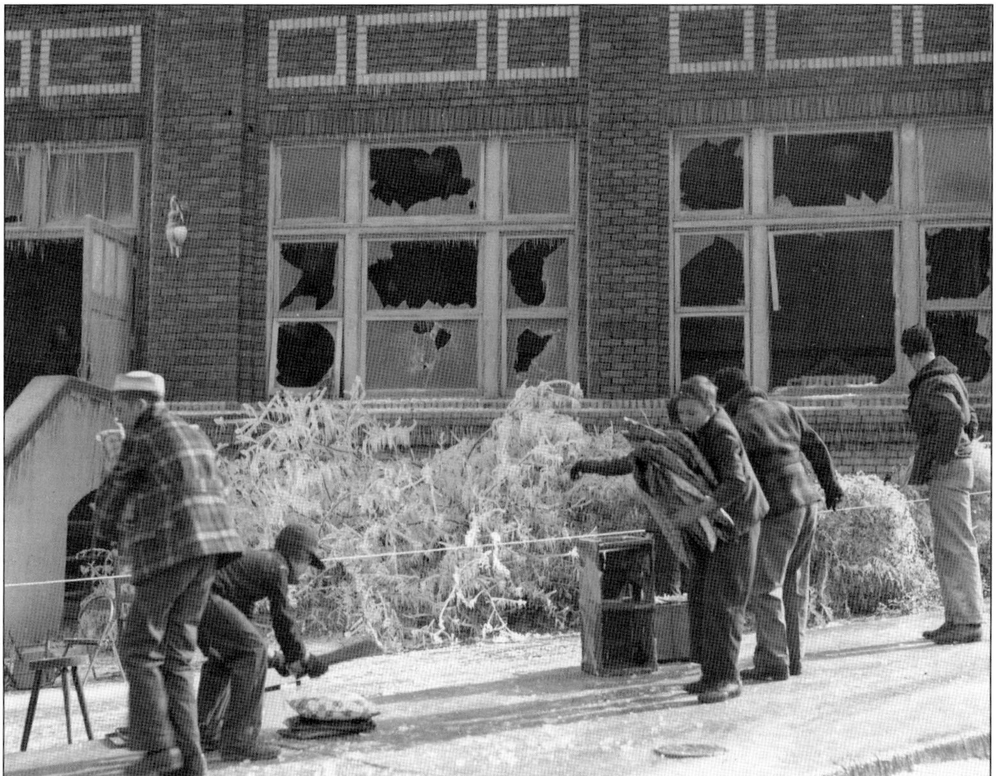

Students sift through the ruins of Harriman High School after a 1945 fire. Overcrowding had been a problem before the fire, and the destruction of the building left administrators scrambling for classroom space. Classes would resume at Harriman Methodist Church, Trenton Street Baptist Church, First Christian Church, and First Presbyterian Church.

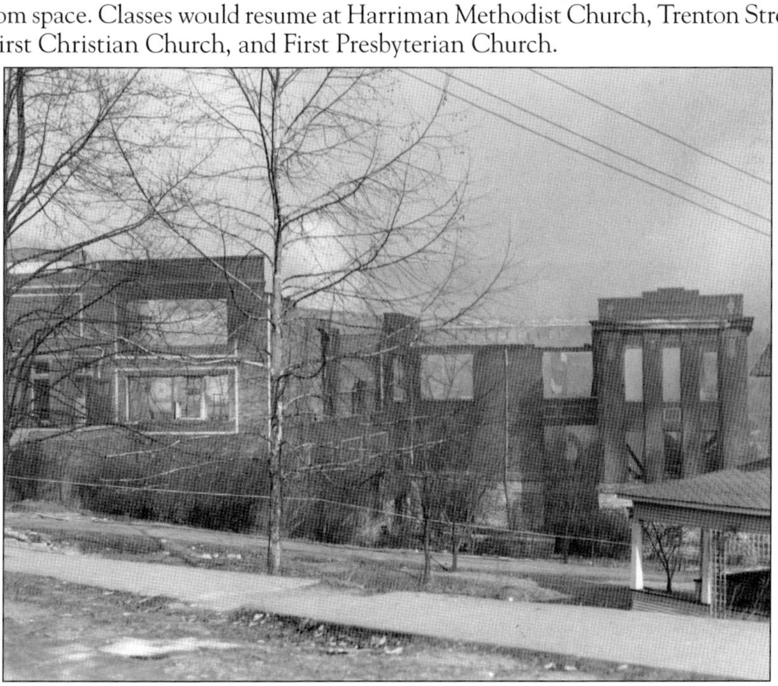

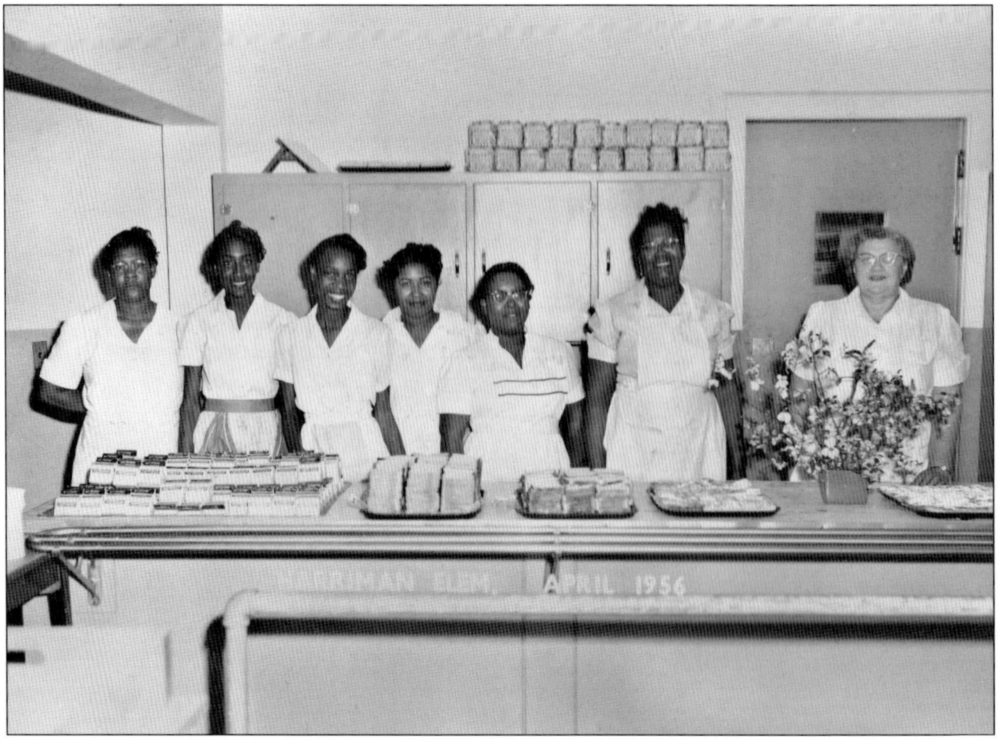

Harriman Elementary cafeteria workers are pictured here in April 1956. Emma Melhorn is on the far right.

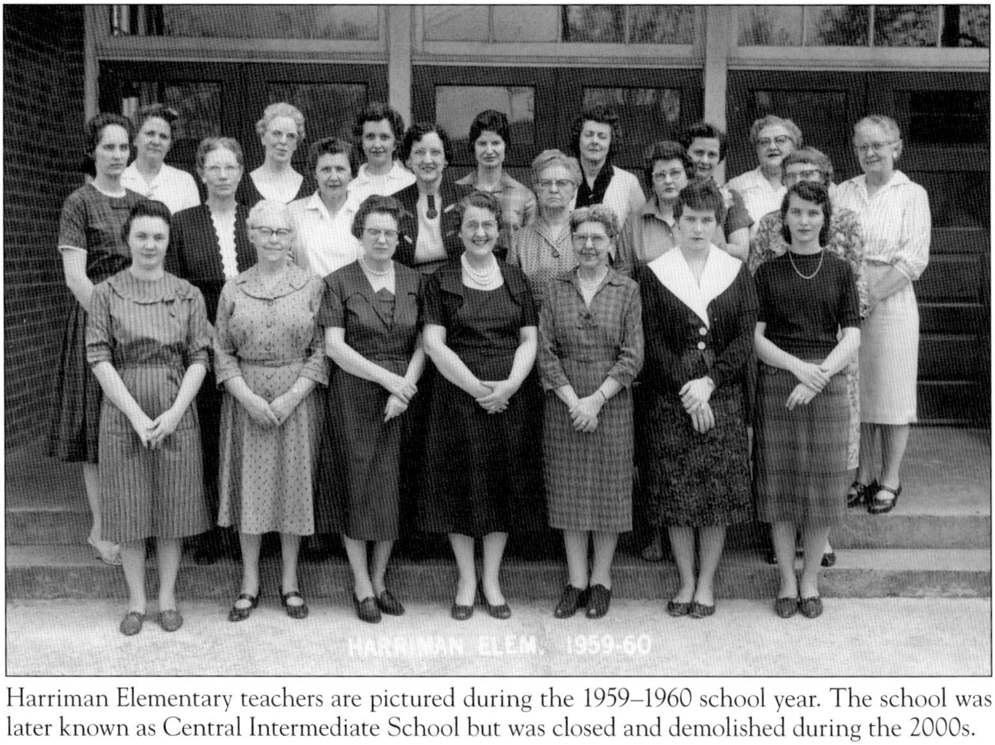

Harriman Elementary teachers are pictured during the 1959–1960 school year. The school was later known as Central Intermediate School but was closed and demolished during the 2000s.

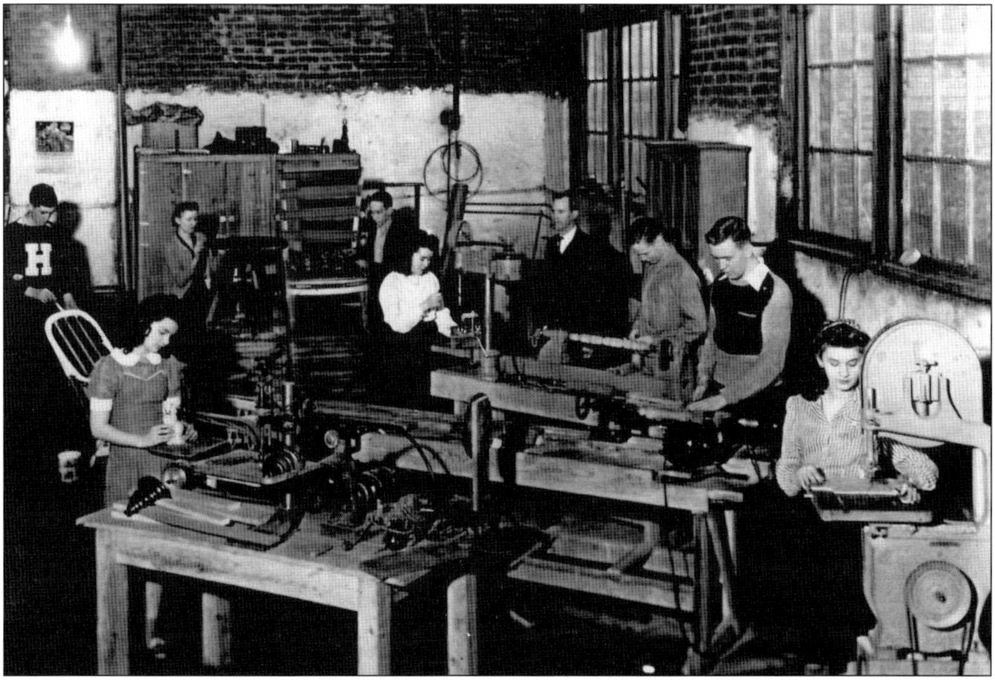

Shop class was offered at Harriman High School, shown here around the 1930s. The class was held in the room underneath the auditorium and was probably taught by J.C. Quinn.

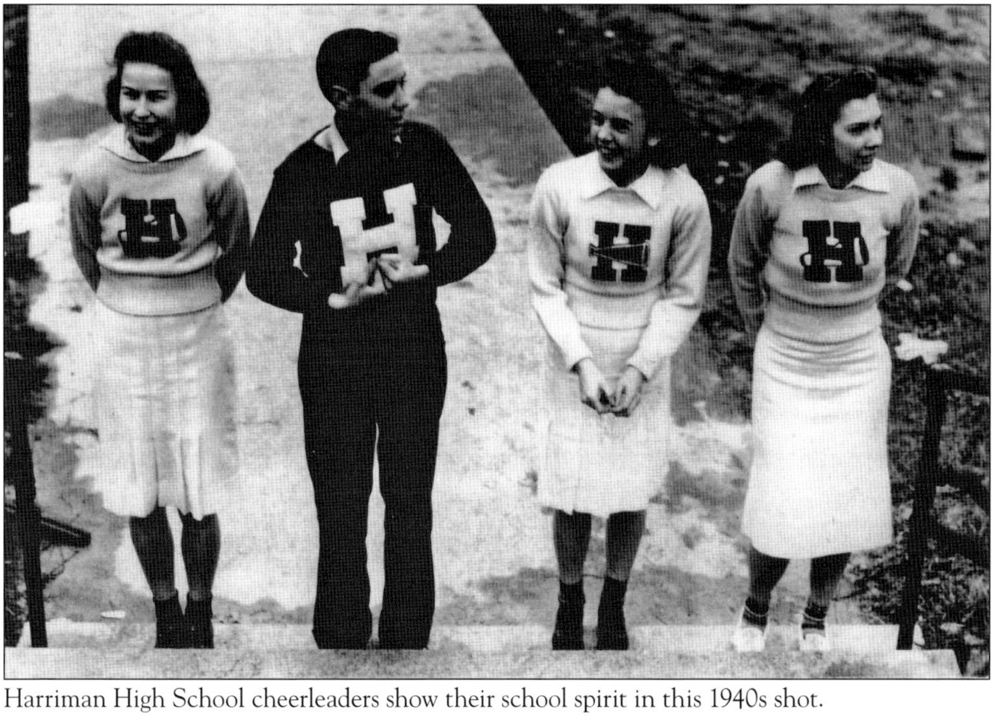

Harriman High School cheerleaders show their school spirit in this 1940s shot.

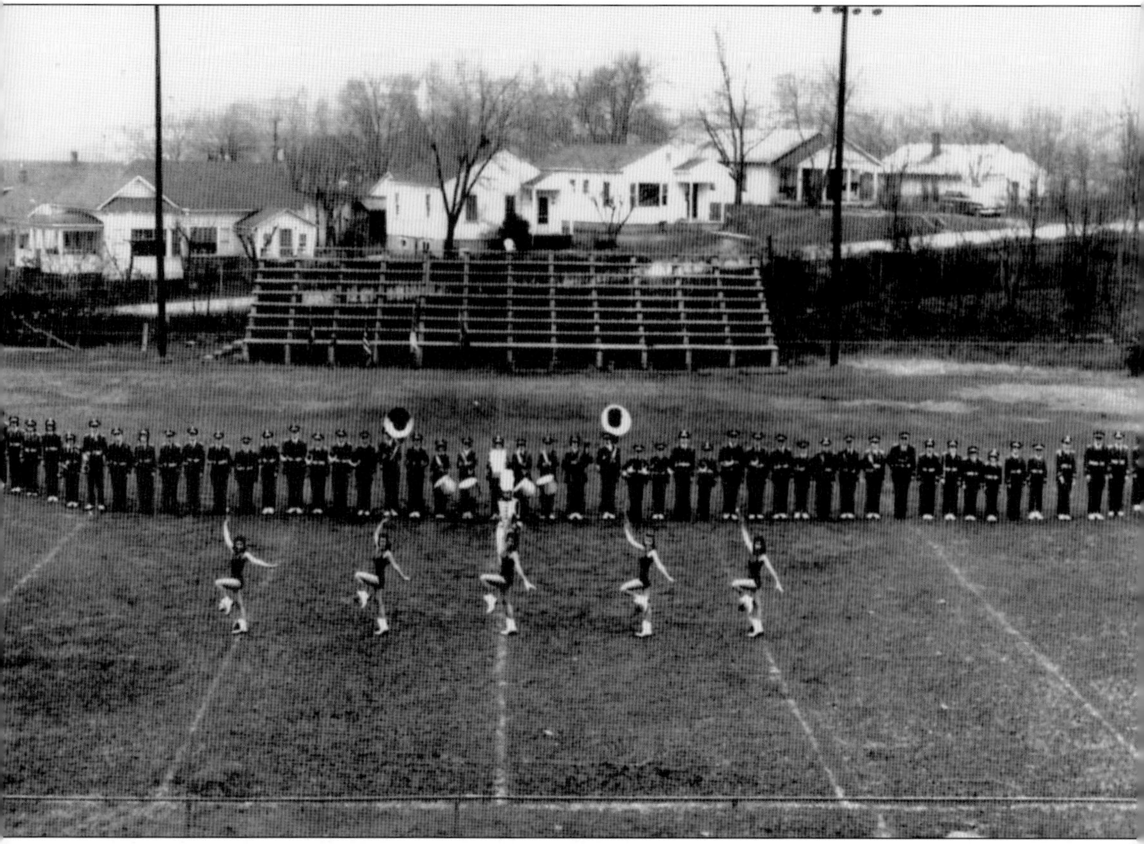

Harriman High School's Rhapsody in Blue Band performs on Wallace-Black field, probably during the 1960s. James "Uncle Willie" Williamson became band director in 1959. Over the years, he became a legend in Harriman, teaching a generation of students the value of music.

Five

Business and Industry

Harriman, founded by a land company, was envisioned from the beginning as an industrial city, intentionally located with river and railroad access for the purpose of business. Even before it was a city, Harriman, then known as Shacktown, was home to several banks and other businesses.

In the 20th century, Harriman became most closely associated with the hosiery industry, which would remain its most prominent industry for many decades. Tom Tarwater, whose father owned a hosiery mill in Rockwood, decided to open a mill in Harriman along with several other business associates, and Harriman Hosiery Mills was chartered in 1912. Production began the following year. Over the next several decades the mill boomed, becoming the second largest manufacturer of seamless stockings in the United States by 1944, when it was purchased by textile giant Burlington Mills of North Carolina.

In 1949, a second hosiery mill was established in Harriman. Roane Hosiery, which was led by the same Tarwater family that had been instrumental in founding and managing Harriman Hosiery, experienced great success in the 1950s. By the 1960s, the mill employed over a thousand workers, the majority of them women.

The third major employer during this time was the Meade Paper Mill, located on the Emory River. Established in 1929, the plant seemingly got off to a poor start when the Flood of 1929 struck just a few days before the plant was slated to begin production. In spite of its inauspicious beginnings, the plant went on to flourish, with an annual payroll of a million dollars to its 145 employees in 1964.

Unfortunately, none of these plants remain in Harriman today. Harriman Hosiery closed in 1985 at the cost of 1,200 jobs. Roane Hosiery and Meade followed suit in the 1990s, greatly diminishing Harriman's industrial base.

Today, the former sites of Harriman Hosiery/Burlington, Roane Hosiery, and Meade lay abandoned—remnants of a once vibrant manufacturing sector.

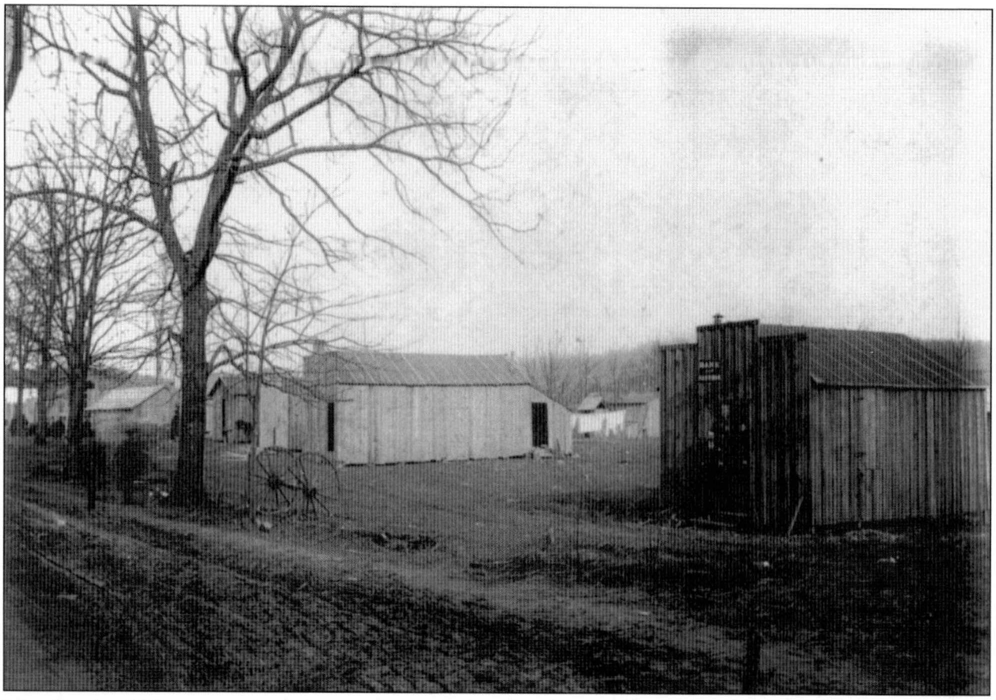

The Bank of Harriman (right) was the city's first bank. Established in a shack in March 1890, it had a capital stock of $50,000. Walter C. Harriman served as the first president.

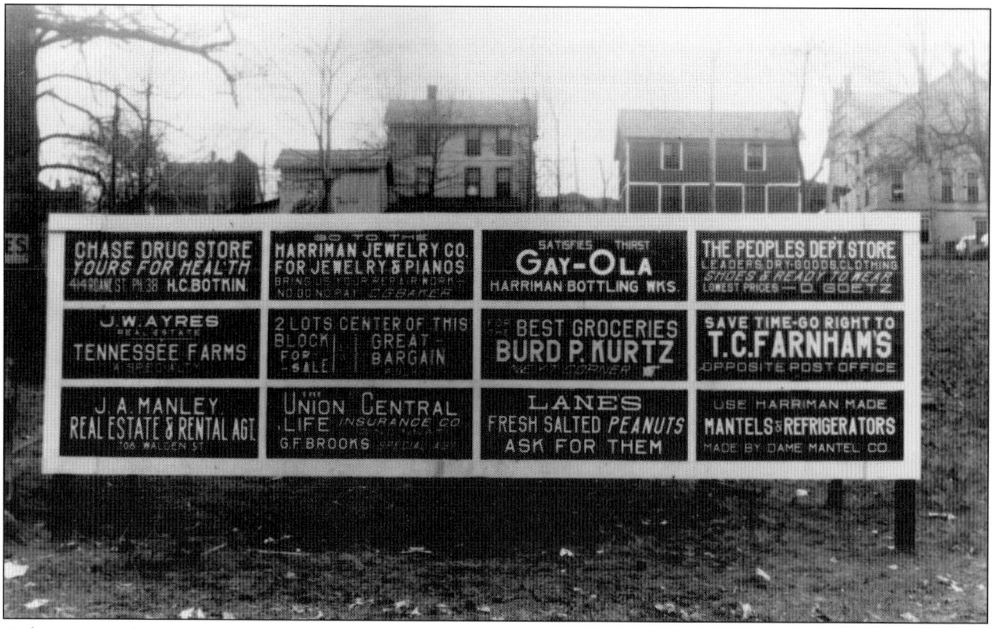

Advertising for various Harriman businesses is shown in this photograph, probably taken around 1920. Many of Harriman's most prominent early businesses are represented here, including Chase Drug Store, Harriman Jewelry Company, T.C. Farnham's, Burd P. Kurtz's Groceries, and others.

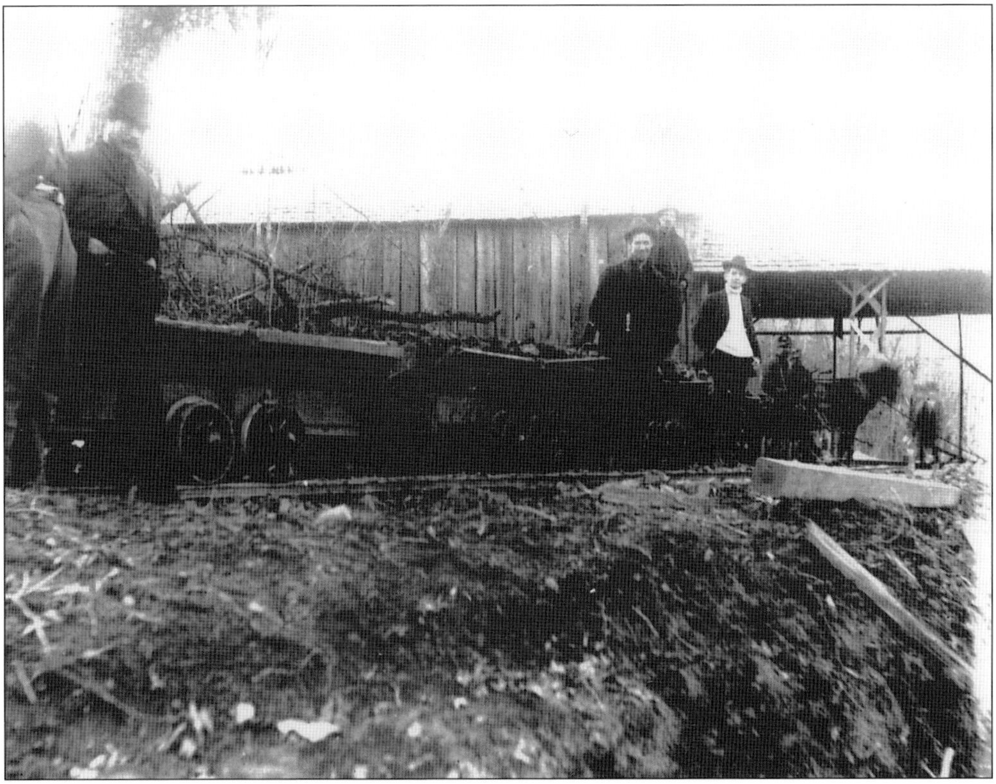

Byrd Mines, near West Hills, is pictured here. In the early 1890s, the East Tennessee Mining Company was established as a subsidiary of the East Tennessee Land Company to mine iron in Harriman. Harriman's founders were so optimistic about mining they promoted it as a potential "iron city" and envisioned a second city at Deermont (near Camp Austin in Morgan County) to accelerate the mining. The company claimed to have an "inexhaustible" amount of coal and iron ore, using this to lure potential buyers. The Byrd Mine closed in 1904.

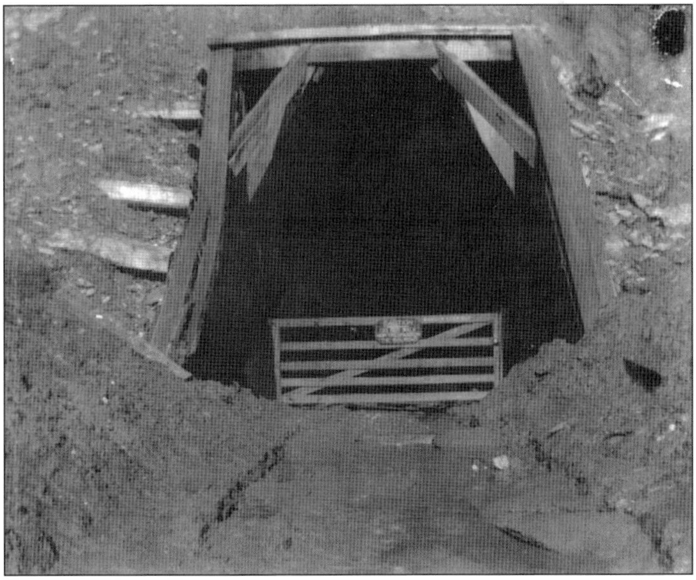

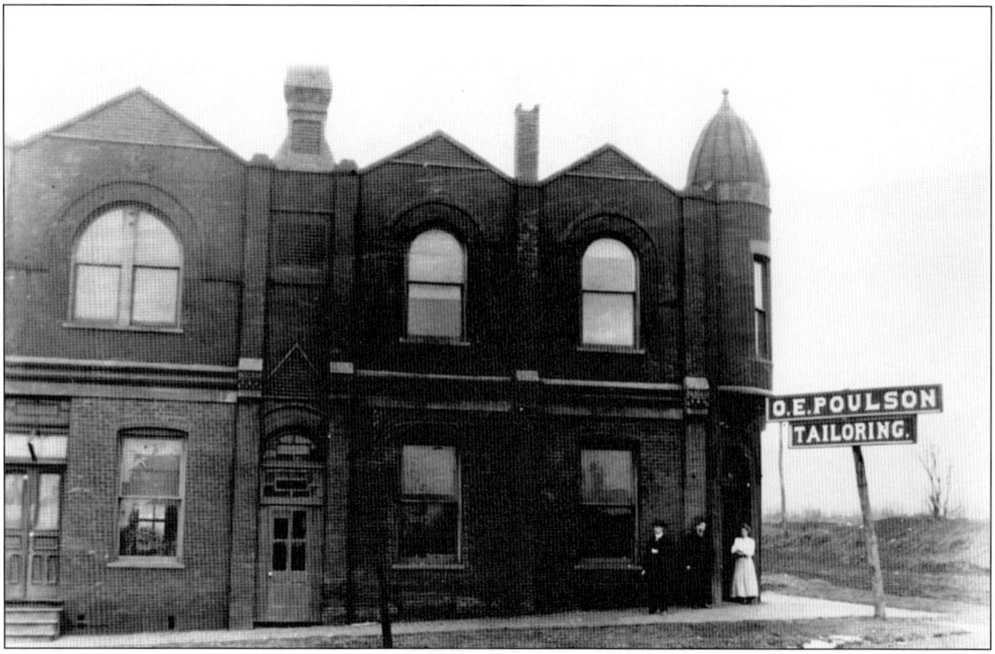

This photograph, probably taken around 1907, shows the building on the corner of Walden and Devonia Streets, which was occupied by O.E. Poulson Tailoring at that time. Later, it would be home to Simmons Photo Studio, Dr. Jay Sadler, and others. The building no longer stands; formerly, it was the parking lot of Drs. Greene, Greene, and Gunter.

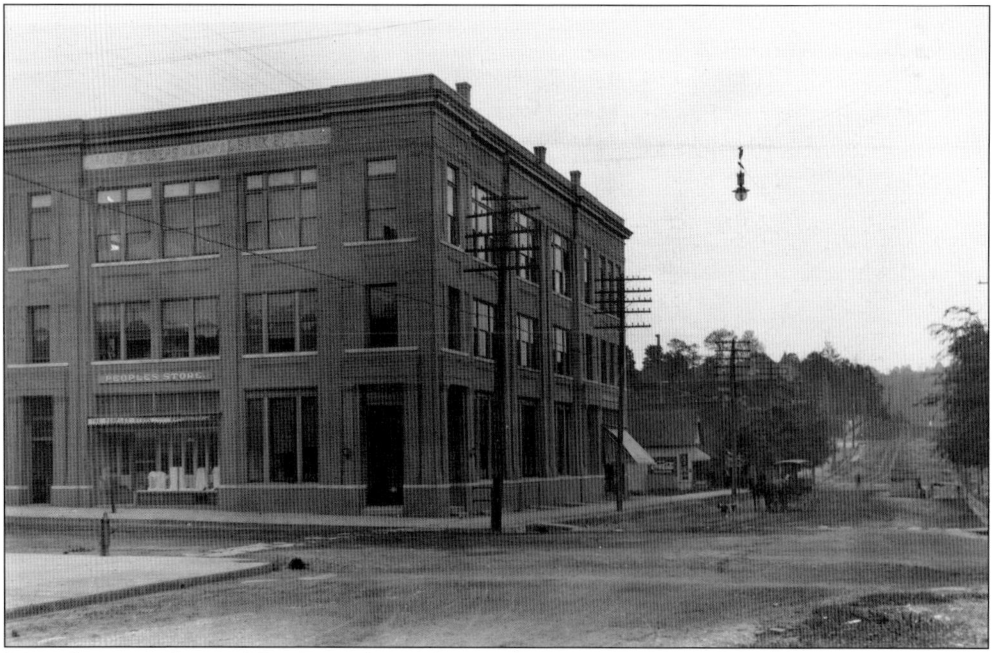

Manufacturers National Bank was located at 402 Roane Street and is shown here around 1907. One of the earliest banks in Harriman, it was established in the early 1890s and continued to operate into the 1920s. Later the site of Bilbrey's Furniture, and currently the parking lot of Regions Bank, the building no longer stands.

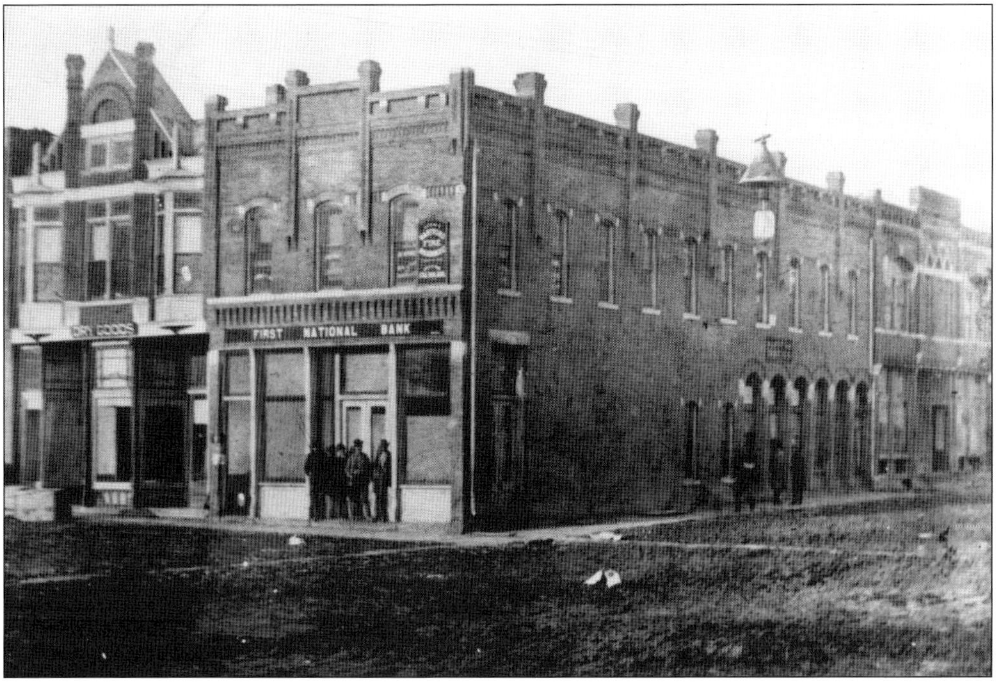

This photograph, most likely taken during the 1890s, shows First National Bank of Harriman. Established by 1891, First National was one of Harriman's first financial institutions. Walter C. Harriman, after whose father Harriman was named, served as the president.

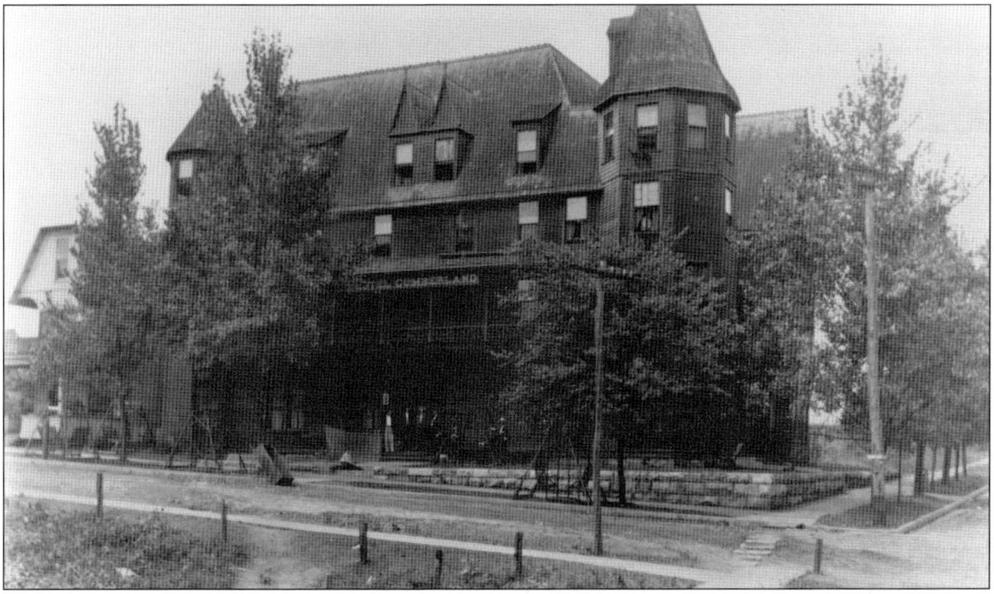

This is what the exterior of the Cumberland Hotel looked like in 1909. Construction on the Cumberland began in 1890 by private financiers but was taken over by the East Tennessee Land Company, which completed it and opened it to the public in 1891. A luxurious hotel with steam heat and baths, Cumberland advertised itself as "Everything First-class." The hotel remained in business until the 1920s. The building, no longer standing, was at the corner of Devonia and Queen Streets (later the site of Harriman Hospital).

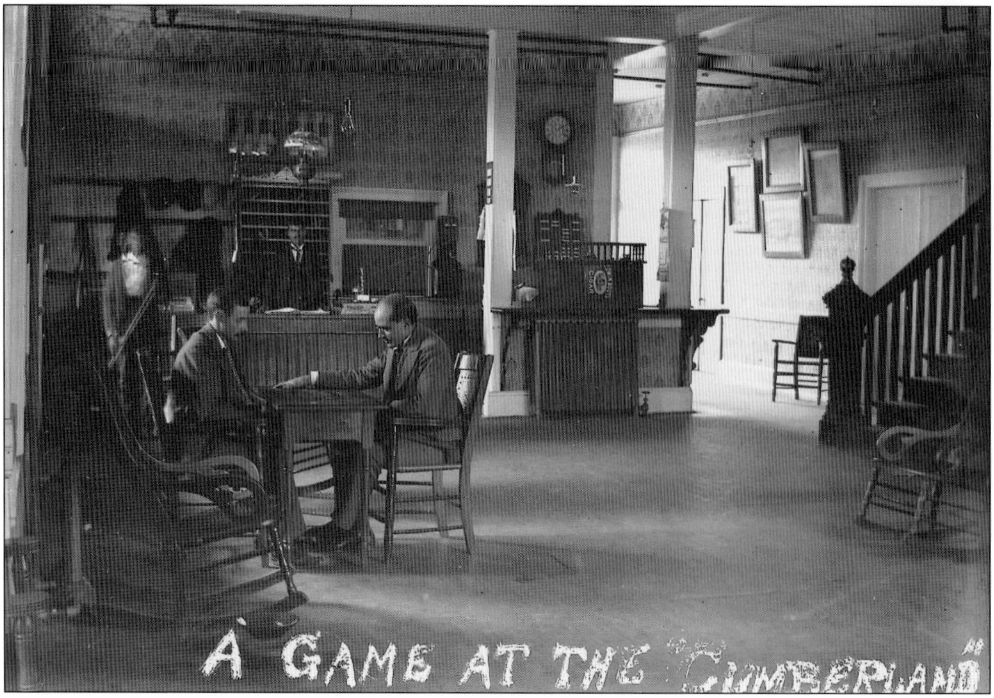

The inside of the Cumberland Hotel was a swanky center for social activities during Harriman's early years. In the photograph above, taken around 1906, two patrons enjoy a game of checkers. Below, the dining room is decorated for the holidays around Christmas 1908.

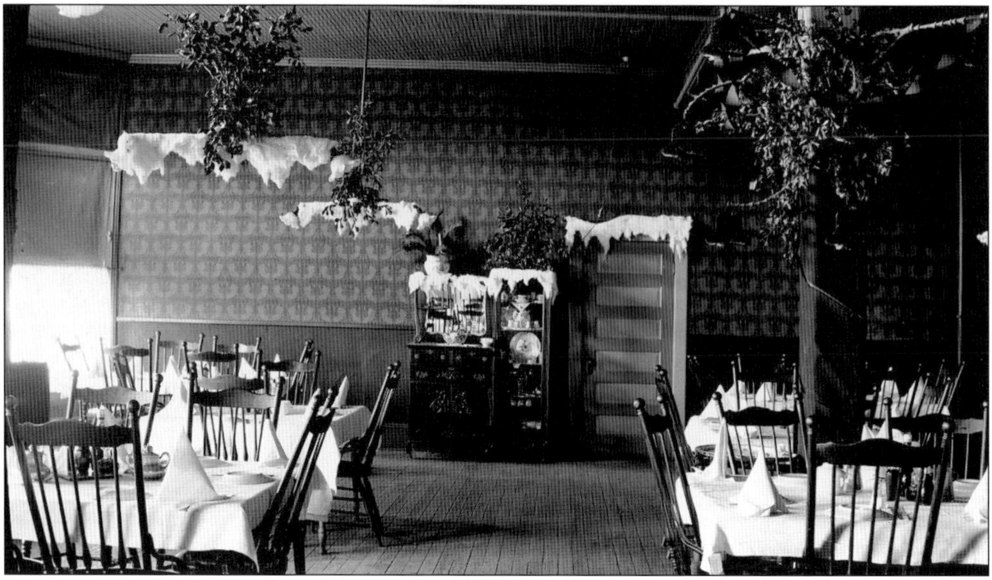

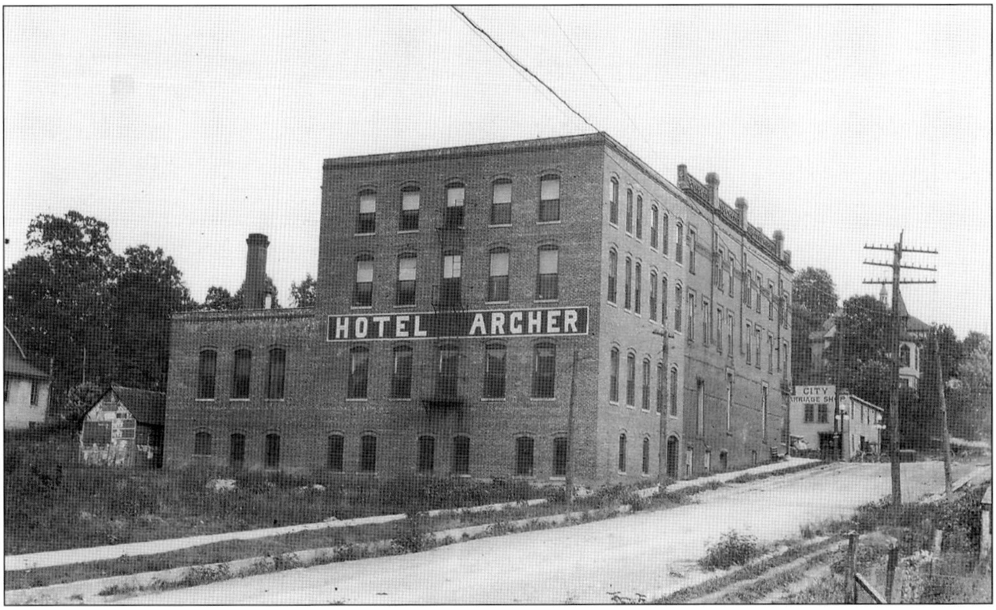

Hotel Archer was located at the corner of Roane and Crescent Streets. Originally established in 1893 as the Virginia Hotel, it was advertised as the "only brick hotel in the city" and claimed to be "ABSOLUTELY fire-proof." It became known as the Archer Hotel (after its then-owner) in the early 1900s.

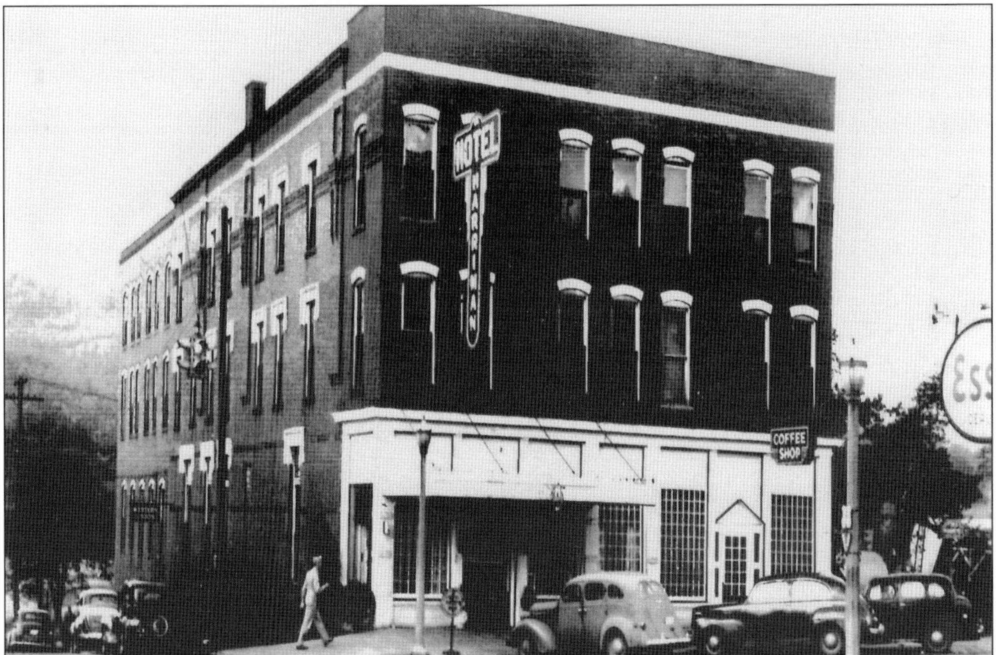

The Harriman Hotel was formerly the Hotel Archer (located on the corner of Roane and Crescent Streets). The hotel assumed its name on August 1, 1920, when it was purchased by a group of businessmen who formed the Harriman Hotel Company. It remained open until the 1970s. This photograph was probably taken in the early 1940s.

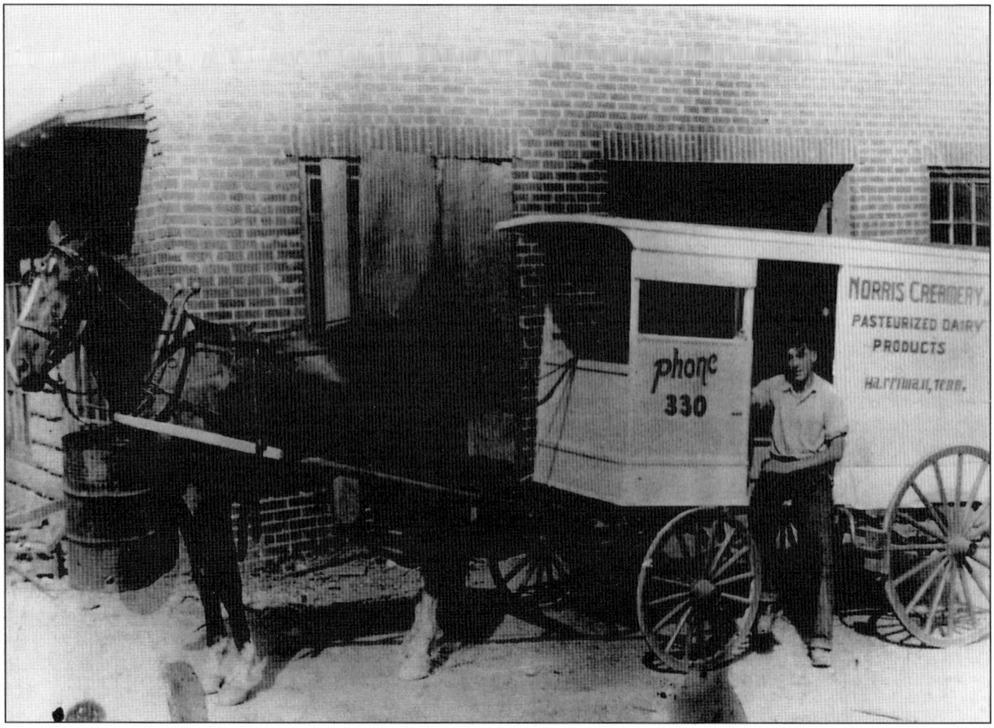

Norris Creamery provided milk and dairy products to generations of area residents. Located at the corner of Roane and Crescent Streets (formerly the site of the Goodyear Store), Norris Creamery remained in business until around 1980. This early 1940s photograph shows a horse-drawn delivery car, which became necessary due to gasoline rationing. The driver is Frank Bowman, and the horse was named Prince.

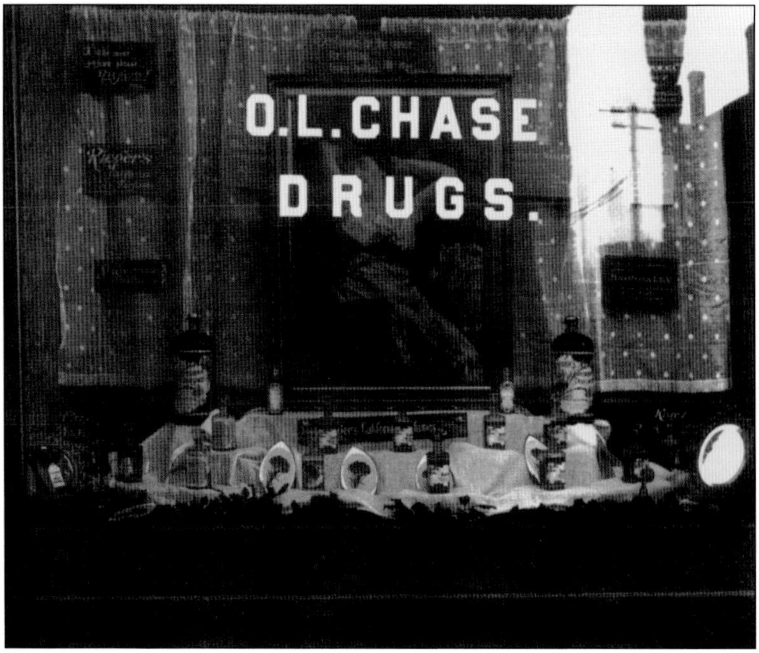

Chase Drug Store opened its doors in downtown Harriman in 1891 and is still in business there today. This photograph shows a display window of the store and was probably taken in the late 1890s or early 1900s.

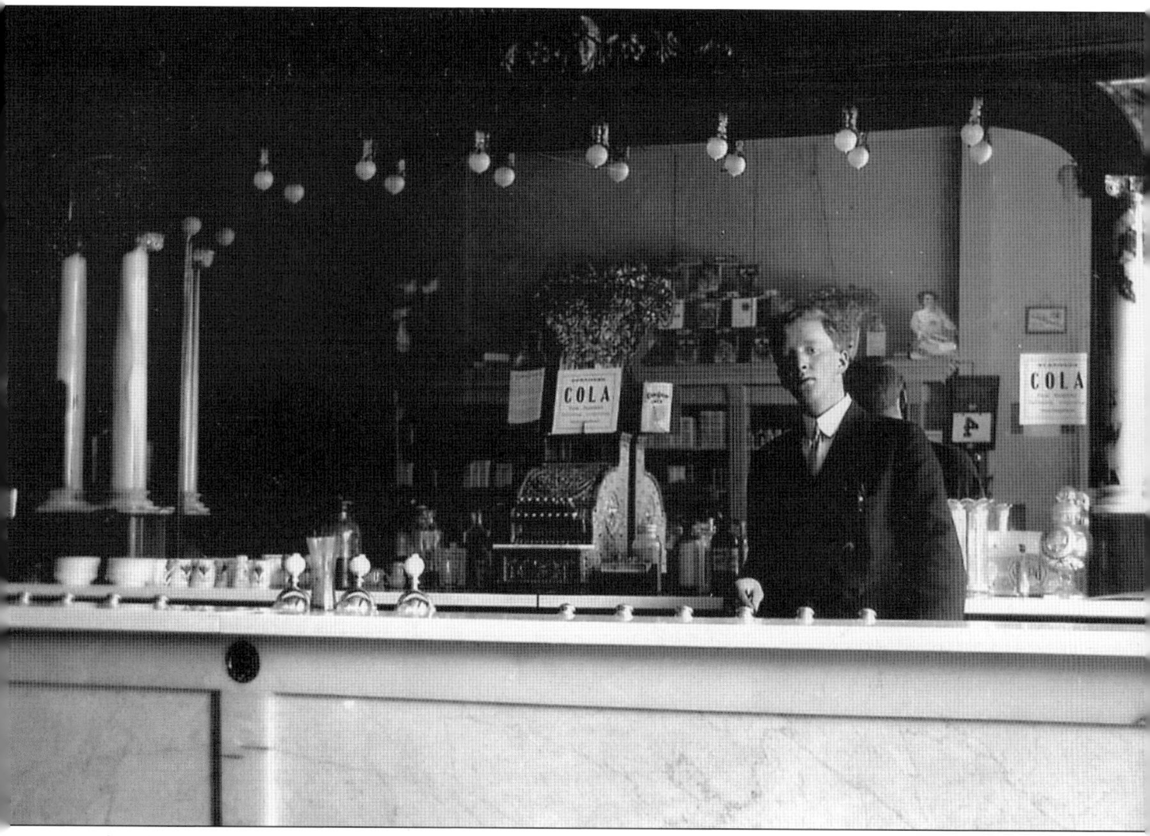

Before being destroyed by a fire, Chase Drug Store was home to a popular restaurant. This 1930s photograph shows the popular soda fountain.

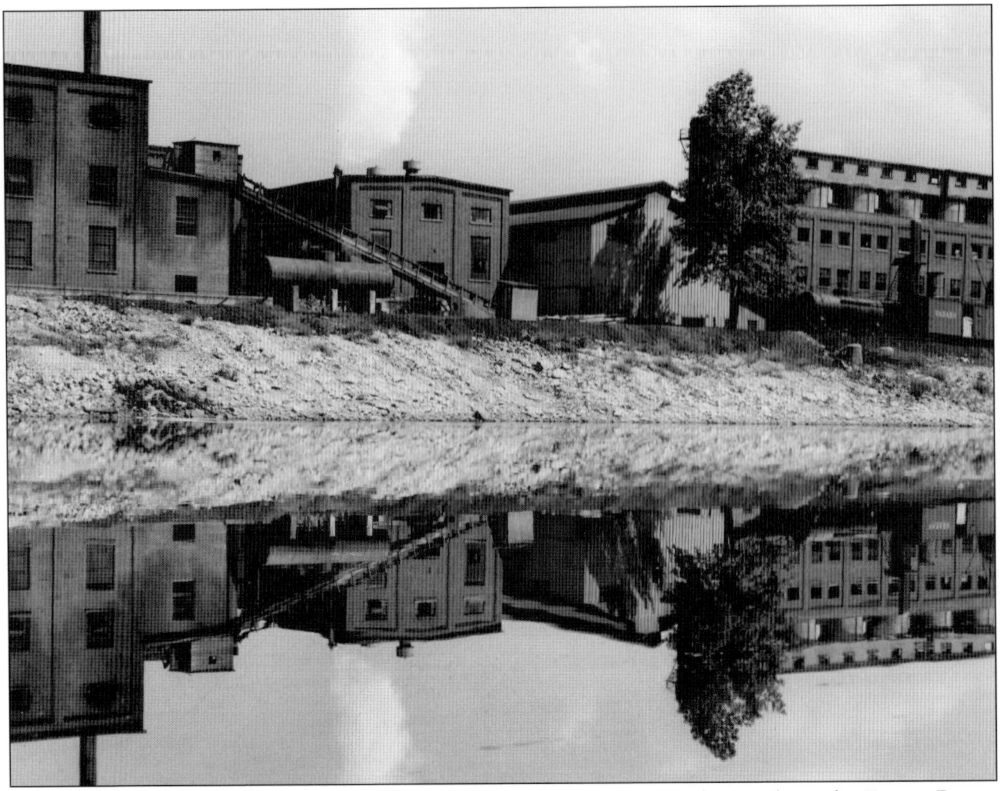

This photograph, probably taken in the 1920s, shows Harriman's industry along the Emory River. Sadly, most of it was destroyed by the Flood of 1929, which, coupled with the stock market crash of the same year, did unspeakable damage to the city.

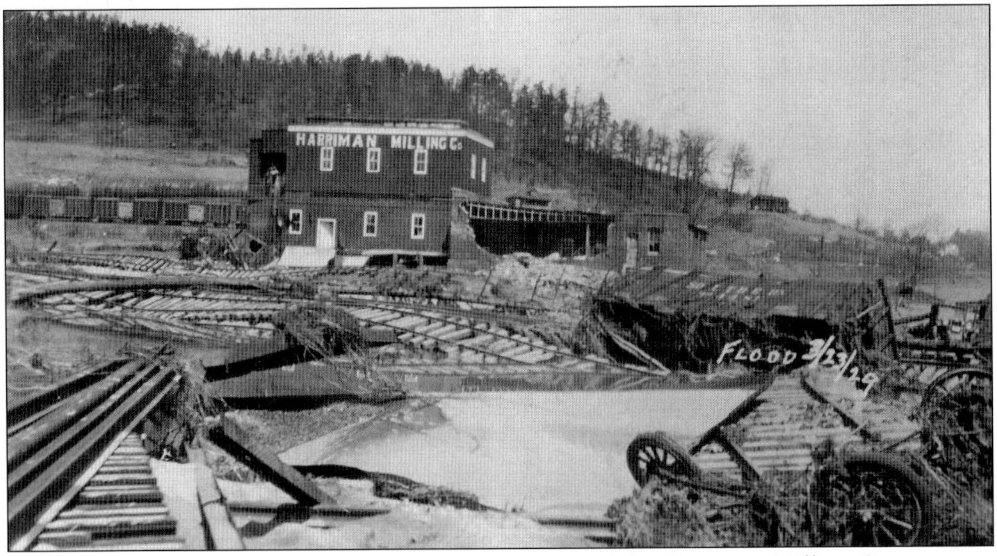

The aftermath of the Flood of 1929 is pictured in front of the Harriman Milling Company on March 23. Originally opened in 1899 as the Emory River Milling Company, and later known as Robinson-Evans, this business recovered from the flood and later from a 1942 fire. It remained in operation until 1965. The building was demolished in 1977.

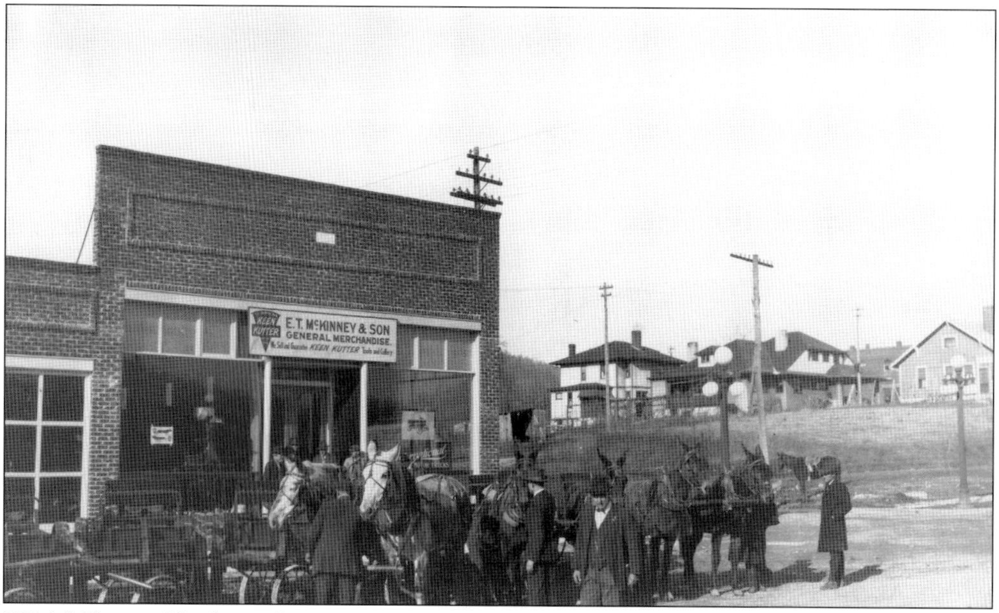

E.T. McKinney Hardware Store was on Roane Street around the turn of the 20th century, at what is presently the site of Christmas Lumber Company. E.T. McKinney served as postmaster in 1909 and was instrumental in securing a post office for Harriman. He also became a charter member of the Harriman Rotary Club in 1919.

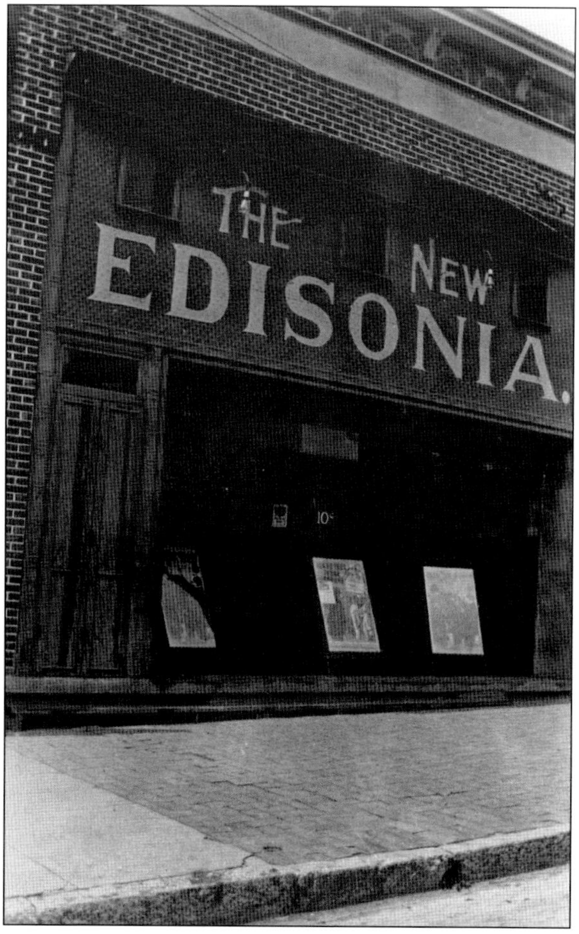

The New Edisonia Theater was on the 500 block of Walden Street. Early motion pictures were controversial, particularly in a city like Harriman. An early penny arcade operator publicly apologized for offending "the sensitivities" of the city, apparently with an inappropriate moving picture. The Edisonia was one of Harriman's first theaters, showing movies on a regular basis by 1909. It would continue to do so into the 1920s.

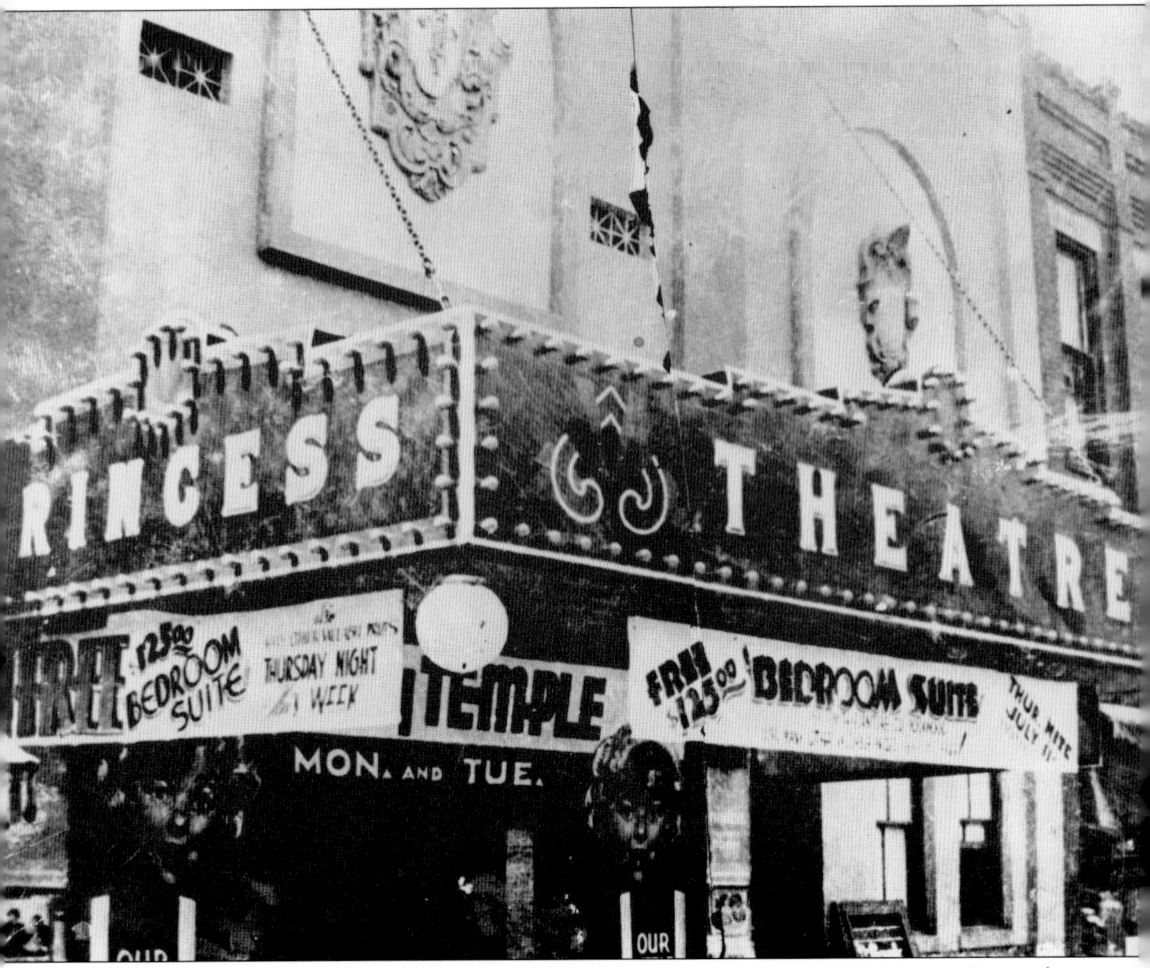

Harriman's most famous theater is the Princess Theatre, which opened for business in September 1926. This 1938 photograph captures the theater not long before a fire destroyed it the following year. The Princess was rebuilt and reopened in November 1939, showing movies for another 60 years. Now owned by the City of Harriman and operated by Roane State Community College, the Princess Theatre remains an important part of Harriman's cultural life.

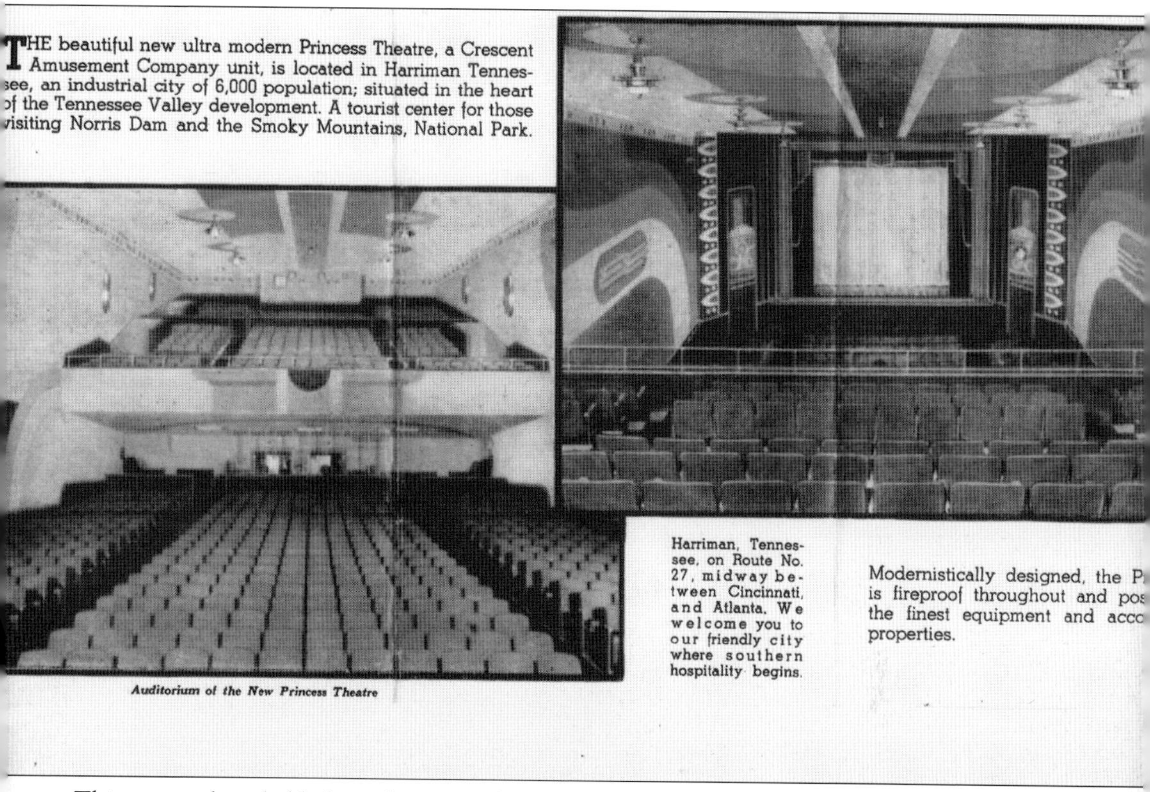

This postcard, probably from the 1940s, depicts the layout of the interior of the Princess Theatre and encourages tourists to visit Harriman. African Americans were required to sit in the balcony during the Jim Crow era, but following its end, the balcony became a popular place for all patrons. By the 1990s, the balcony was closed.

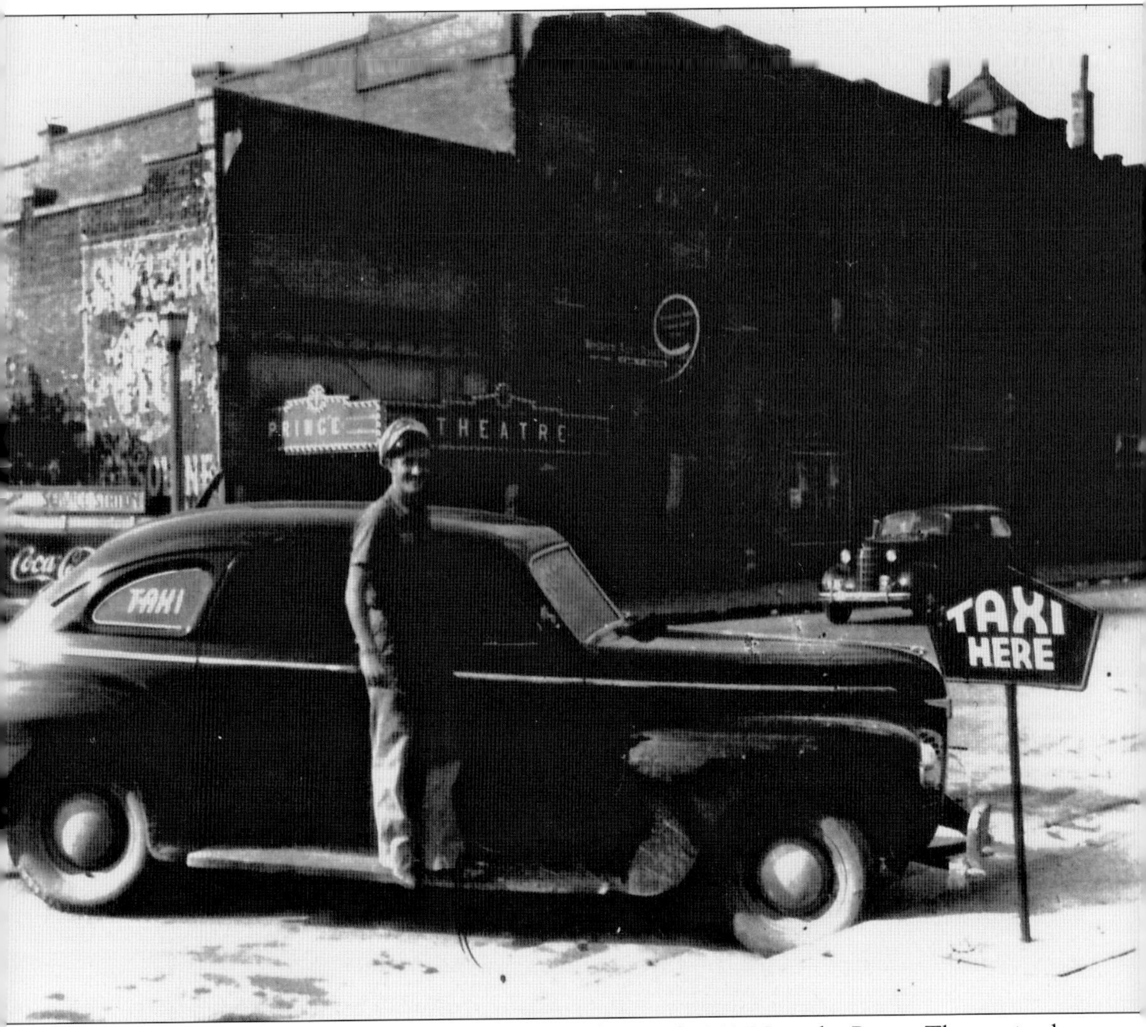

This taxi stop on Roane Street was photographed around 1940. Note the Prince Theatre in the background. The Prince was a popular place to take in a movie during World War II.

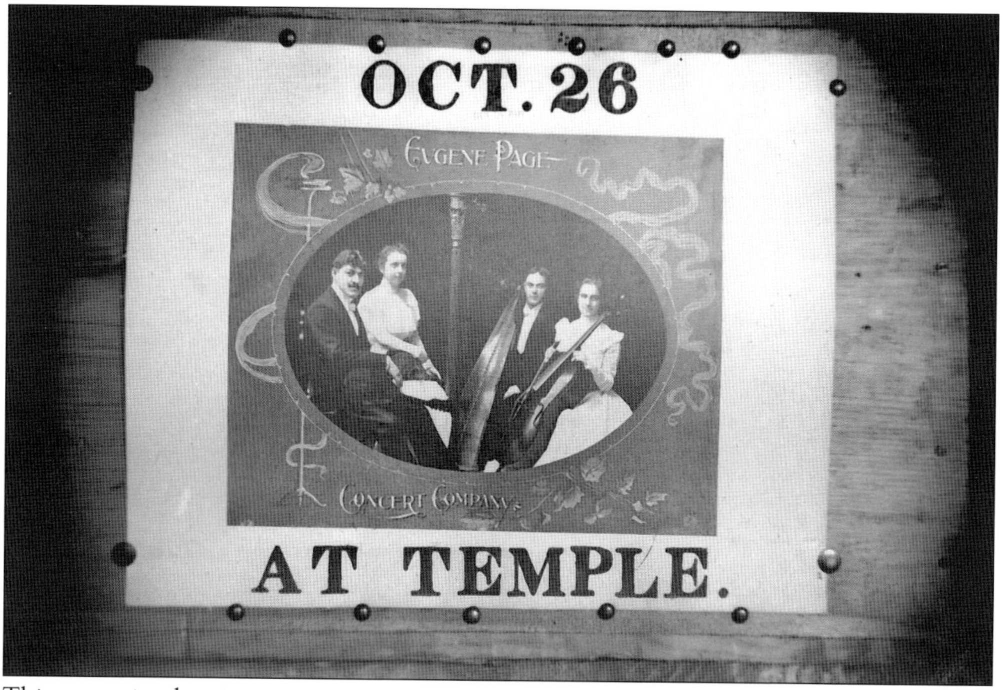

This poster is advertising an upcoming appearance by Eugene Page Concert Company at the Women's Temperance Christian Union Temple. The photograph was probably taken between 1900 and 1905.

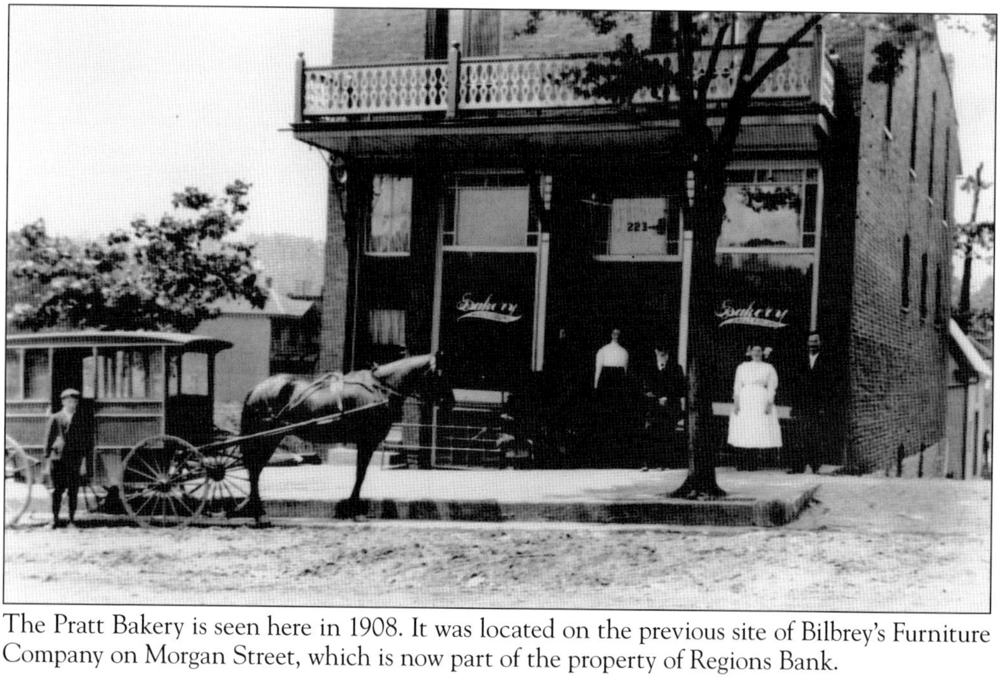

The Pratt Bakery is seen here in 1908. It was located on the previous site of Bilbrey's Furniture Company on Morgan Street, which is now part of the property of Regions Bank.

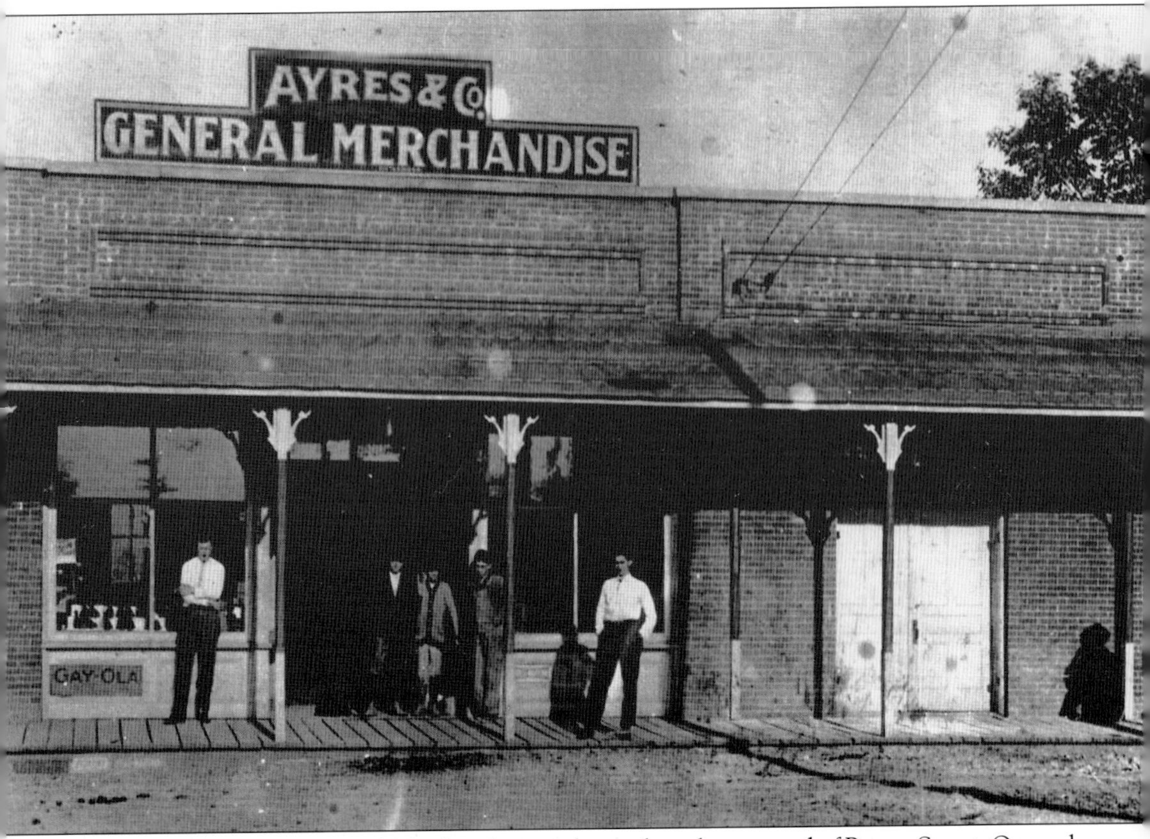

Ayers and Company General Merchandise was located on the east end of Roane Street. Opened in 1912, the building was demolished in 1967 to make way for an extension of Roane Street.

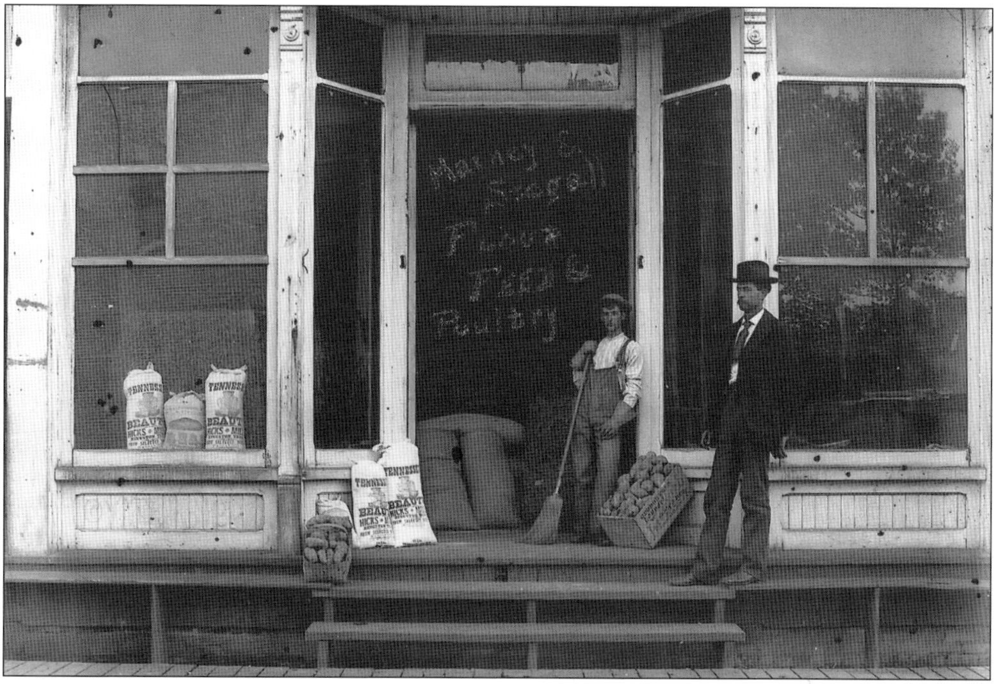

Marney and Stegal Flour, Feed, and Poultry was photographed around 1900. The store was located on Morgan Avenue near Clinton Street and was operated by R.C. Marney in 1900. The business was later located on the second floor of the First National Bank, where it remained until closing around 1960.

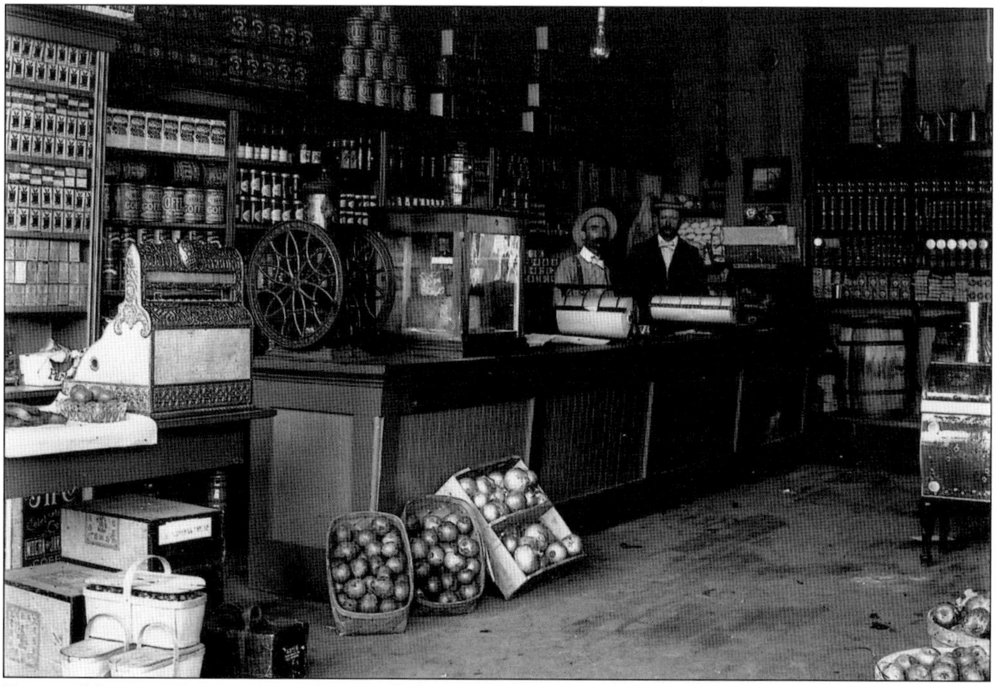

Pictured here is the interior of an early Harriman grocer around 1900. It could be Marney and Stegal Flour, Feed, and Poultry, or perhaps A.R. Davis Grocery. Both operated at that time.

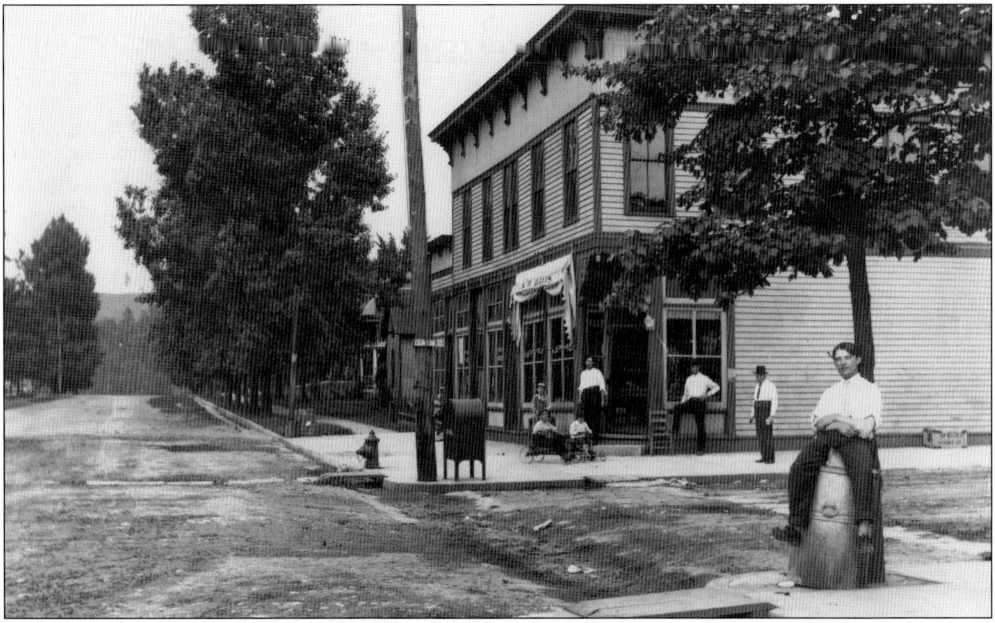

A.R. Davis Grocery is pictured here around 1905. Later, the store was known as New Harriman Grocery and was managed by a Mrs. Barnawell. Located at the corner of Clinton and Morgan Streets, the building burned in 1961.

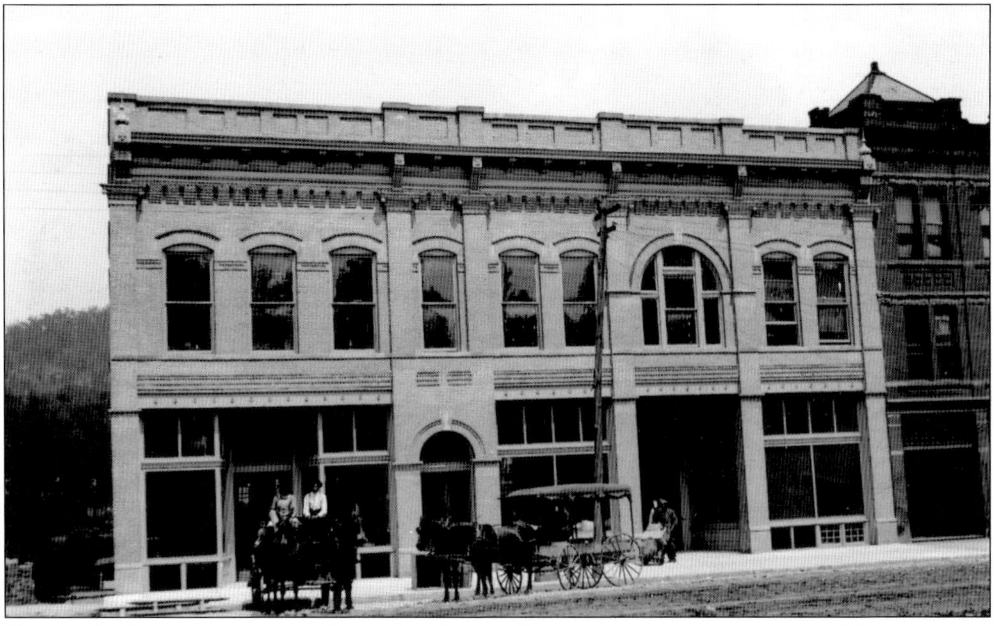

Carson Brothers Groceries was located on Roane Street and is seen here around 1908.

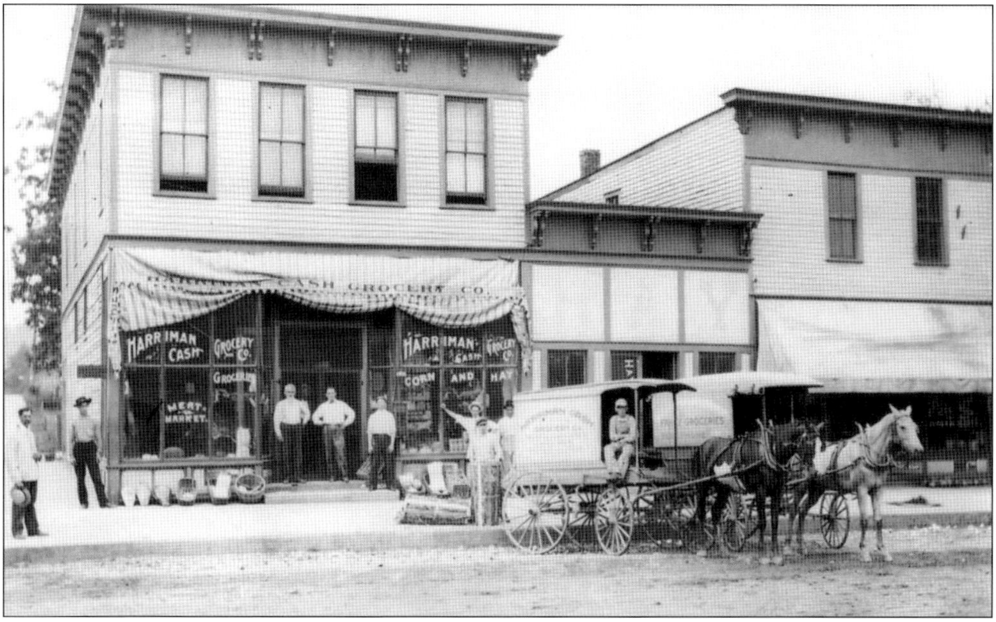

Harriman Cash Grocery Company was known as the best place in Harriman to buy groceries. This photograph was probably taken around 1915.

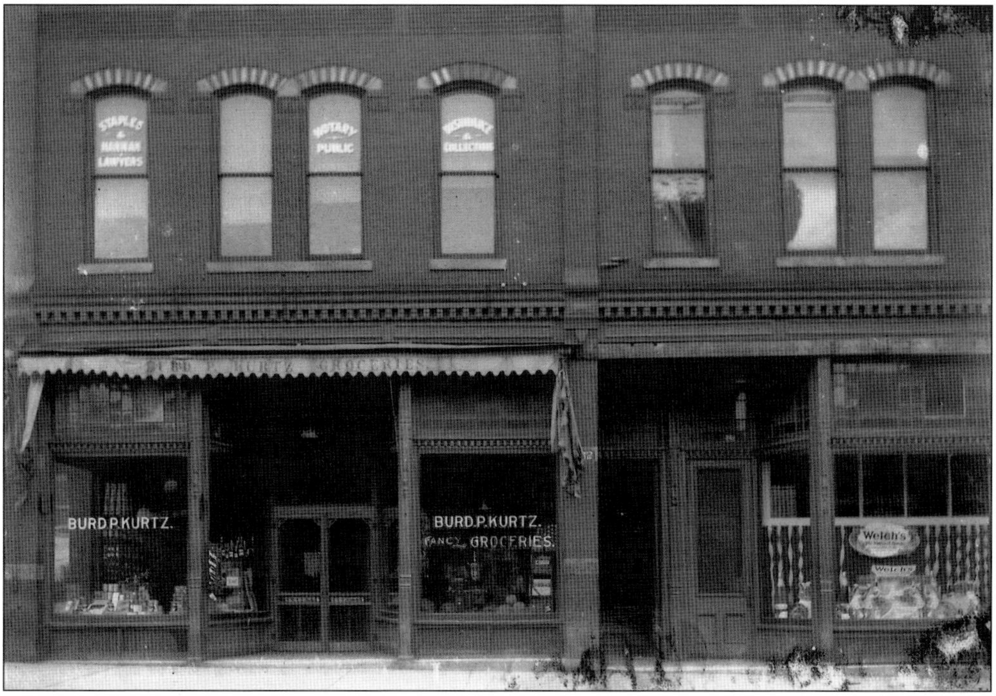

Burd P. Kurtz Fancy Groceries was located on the Caldwell Block on Roane and Queen Streets and is seen here in about 1910. Burd P. Kurtz was an 1899 graduate of the American Temperance University. He also worked in the insurance industry, according to the 1900 *Business and Professional Directory* for Harriman.

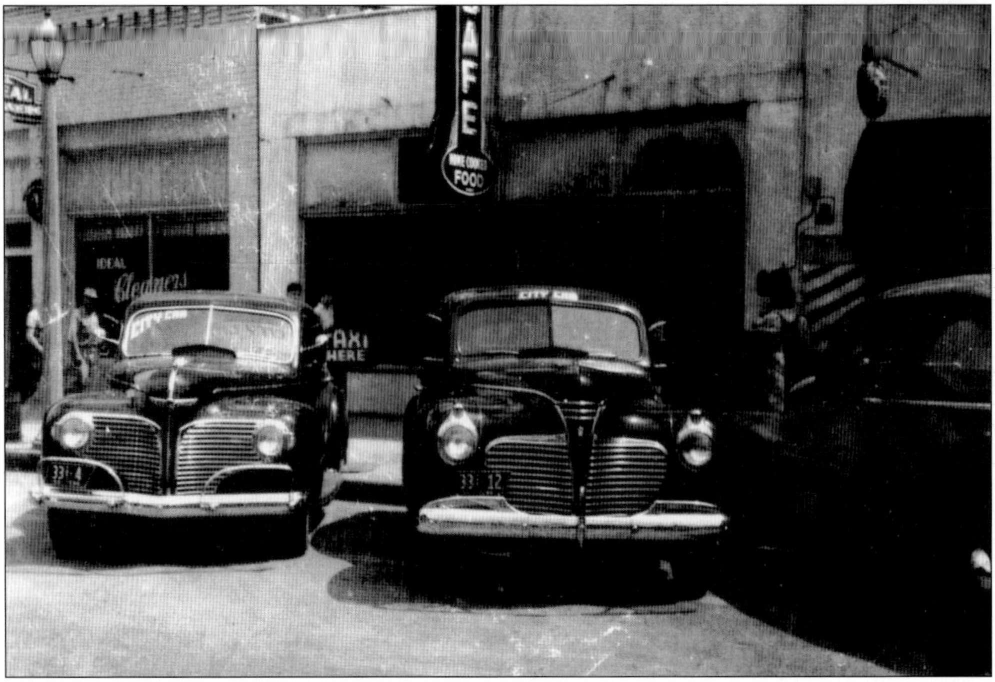

Taxis are lined up on Roane Street in front of Ideal Cleaners just north of the post office (near Edward's), probably during the 1940s.

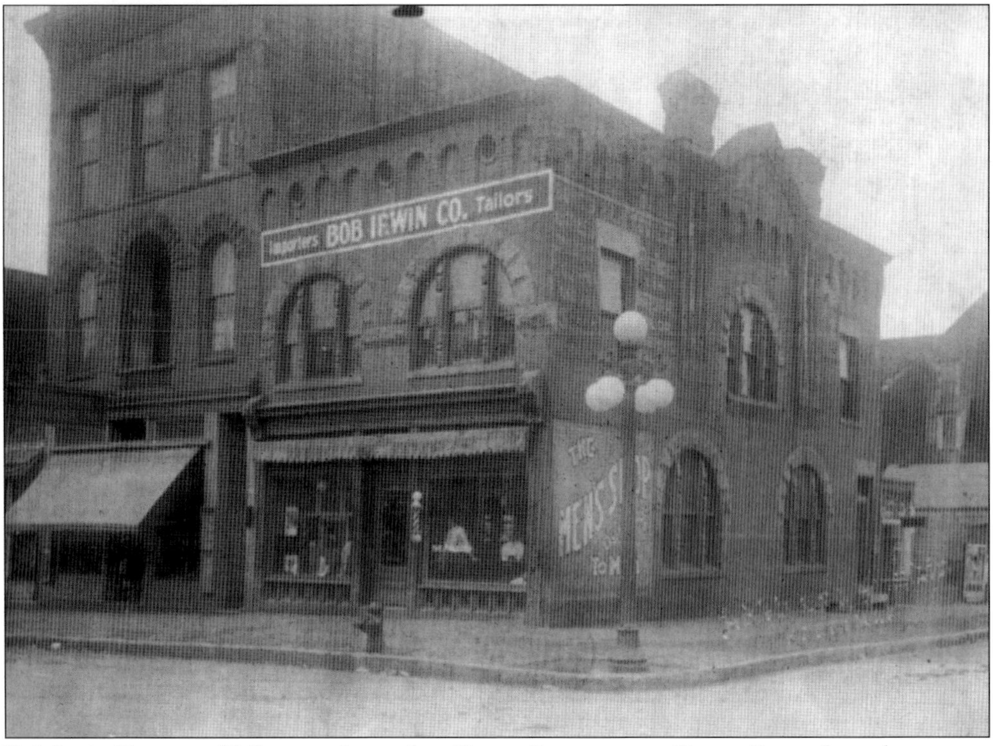

Bob Irwin Company Tailors was located on Roane Street, across Queen Street from the current site of Adkisson's Flowers and Gifts.

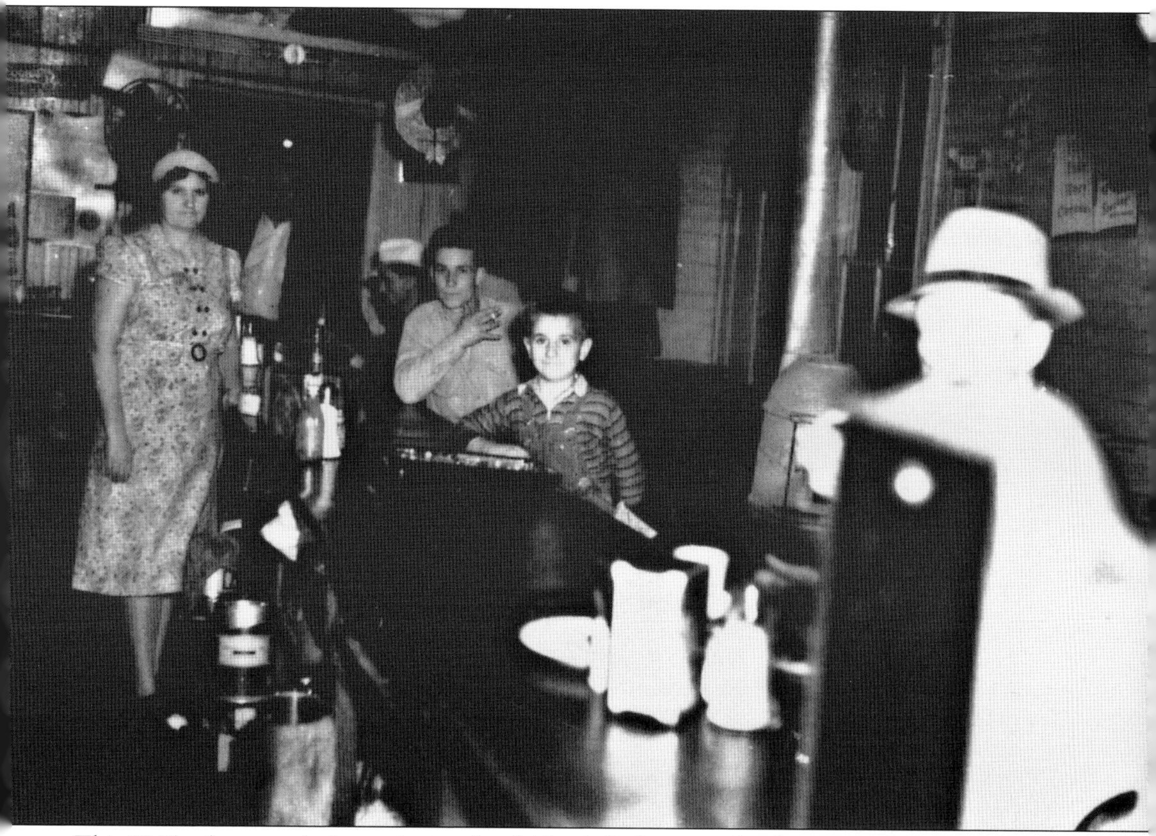

This 1940s photograph shows the inside of Alice's Café, a popular downtown diner. Alice's was on Walden Street, across from the public library. The restaurant remained open until around 1970. A parking lot now occupies the former site.

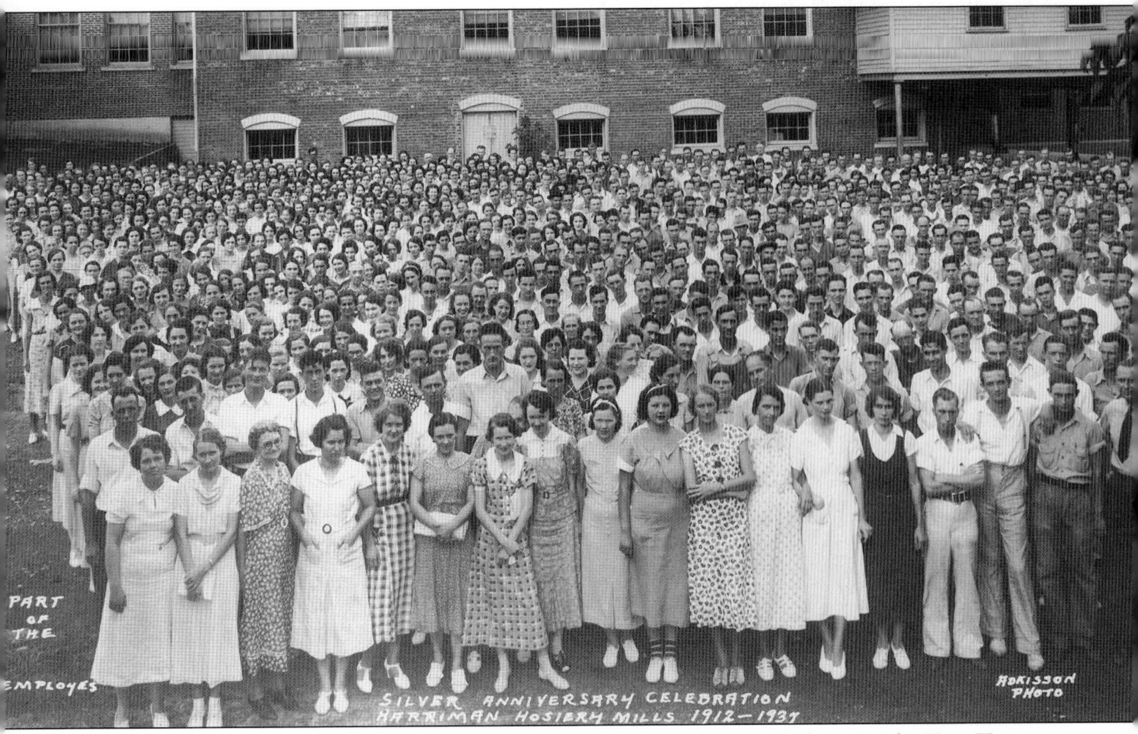

Harriman Hosiery Mill celebrated its 25th anniversary in 1937. Founded in 1912 by Tom Tarwater, the company manufactured seamless cotton hose for women and employed mostly women. The mill was purchased by Burlington Industries just after World War II and remained in operation until 1985. When it closed, 1,200 workers lost their jobs. (Courtesy of David Webb.)

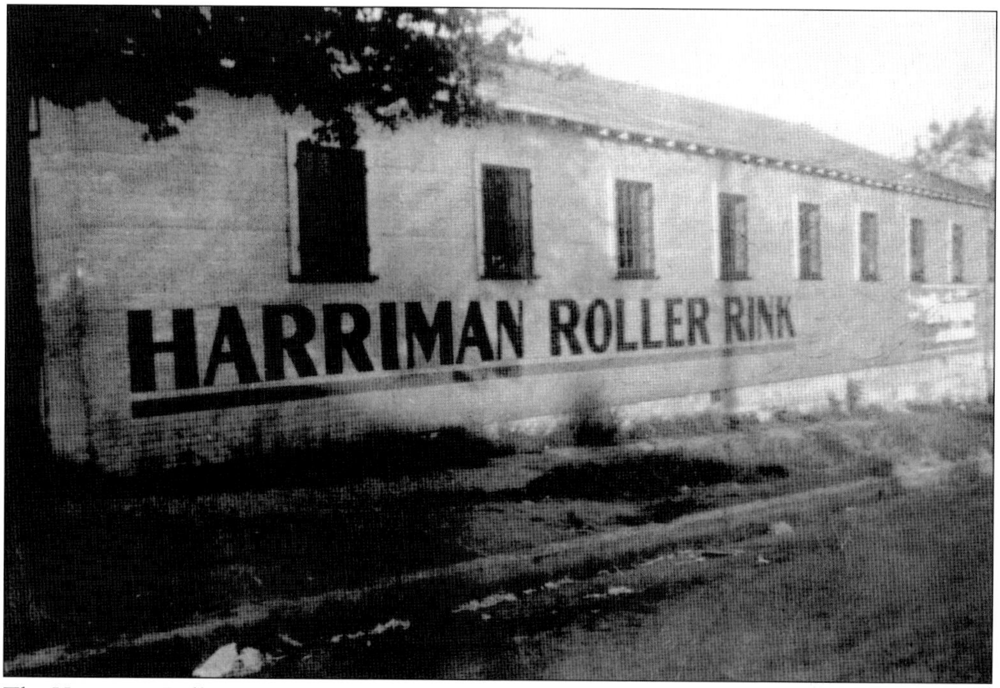

The Harriman Roller Rink is pictured here, probably during the early 1940s. Located on Queen Street (later the site of the former hospital addition), the establishment also served as a bowling alley at other times. Julian Ahler recalls visiting the roller rink with his family as a boy during World War II. The establishment closed in the early 1950s and later burned down.

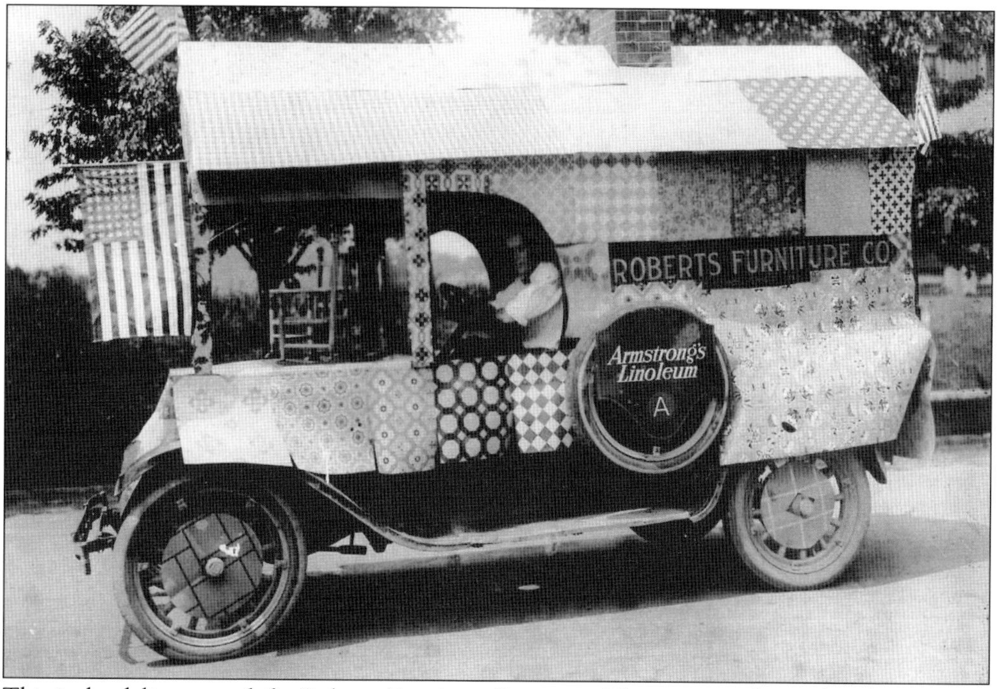

This is the delivery truck for Roberts Furniture Company. The store was located at the corner of Roane and Walden Streets, site of the current Chase Drugs parking lot.

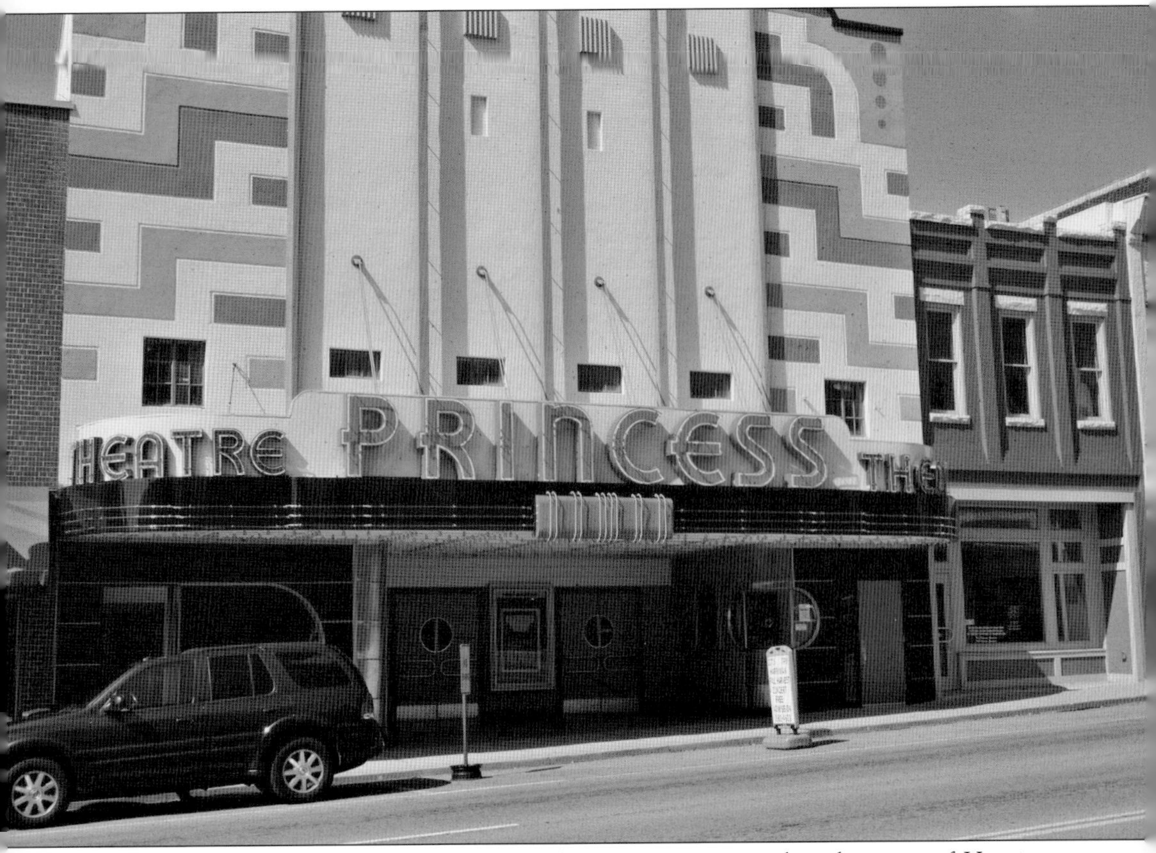

After more than 80 years, the Princess Theatre remains a cultural center of Harriman. (Author's collection.)

Six

Clubs, Civic Organizations, and Institutions

From the beginning, Harriman residents have been civic-minded. The 1892 city directory lists the following three lodges for men: Southgate Lodge, Free and Accepted Masons; Harriman Lodge No. 56, Independent Order of Odd Fellows; and Fisk Lodge No. 71, Knights of the Pythias. This last society purchased a building on Morgan Street and remained active in Harriman until relocating to Oak Ridge in the 1940s.

Another early organization, the Babahatchie Social Club (Babahatchie was a Native American name for the Emory River), was organized in 1902 and held periodic dinners, dances, and other social events for the community.

The city's early history also boasted the Merchants Association (described as "most progressive"), the Walter Harriman Post No. 94 of the Grand Army of the Republic, two labor unions, and—of course—a Prohibition Club, which met in the Women's Christian Temperance Union Temple.

The Harriman Rotary Club was established in 1919 with Dr. Reagan Yeargan, owner of Acme Drugs on Roane Street, serving as the first president. The Rotary Club played an important part in Harriman's early history by lobbying strongly for both a hospital and for the formation of the Mossop School for Girls.

The Kiwanis Club was chartered in July 1940 with John Winston as its first president. For many years, Kiwanis sponsored Law Day to recognize peace officers, as well as a Key Club for Harriman High School students. Kiwanis also built two gateway welcome signs—one on Pansy Hill Road (then Highway 27) and another on Oakdale Highway.

The Harriman Lions Club was chartered in December 1948 with Tom Sain, manager of the Harriman Hosiery Company, serving as the first president. Shortly thereafter, the club began work on establishing a park on Watts Bar Lake, a project that would result in Roane County Park.

These are only a few of the organizations that were and continue to be active in Harriman. Because of civic-minded residents, Harriman was able to establish a library, a post office, a hospital, and other necessary institutions in its early years, institutions still serving the city today.

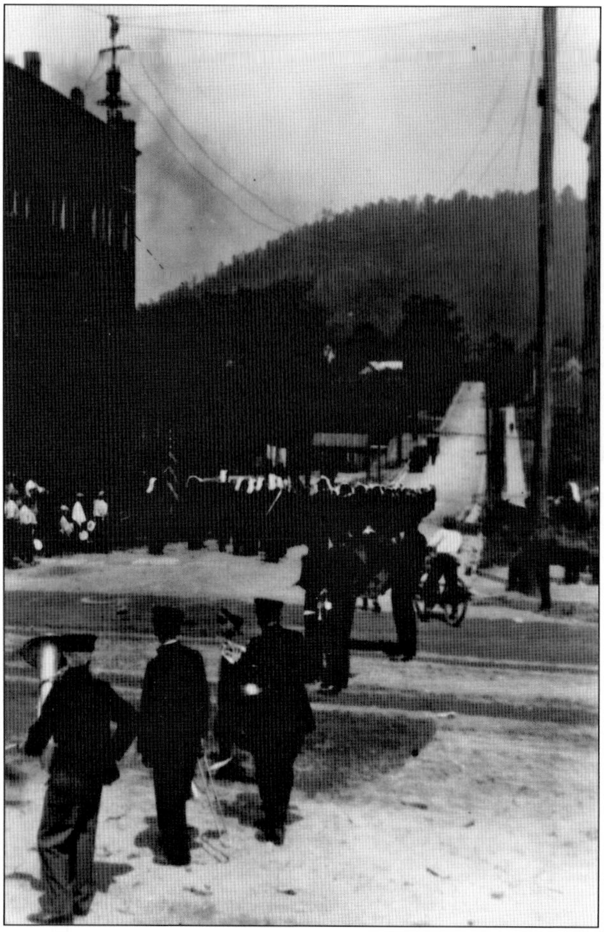

The Mason parade is pictured in a view down Crescent Street between the old Harriman Hotel and Miller-Brewer building. Lodges played an important role in the city's early history, as there were at least three active in Harriman as early as 1892. This photograph was likely taken around the turn of the 20th century.

The ground breaking ceremony for Harriman Public Library was held October 1, 1909. The Harriman Library Association was incorporated in January 1898 and lobbied for a new public library for Harriman. In 1908, the association won a grant from Andrew Carnegie to build a library, which would open the following year.

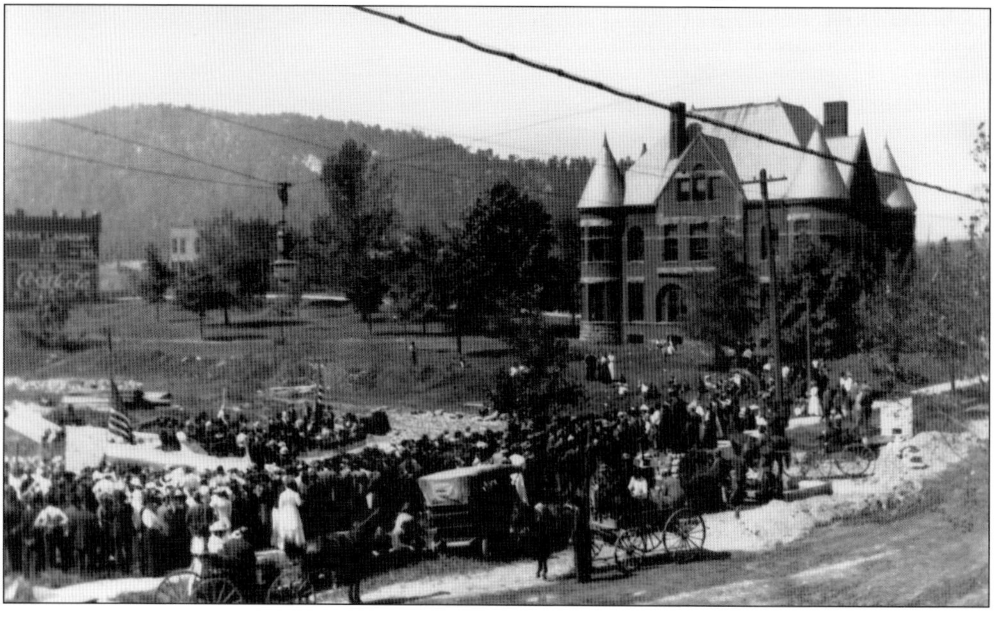

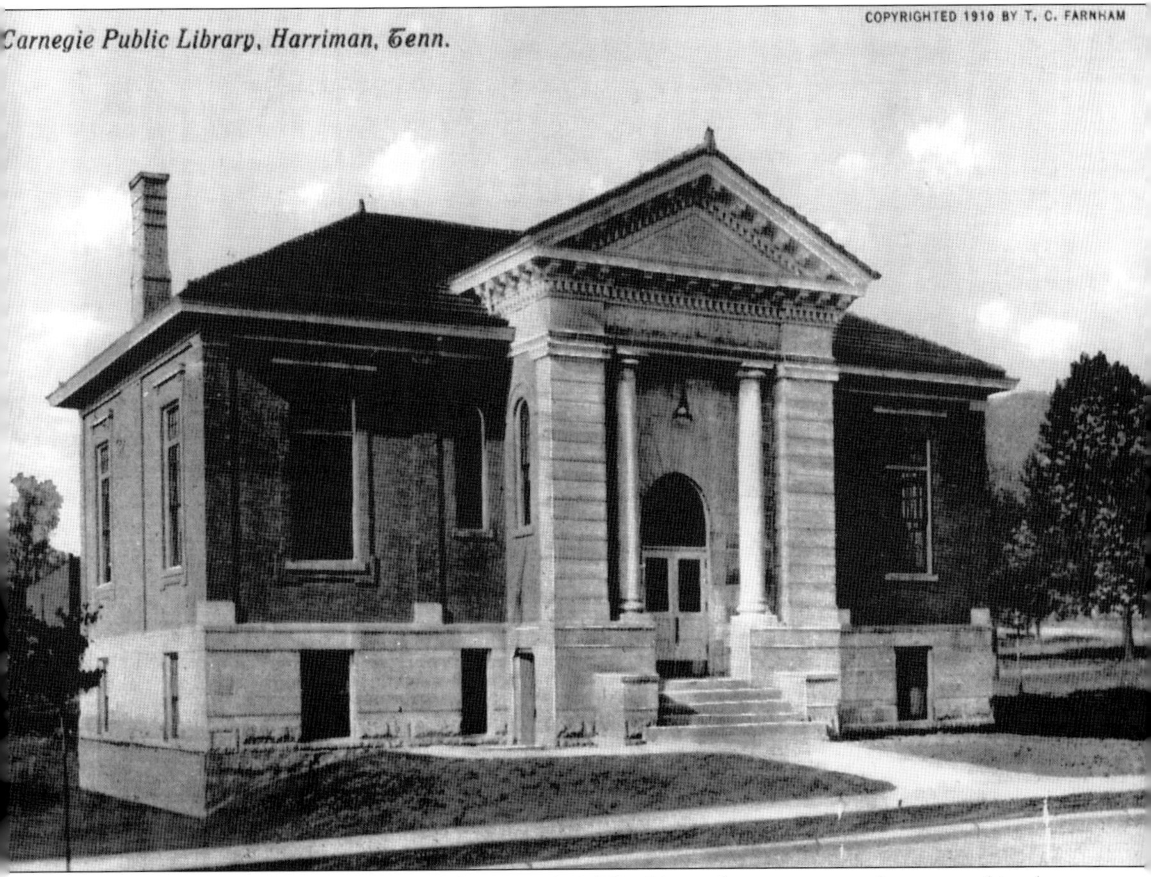

The Harriman Public Library is seen here in 1910. The library has continuously operated in the same building on Walden Street since 1909, providing resources for adults and fostering a love of reading in children for generations of residents.

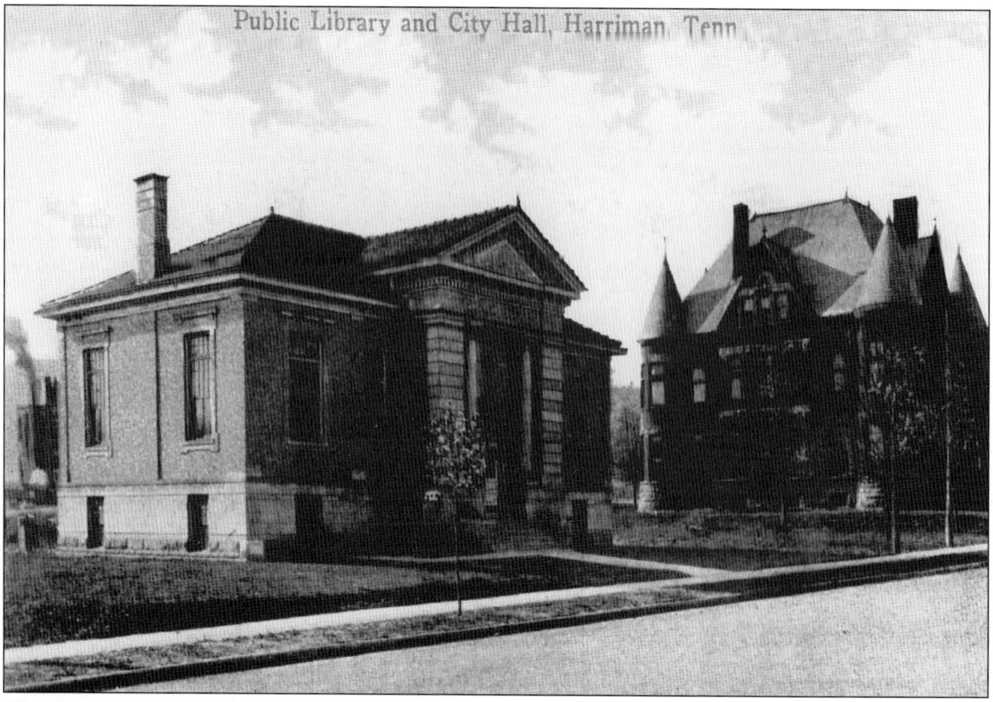

The Temperance Building is seen to the right of the Carnegie Public Library in Harriman, probably around 1920.

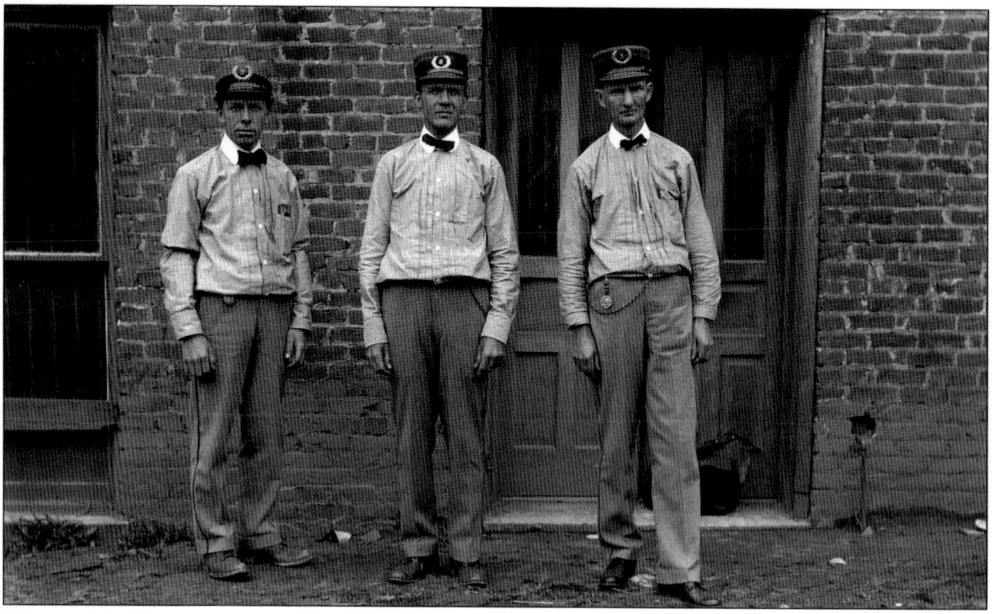

These early Harriman postal workers are, from left to right, Harley Harsh, D.T. "Doc" Jones, and Herman Abby, around 1905. At the time, Harriman did not have a regular post office, but operated out of store buildings.

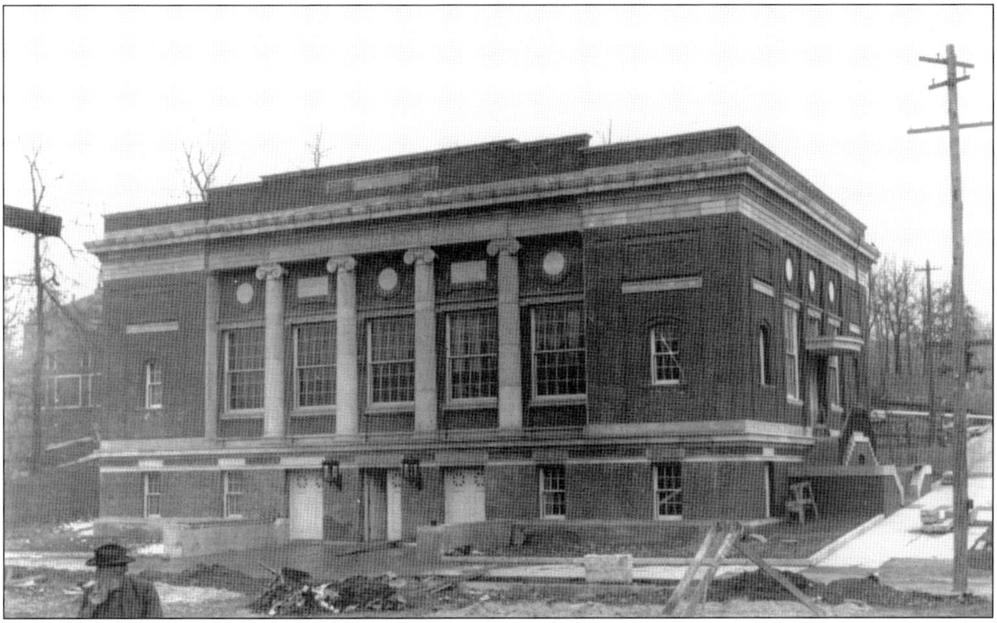

The United States Post Office building on Roane Street is under construction in 1912. By 1909, efforts were underway to land Harriman a permanent post office building. In 1912, the post office opened on the corner of Roane and Queen Streets, and would remain at that location for over 65 years before moving to its current location in South Harriman.

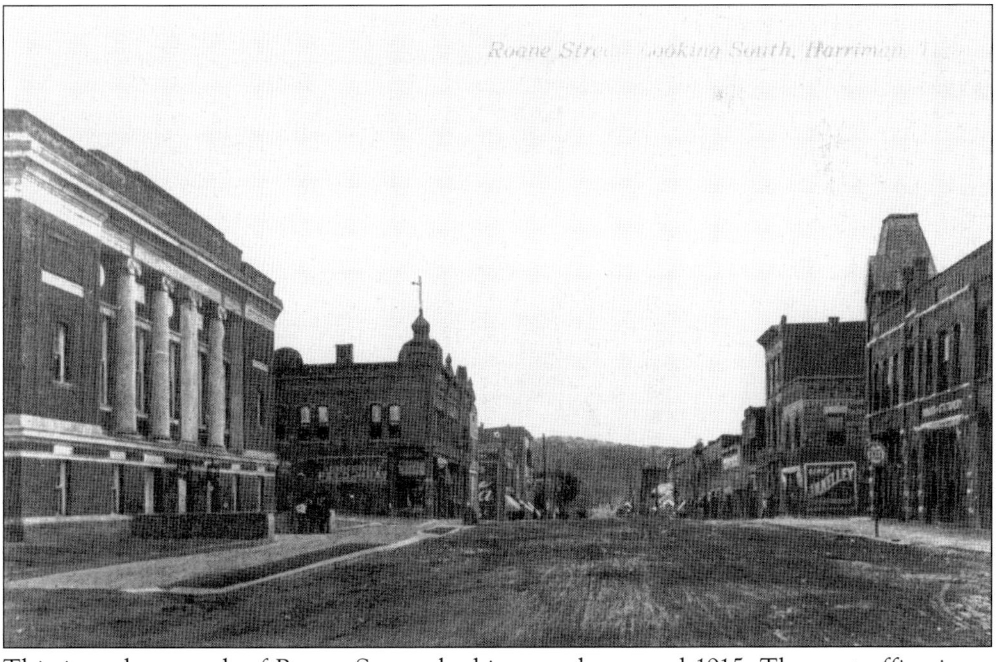

This is a photograph of Roane Street, looking south, around 1915. The post office is on the left.

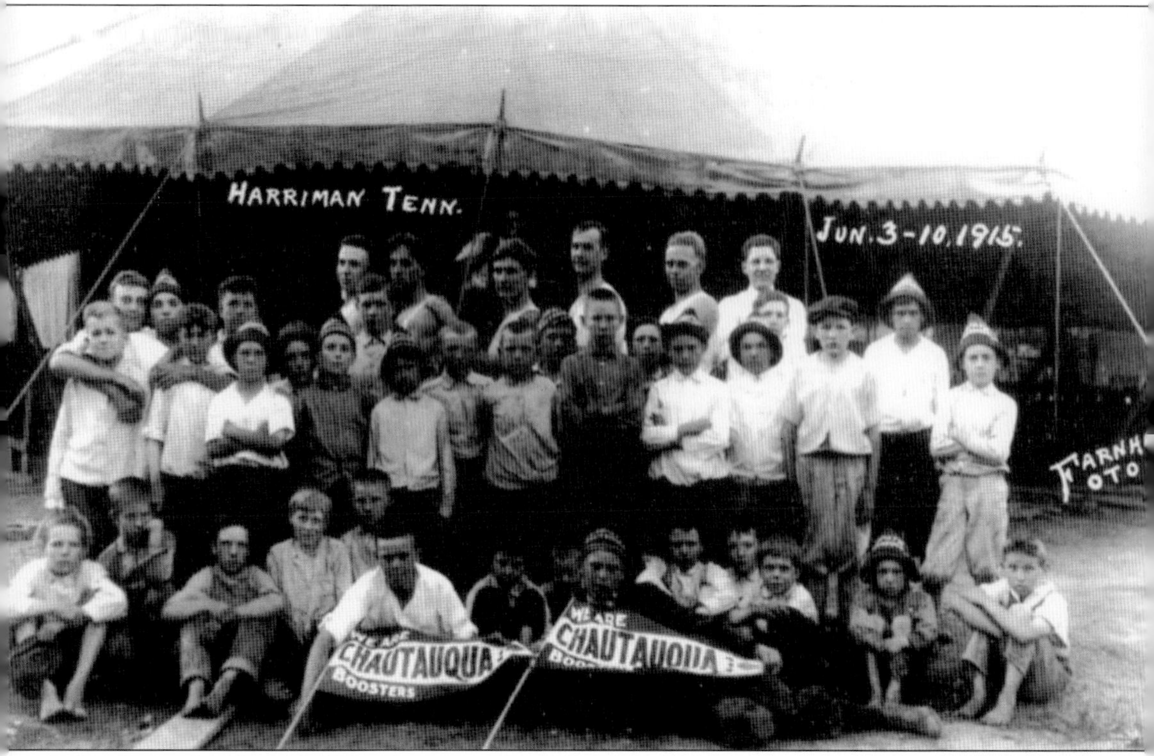

The Red Path Chautauqua Tent Crew is pictured on a then-vacant lot at the corner of Roane and Walden Streets in June 1915. Between 1913 and 1929, the annual summer appearance of the Redpath Chautauqua was one of the most highly anticipated events of the year. Redpath was one of the most well known Chautauquas and toured throughout the South, telling stories, performing music, acting, and lecturing. Among those to lecture in Harriman were Jeanette Rankin, the first woman elected to Congress, and Ruth Bryan Owen, daughter of William Jennings Bryan.

Pictured here is Harriman Hospital in the 1940s. First publicly suggested by the Rotary Club in 1923, Harriman General Hospital opened its doors in 1939. Later known as Roane Medical Center, it would continue to operate downtown until relocating to Midtown in 2012.

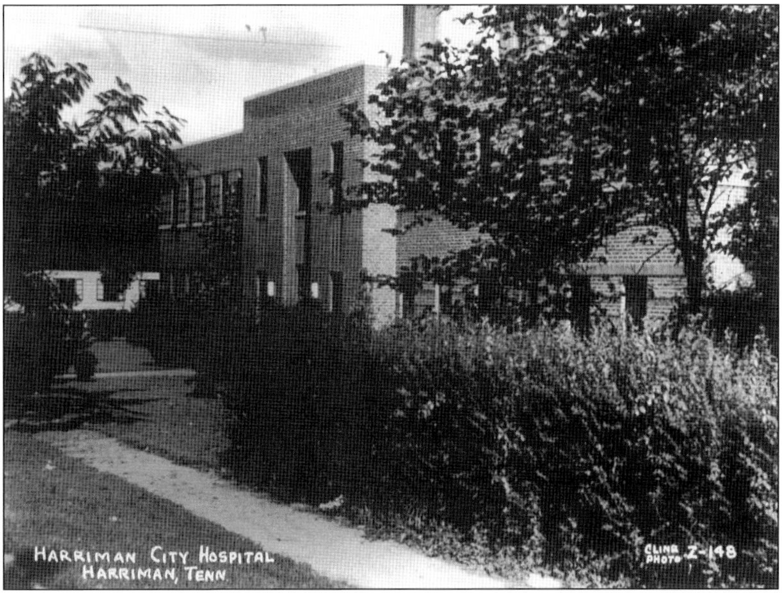

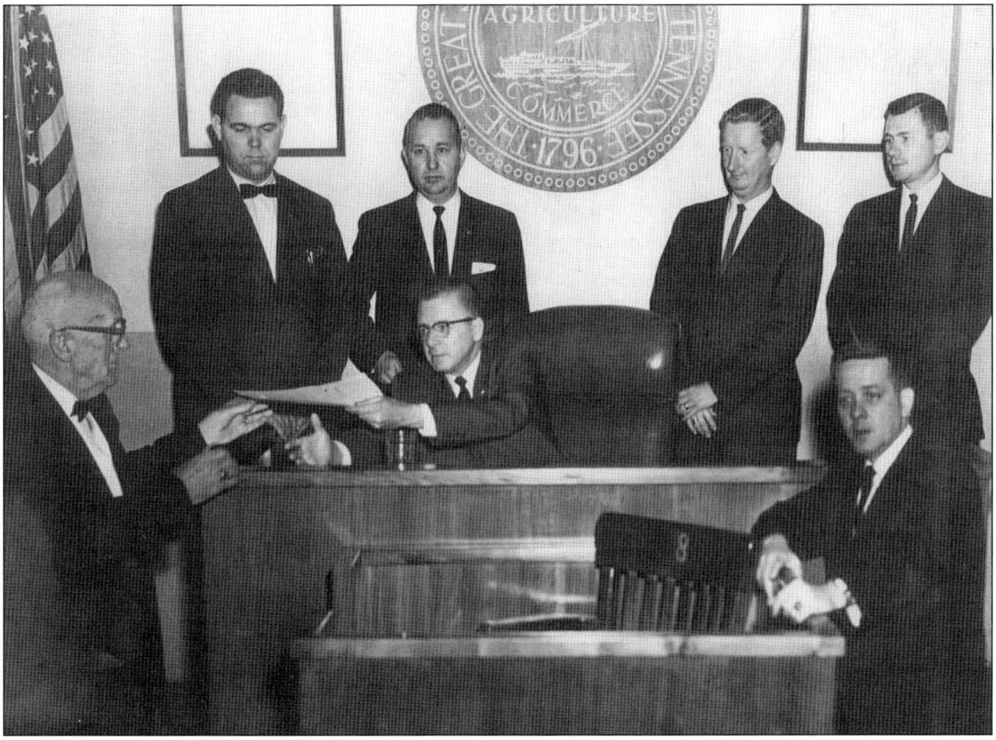

Members of the South Harriman Ruritan Club honor Elmer L. Eblen, a long-time attorney, county judge, and mayor of Harriman, around 1957. The men include Rex Walls, vice president; Noah E. Howard, past president and governor of Cherokee District, Tennessee; and Jim Littleton, member. (Courtesy of Noah Howard.)

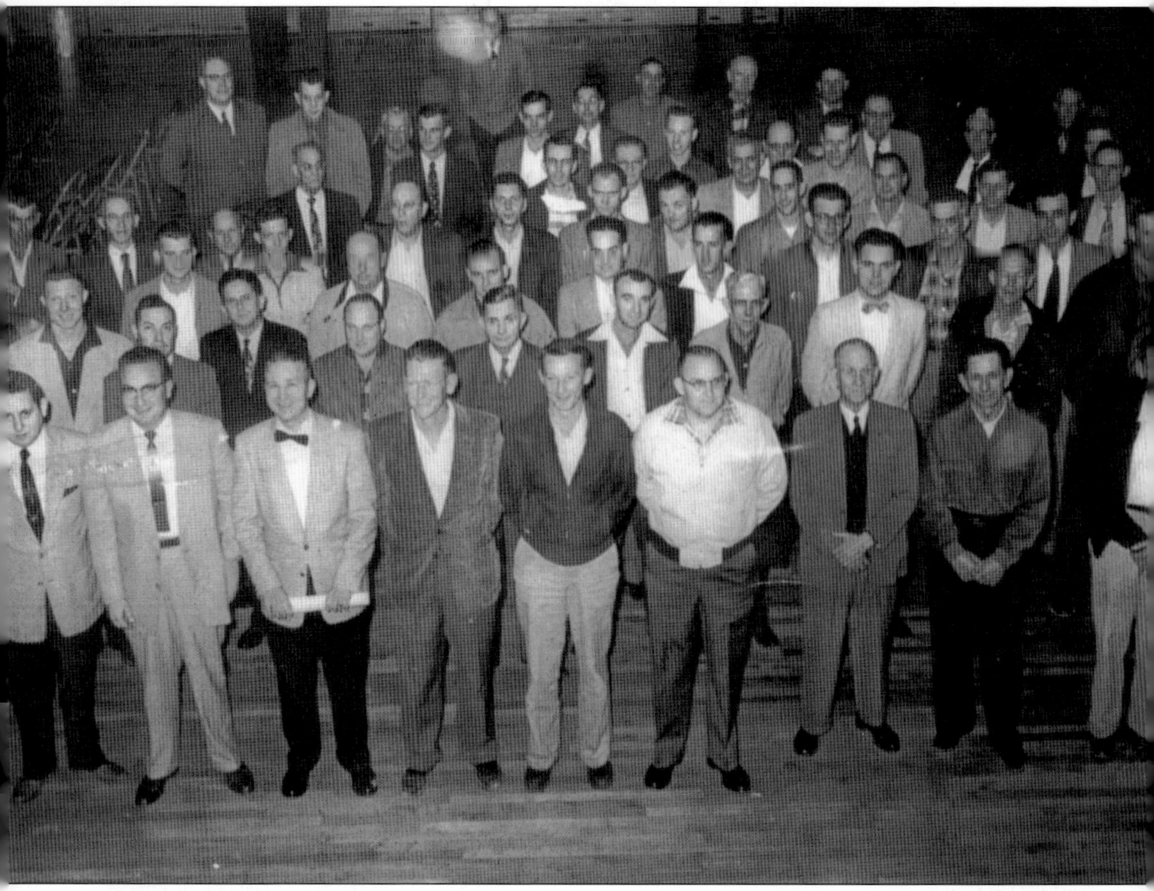

Pictured here is a late 1950s meeting of the South Harriman Ruritan Club honoring Elmer L. Eblen. This chapter of the Ruritan Club was chartered in 1957 with Noah Howard as the first president.

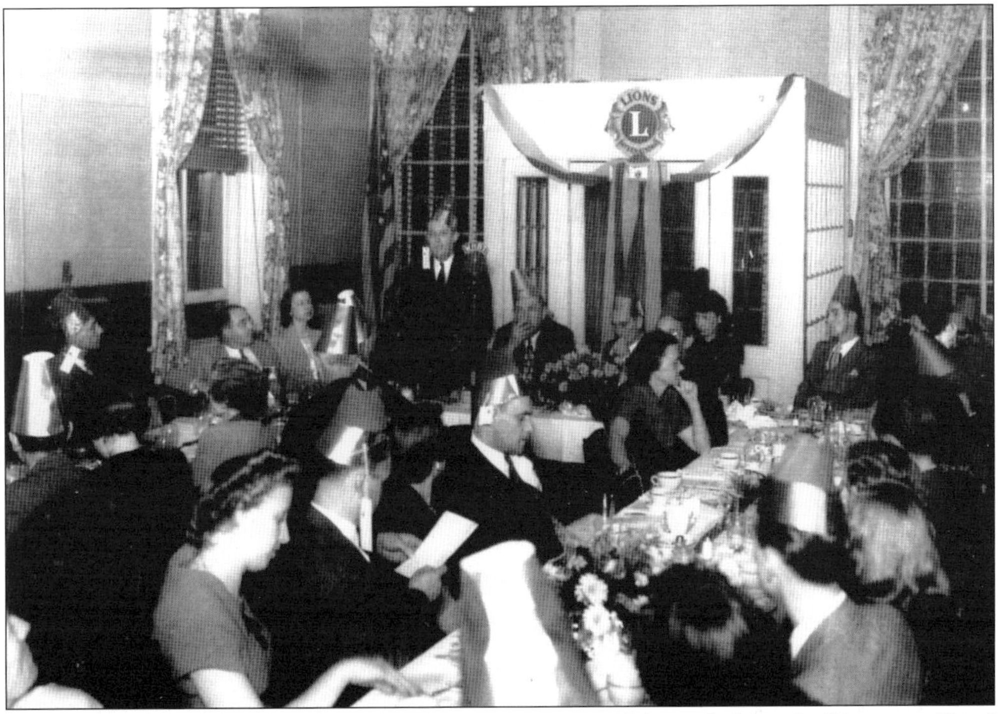

The charter presentation banquet of the Harriman Lions Club was held at the Harriman Hotel on December 13, 1948. Tom Sain was the first president.

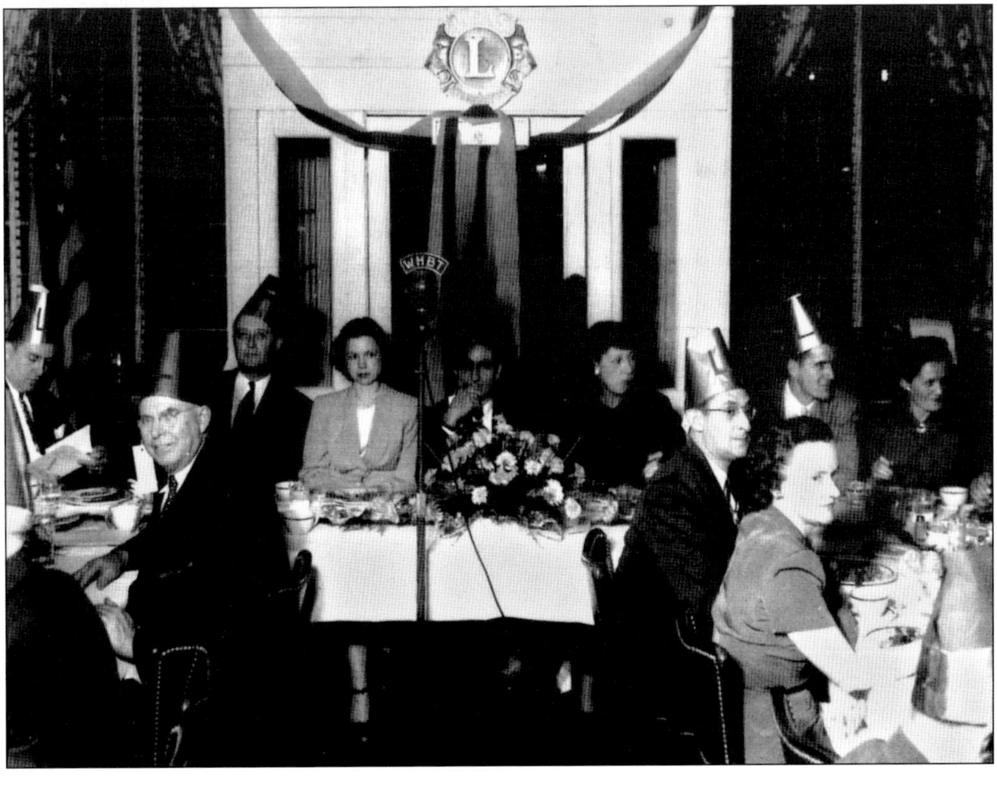

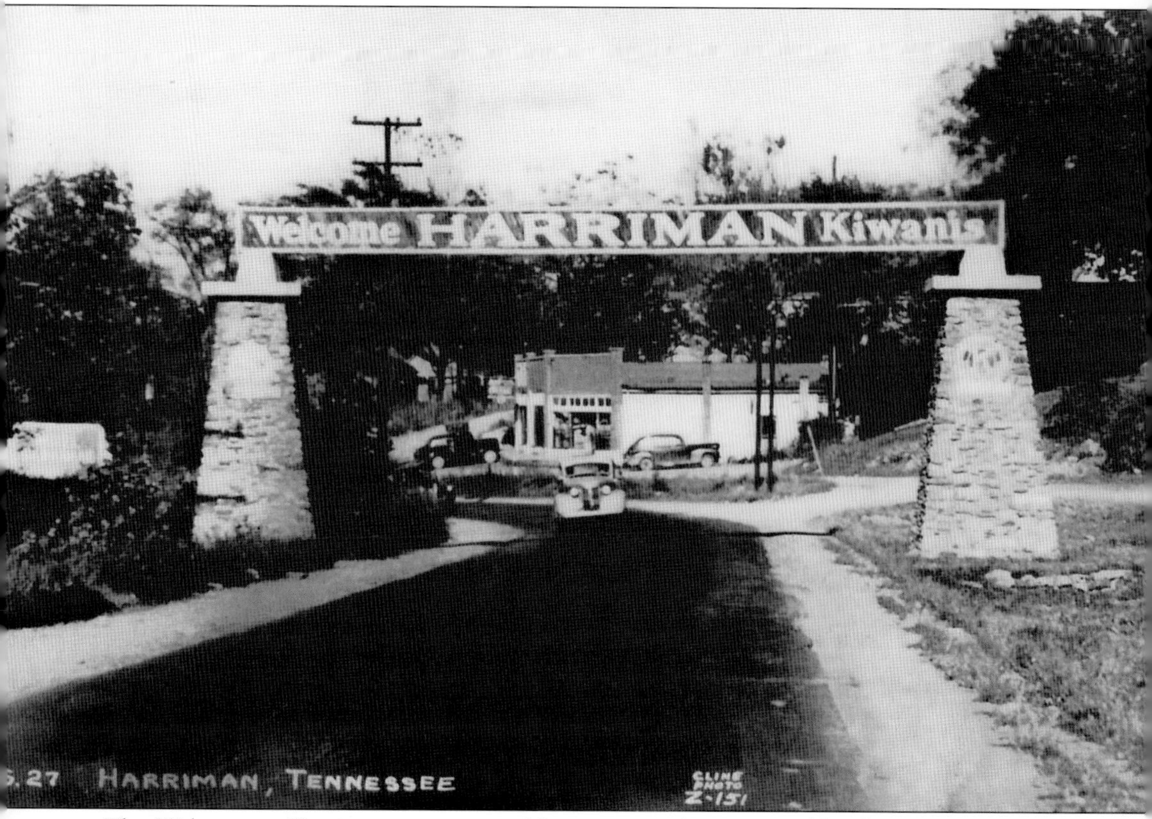

The Welcome to Harriman sign pictured here is one of two erected by the Harriman Kiwanis Club around 1940. This photograph shows the sign on what is now Pansy Hill Road, but was then Highway 27. The other sign was on Oakdale Highway.

Seven

RELIGION

As a city founded on Victorian values, it is no surprise that Harriman promoted its churches from the very beginning. In fact, the East Tennessee Land Company offered free land to churches wishing to build. Because of this, churches sprouted up nearly overnight in the new city.

The first church appeared in Shacktown in March 1890, meeting in a primitive shack built from planks. It was known as Pilgrim's Tabernacle, a Congregationalist church, though other religious groups also used the building during that time.

Two Years of Harriman, a promotional booklet of the East Tennessee Land Company, states that there were nine different church organizations operating in Harriman in 1892, including two African American churches, though the Christian Church was the only one to have a permanent building. Church denominations included Baptist, Congregational, Episcopal, Methodist, "Colored," Universalist, Presbyterian, and nondenominational. These churches would serve as predecessors to several churches still active today in the city.

The Universalist Church, described as the most elegant of the early churches, was established in 1892 thanks to the support of Quaker Oats magnate Ferdinand Schumacher. It would be attended by many of the city's early leaders.

Though small in number, Catholics were present from early on in Harriman's history, though it would be 1907 before a permanent Catholic Church would be established in the city. Until then, Catholics had services in private homes.

Through the years, Harriman's churches have been involved in many beneficial services for the city and have served as social institutions for generations of residents in addition to serving the spiritual needs of their members. They are also, in some ways, the most enduring of Harriman's institutions. While very few of Harriman's first businesses still exist, many of the earliest congregations are still active today.

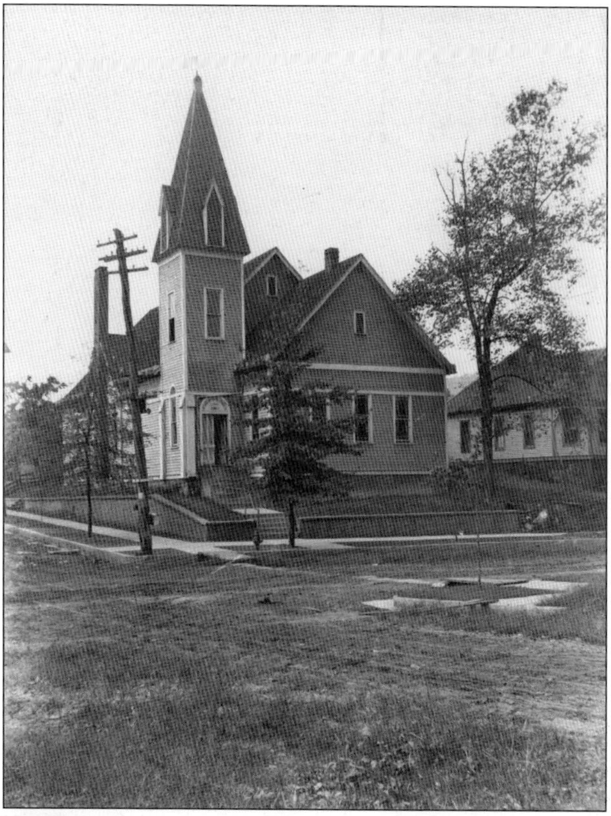

Pictured here are two views of the First Christian Church of Harriman, around 1905. It is believed to be the second church to formally organize in Harriman and the first permanent church building (1890). It is located on the corner of Morgan and Cumberland. This original building is still standing, though in disrepair.

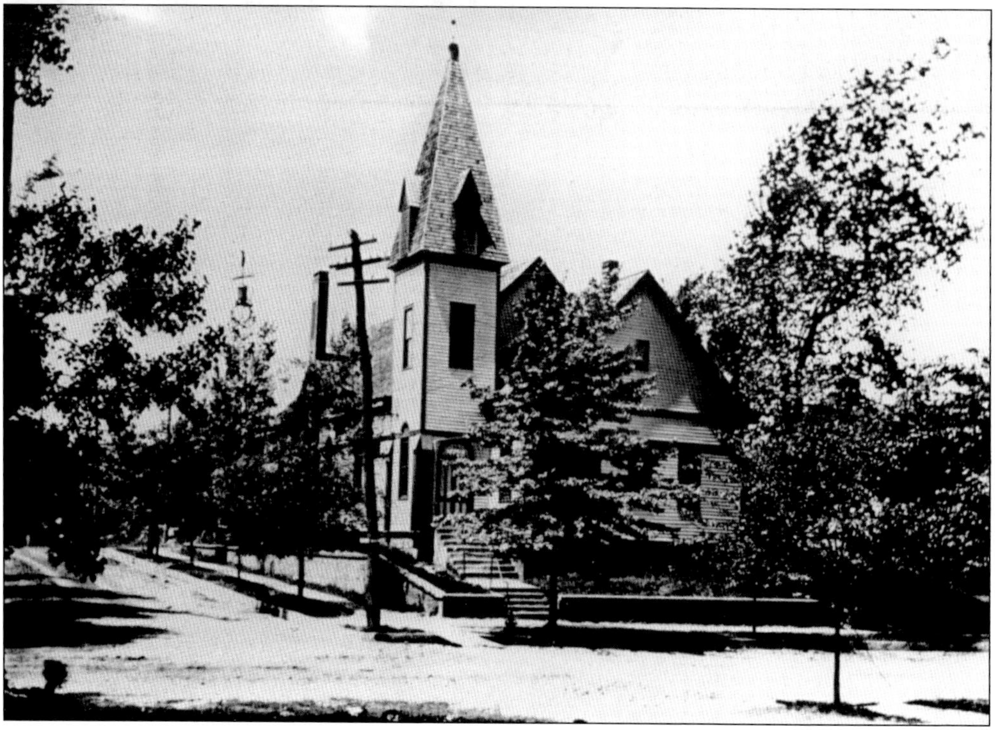

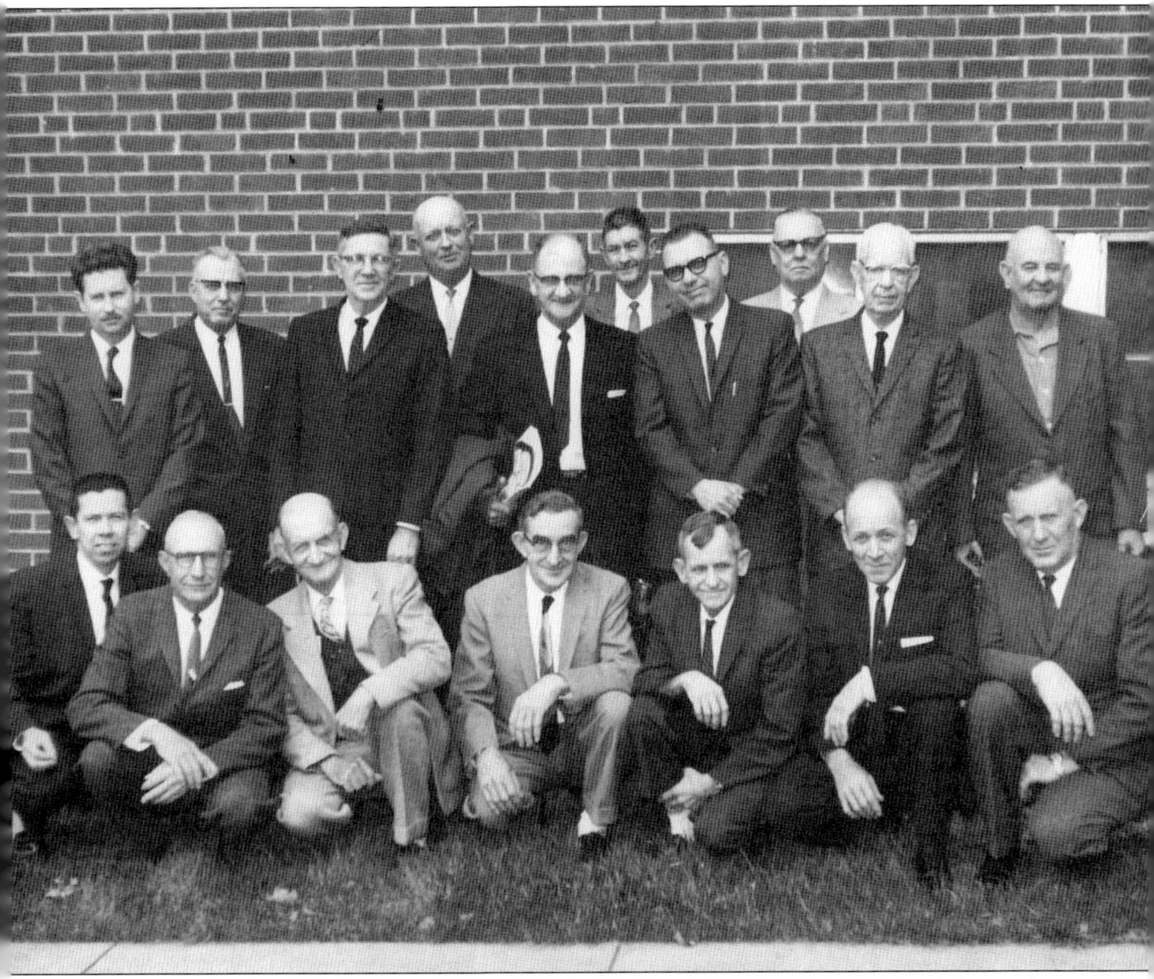

The Loyal Men's Class at the First Christian Church is pictured around 1959. From left to right are (first row) Eugene Ketchen, Hastings Pope, ? Sampson, Albert Hoag, Jesse Adkisson, Lee Swafford, and Carl Stiles; (second row) Bill Adkisson, Joe Gardner, ? Porter, Walter Gilmore, James Overton, Johnson Hyder, William J. Hill, Lewis Poole, Luther Mee, and George McDaniel. Eugene Ketchen and James Overton taught the class.

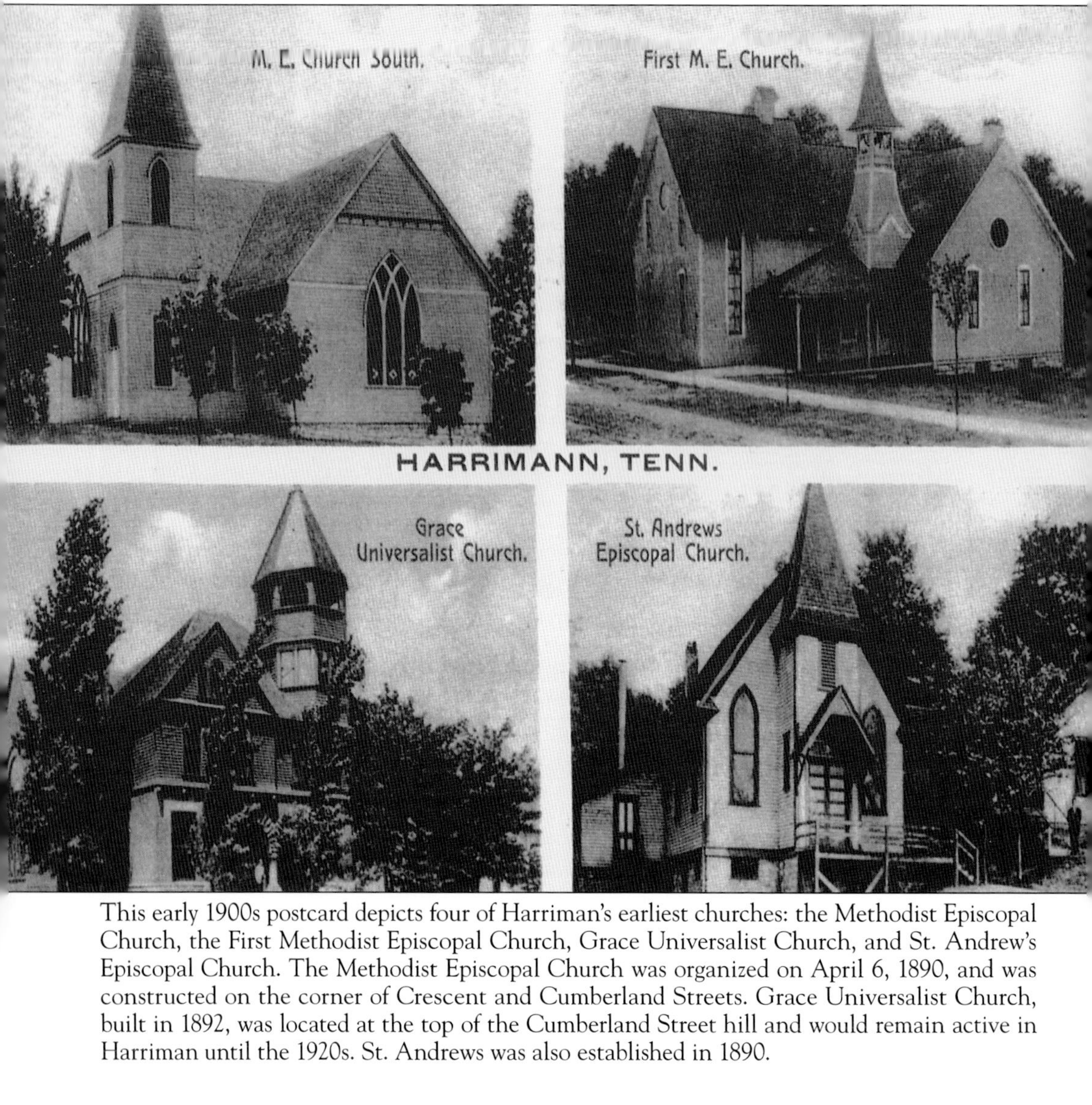

This early 1900s postcard depicts four of Harriman's earliest churches: the Methodist Episcopal Church, the First Methodist Episcopal Church, Grace Universalist Church, and St. Andrew's Episcopal Church. The Methodist Episcopal Church was organized on April 6, 1890, and was constructed on the corner of Crescent and Cumberland Streets. Grace Universalist Church, built in 1892, was located at the top of the Cumberland Street hill and would remain active in Harriman until the 1920s. St. Andrews was also established in 1890.

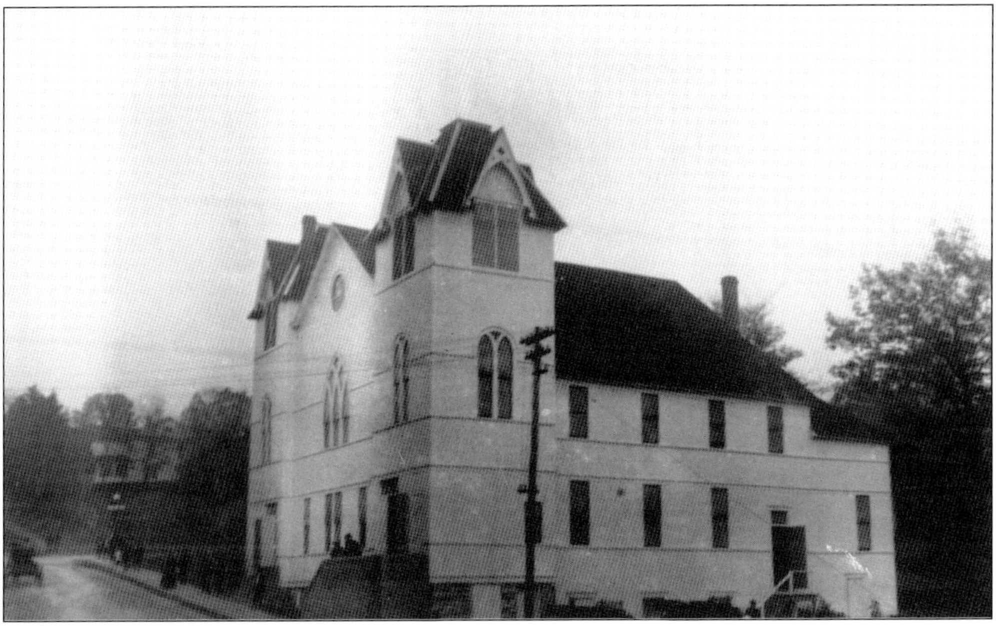

The Women's Christian Temperance Union Temple is shown here in the late 1800s. The WCTU Temple was dedicated April 14, 1892, and located on the 300 block of Clinton Street (behind the present site of Kyker Funeral Home). According to its charter, its purpose was "to educate public sentiment up to the standard of total abstinence, train the young, save the inebriate, and secure . . . the legal prohibition and complete banishment of the liquor traffic." The temple was sold on July 23, 1919, to Temple Building Corporation and was converted into a theater for stage and silent motion pictures. It was then known as Temple Theater. The building was torn down in the mid-1930s.

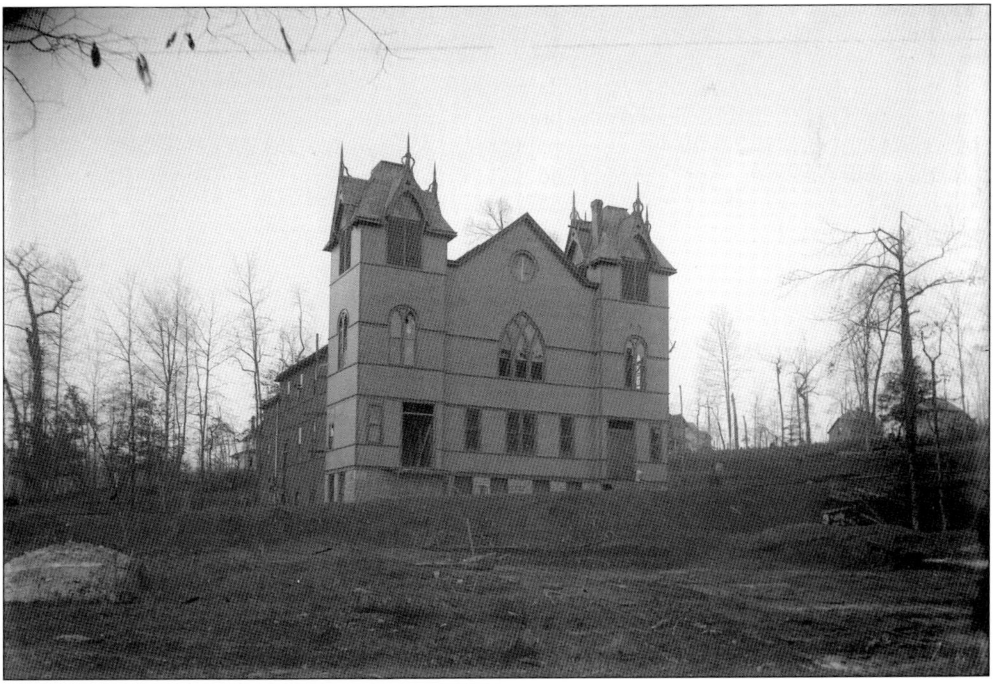

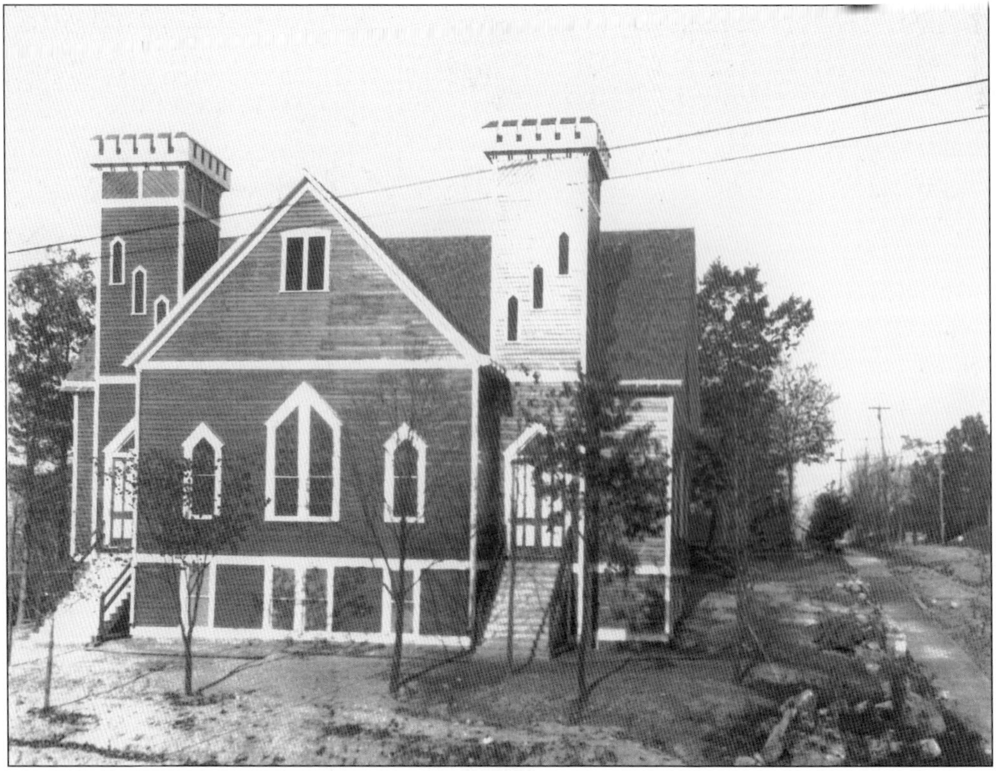

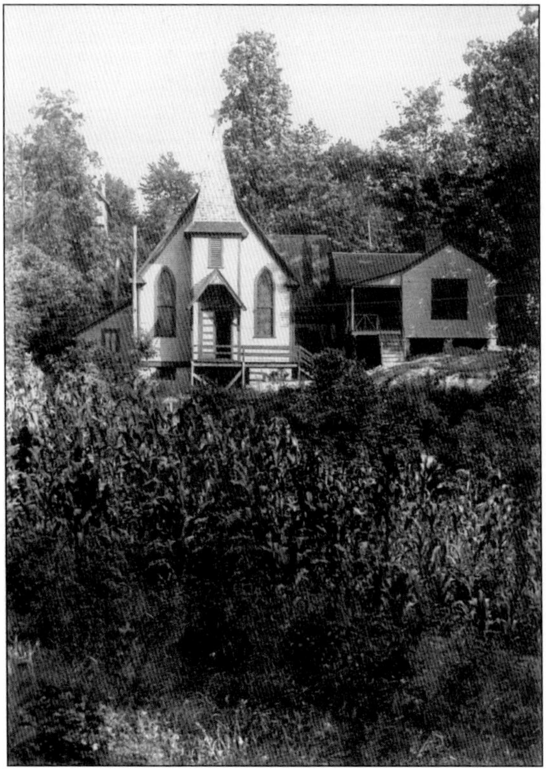

Trenton Street Baptist Church is seen here, probably around 1905. Organized with a congregation of 11 in the fall of 1890, it first met in the WTCU building before moving to a permanent location. Rapid growth required the original structure to be torn down in 1900 and replaced with the one seen here.

This photograph shows the exterior of St. Andrews Episcopal Church, probably around 1910. St. Andrews was built on land donated by the East Tennessee Land Company at the corner of Crescent and Trenton Streets. The building pictured burned down on March 2, 1969.

The interior of St. Andrews Episcopal Church is pictured here, probably around 1925.

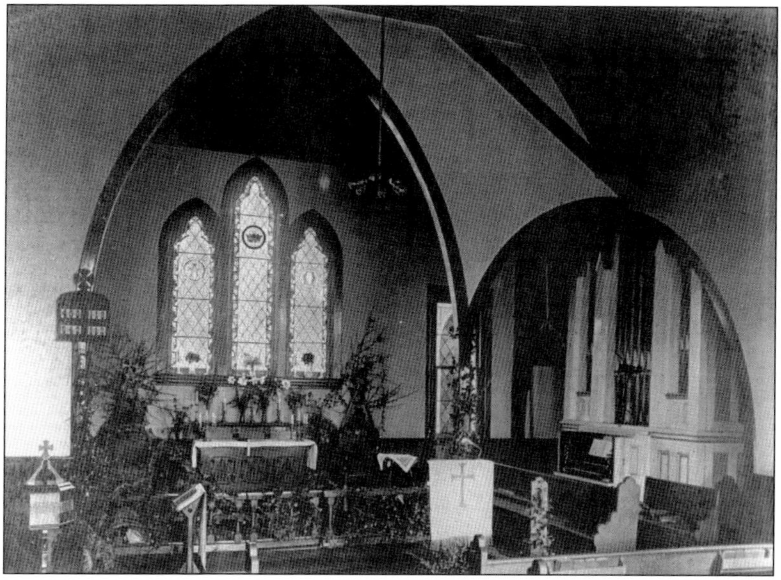

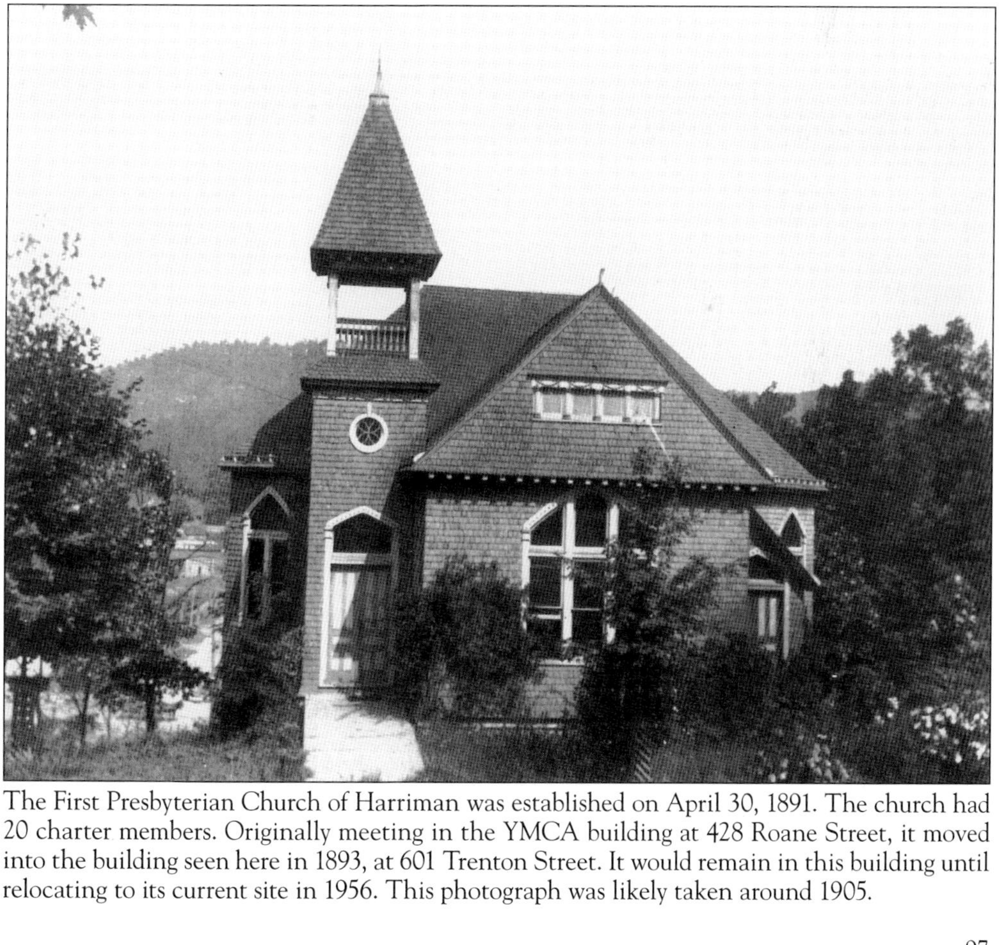

The First Presbyterian Church of Harriman was established on April 30, 1891. The church had 20 charter members. Originally meeting in the YMCA building at 428 Roane Street, it moved into the building seen here in 1893, at 601 Trenton Street. It would remain in this building until relocating to its current site in 1956. This photograph was likely taken around 1905.

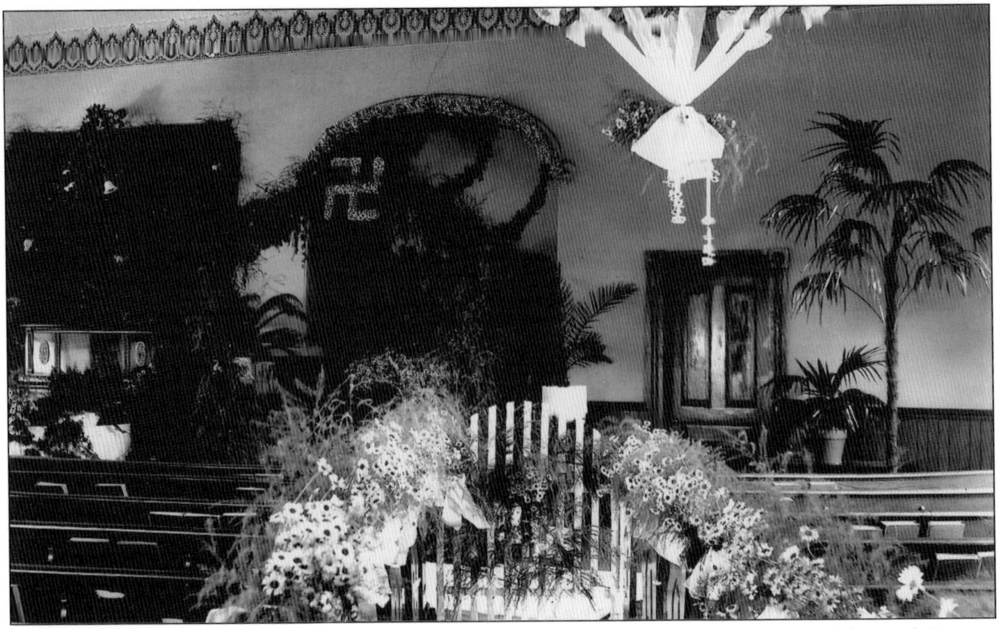

Seen here is the interior of the First Presbyterian Church, decorated for the wedding of George Mayers and Susie Tidwell, probably in the 1920s. Note the swastika, which was used as a good luck symbol in the early 20th century before it was associated with the Nazi party.

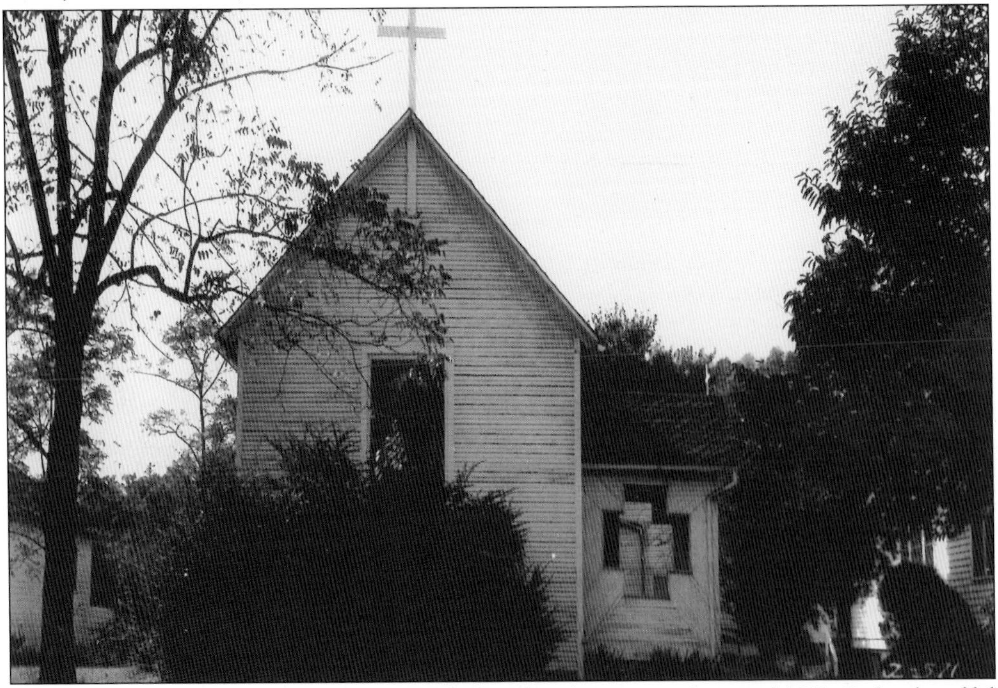

The first building of Blessed Sacrament Catholic Church is pictured around 1910. Only a handful of Harriman's early settlers were Catholic, but the Rev. J. Face arrived in the city in 1891 to minister to them. One of his successors, Fr. Emmanuel Callahan, purchased six lots in block 105 on Margrave Street to build a permanent church building, which was dedicated on December 29, 1907.

The old South Harriman Baptist Church is pictured here around 1940. The church was organized in a field near its present site on September 9, 1907. The original building was behind the old South Harriman school and served the church from 1908 until it was replaced by the building seen here in 1927. This building was in turn replaced in 1970.

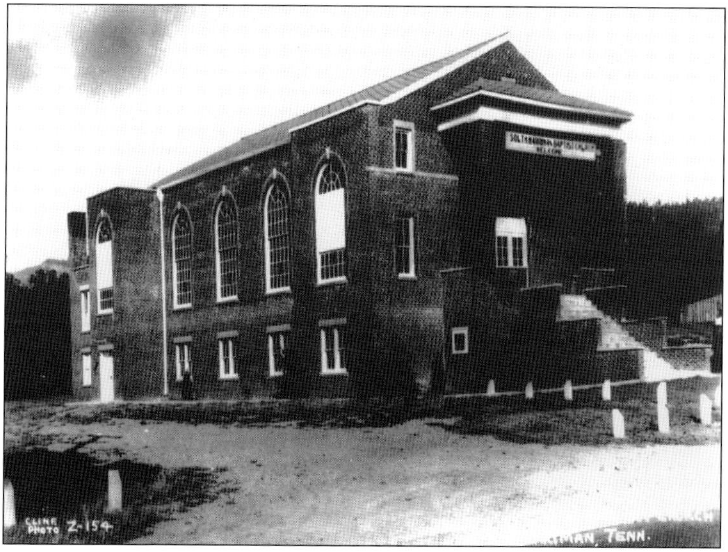

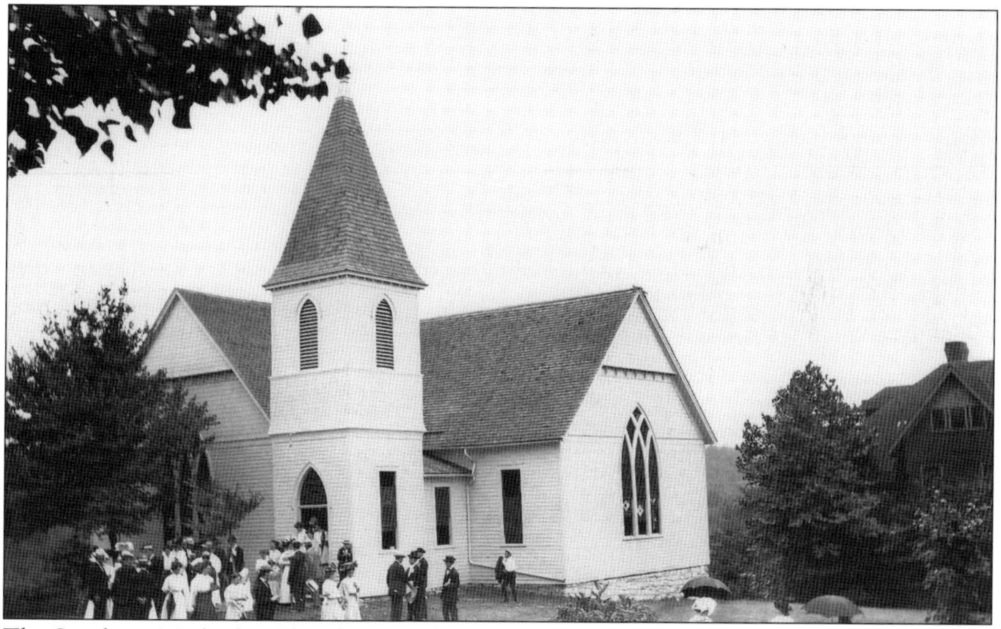

The Southern Methodist Church is seen here around 1910. Organized in May 1890, the church building was dedicated in September 1891. It was one of two Methodist churches in Harriman's early years—the other being the Methodist Episcopal Church—reflecting divisions between Northern and Southern Methodists. A further controversy arose over the issue of supporting political parties favoring legalized saloons, leading to the formation of a third Methodist church, the Independent Methodist Church, founded in 1896 from former members of the Methodist Episcopal Church.

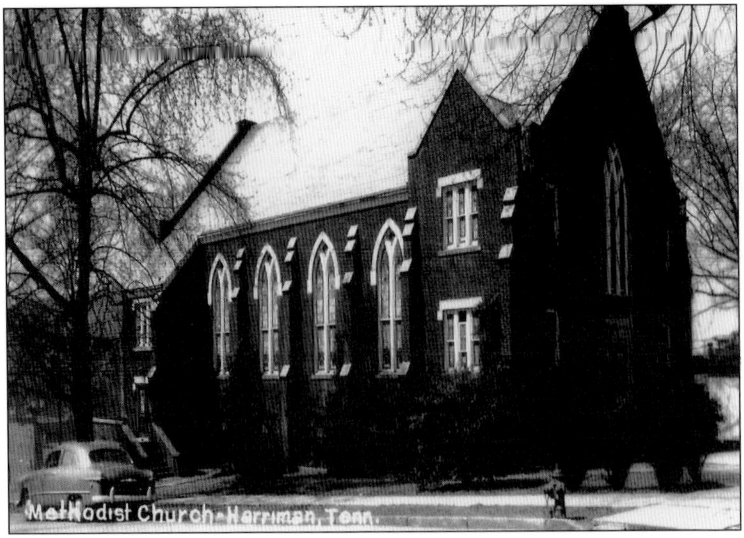

Harriman Methodist Church is seen here around 1940. This church, constructed in 1927, is located at the corner of Queen and Trenton Streets and is still in operation today.

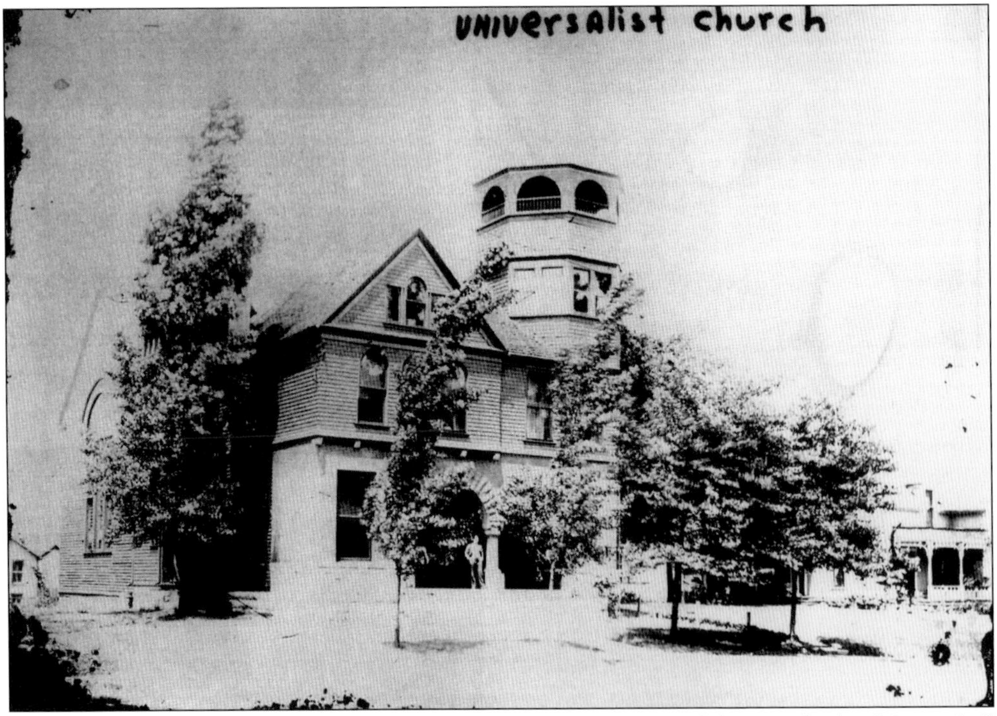

Grace Universalist Church, built in 1892, was located at the top of the Cumberland Street hill (across from the present Cumberland Street Park). One of the first buildings in Harriman, the church's steeple (at 75 feet) was the highest point in Harriman at the time. Many prominent early residents attended the church, which remained active until the 1920s. Unfortunately, declining members necessitated the discontinuation of the church, and the building was torn down in 1932.

Eight

Homes

Harriman's historic homes continue to draw visitors from far and wide thanks to their unique designs. Unlike most towns, particularly in the Appalachian region, Harriman was a planned city, built on a grid over a three-year period. It went from a community consisting of two farms to a city of 4,000 people in just two years. Following the collapse of the East Tennessee Land Company, construction ceased. As a result, many of the homes reflect the Victorian style popular in the early 1890s.

Although some homes from Harriman's early days no longer stand or have fallen into disrepair, many have been maintained or restored over the years. In 1990, the Cornstalk Heights Historical Community Organization (CHHCO) was established to protect the historic home district. Today, the organization hosts periodic tours of many of the homes.

Cornstalk Heights, which was listed in the National Register of Historic Places in 1990 thanks to the efforts of the CHHCO, is home to many painstakingly maintained Victorian homes dating to the 1890s. Harriman's earliest leaders lived in these homes, which serve today as the clearest visual link to the city's Victorian past.

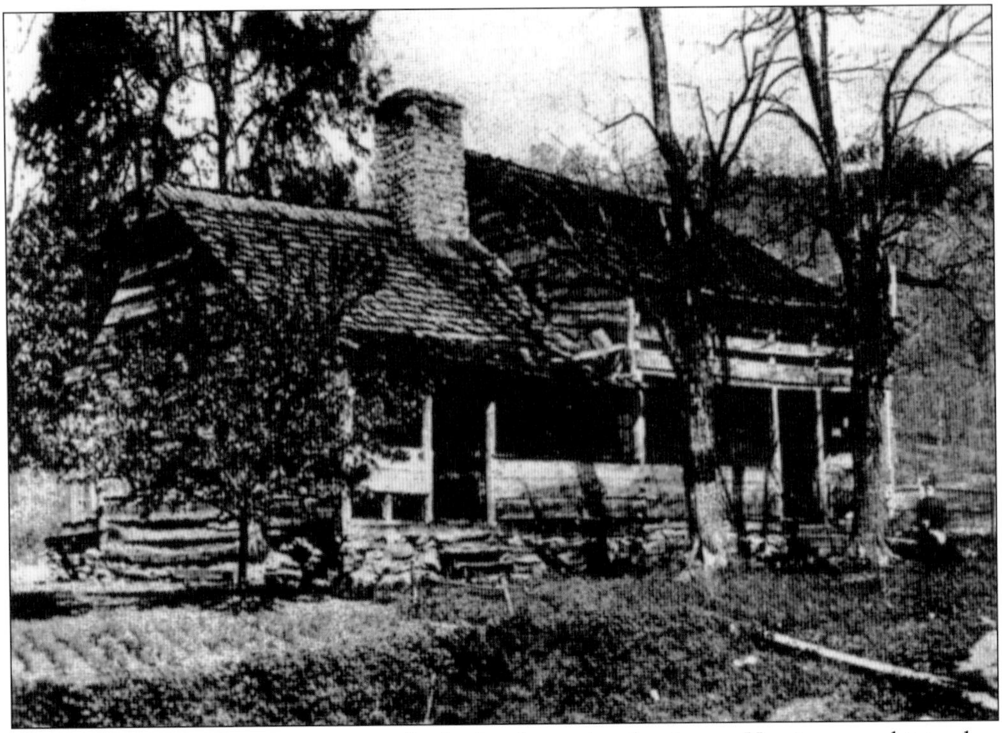

The Old Margrave House was reportedly the first house in what is now Harriman, and it is a key landmark in the city's early history. Dating back at least to the 1860s, and perhaps to the 1810s, it was in this area that Union general Walter Harriman camped during the Civil War. While here, he encountered the disabled resident of the house, mentioning to him the area "would make a fine place for a town." Years later, the man would recount this to the founders of Harriman who would then choose to name the city after General Harriman, instead of the previously suggested Fiskville. This photograph was probably taken in the early 1890s.

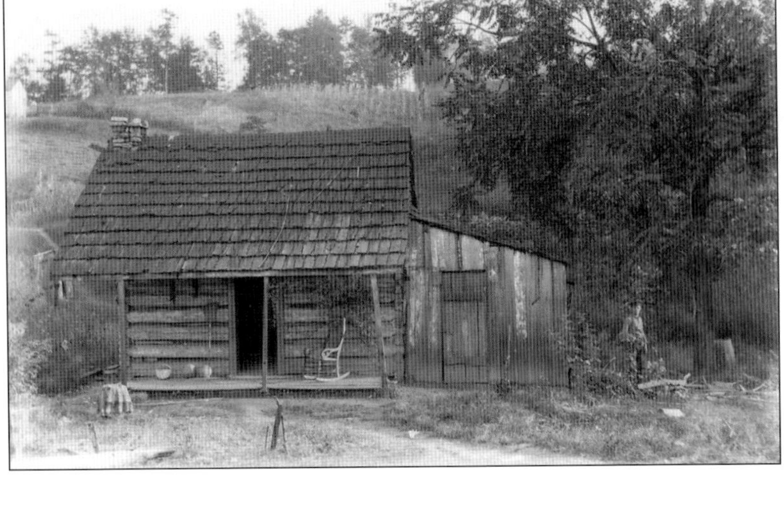

Known as the "Little Old Log Cabin in the Lane" at Walnut Hill, this was another early Harriman home, probably from the early 1890s.

This photograph of Dr. John Rockwell's home at Ridgeview on Walden's Ridge, overlooking the city, was taken around 1910. This was Rockwell's country home, as he also had a house at 413 Cumberland Street. Rockwell served on the faculty of the American Temperance University. The house stood near Balanced Rock, about a quarter mile southwest from where the Roane State Community College president's house now stands. The house may have burned, and was no longer standing in 1930.

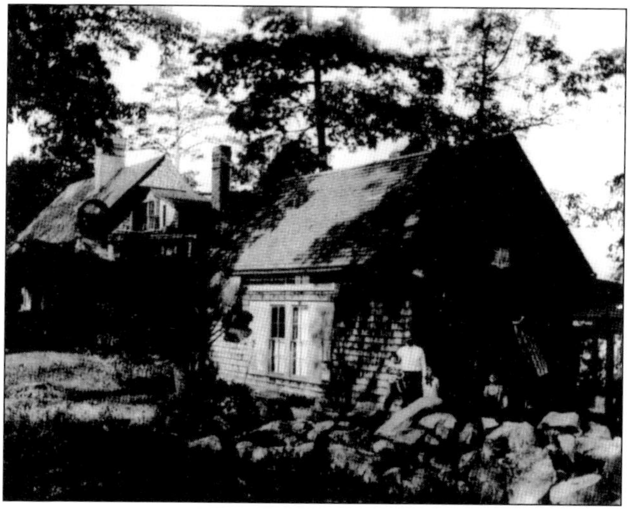

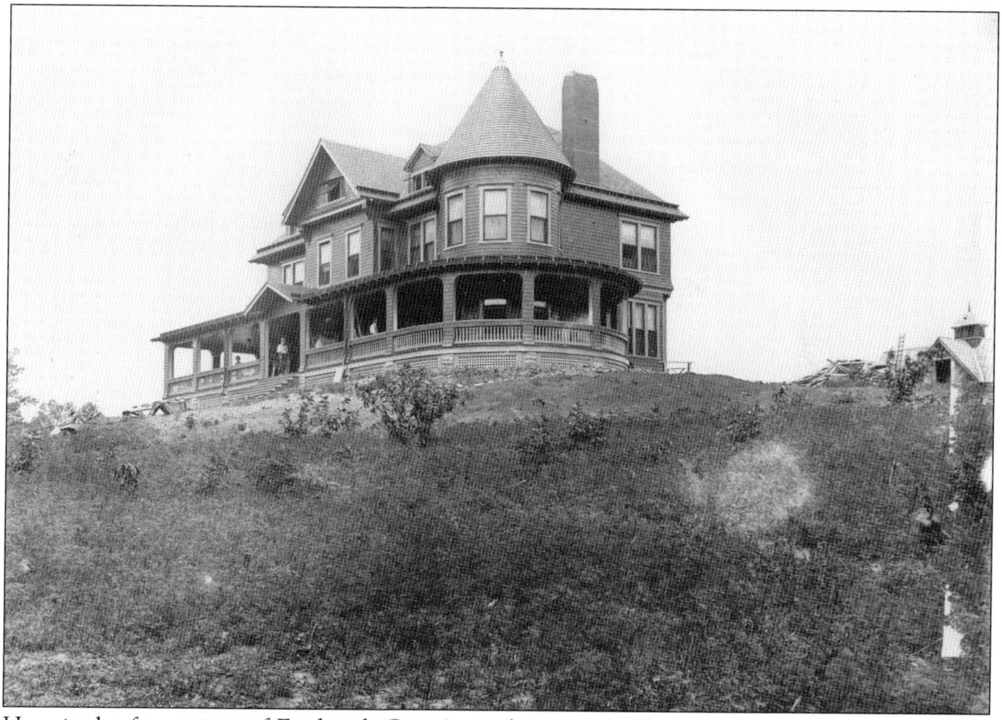

Here is the front view of Frederick Gates's residence, around 1895. Gates was the founder of Harriman, a former Methodist minister who believed that temperance "could be commercialized to the betterment of mankind and to business profit," according to Walter Pulliam. A native of New York, Gates believed so strongly in this vision that he helped build a city based on it. Torn down in the mid-1950s, the Gates home was located on the former site of Harriman Middle School on Cumberland Street.

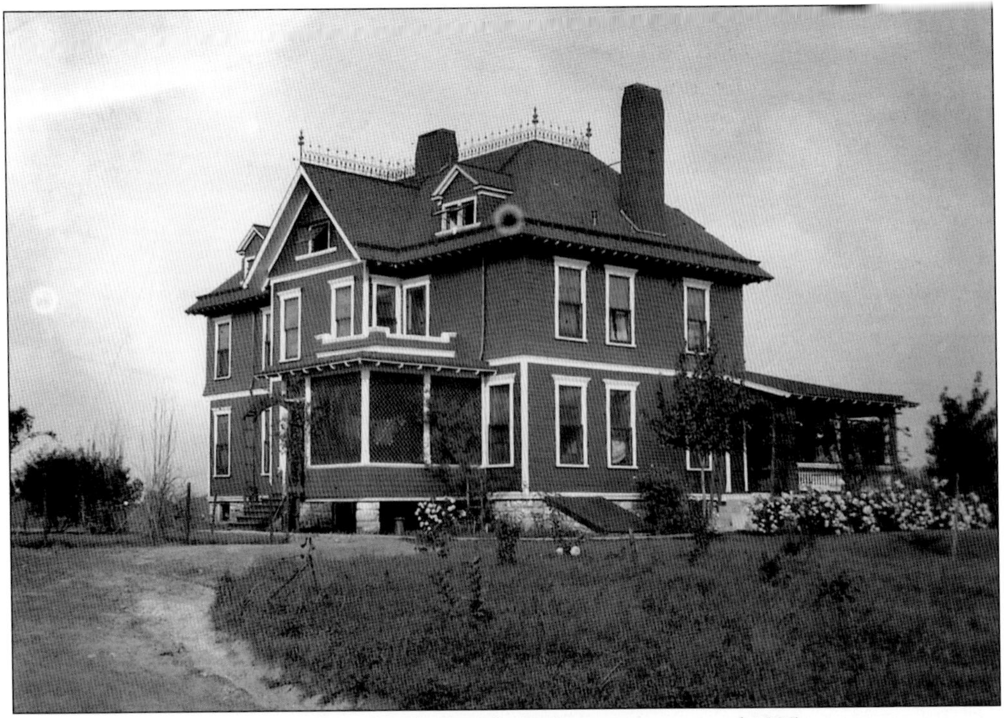

Shown here is the rear view of Frederick Gates's residence, also around 1895.

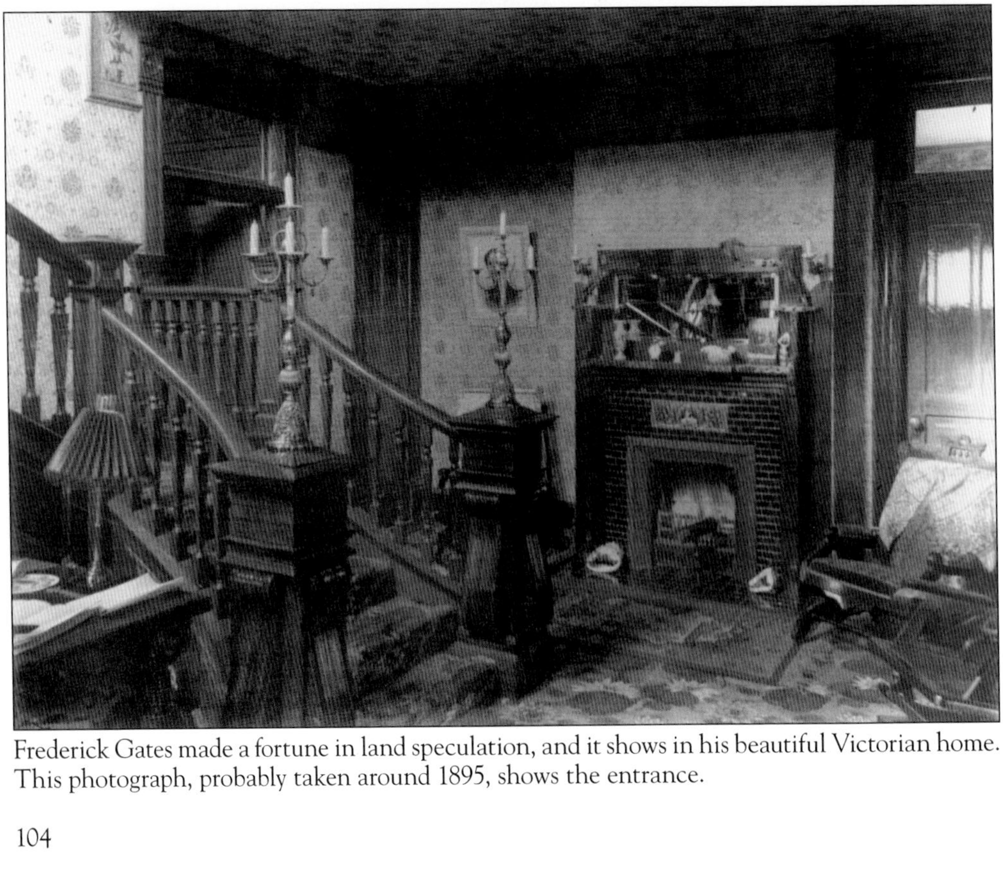

Frederick Gates made a fortune in land speculation, and it shows in his beautiful Victorian home. This photograph, probably taken around 1895, shows the entrance.

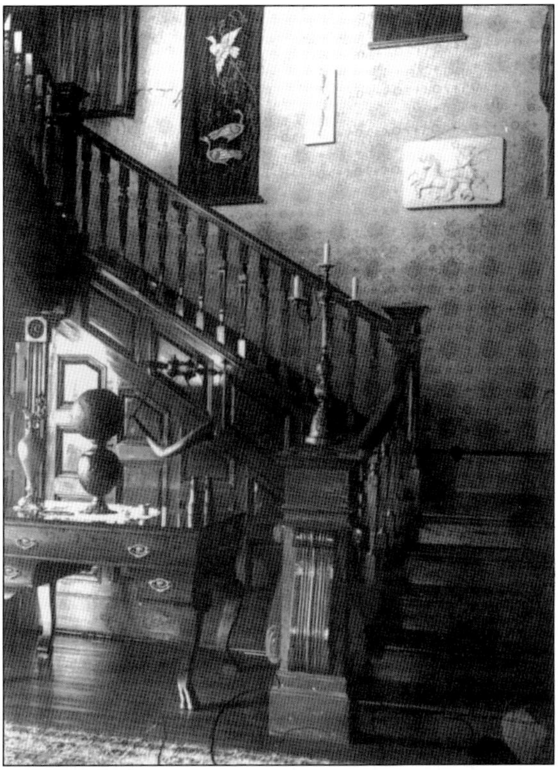

The staircase inside the Gates home is pictured here around 1895.

The residence of Walter C. Harriman is on the left, around 1895. A former New Hampshire congressman, the city was named for his father, a Union general who camped in the area during the Civil War. Walter C. Harriman served as managing director of the East Tennessee Land Company and later worked for the First National Bank. His home was located at 449 Margrave Street. It was torn down in the 1960s.

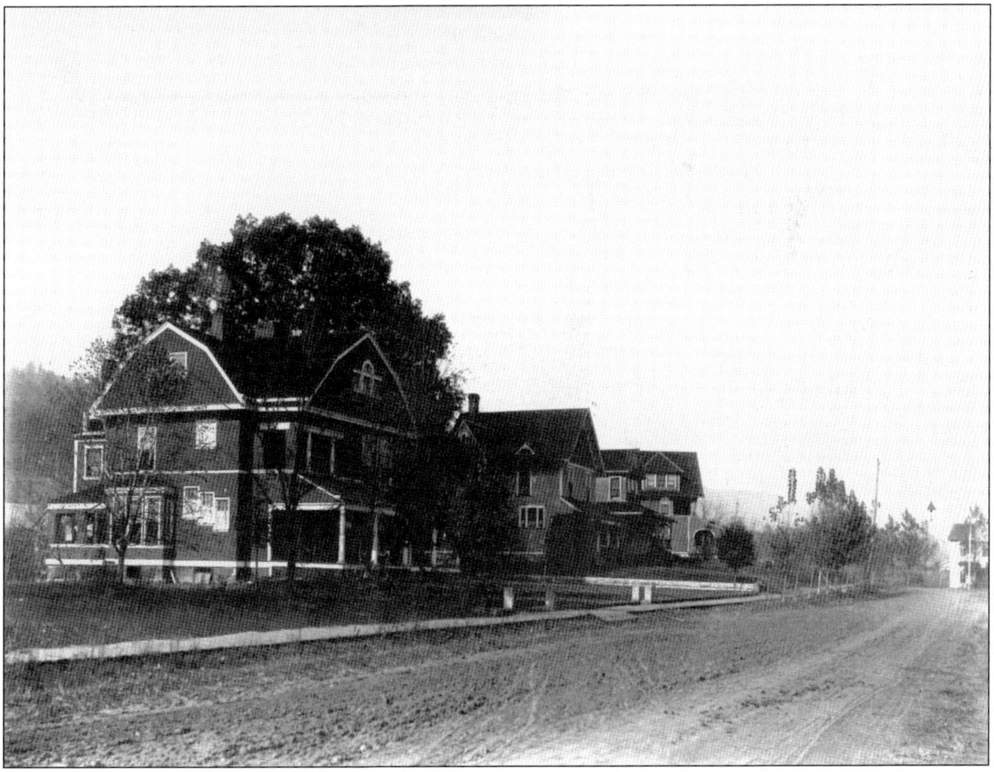

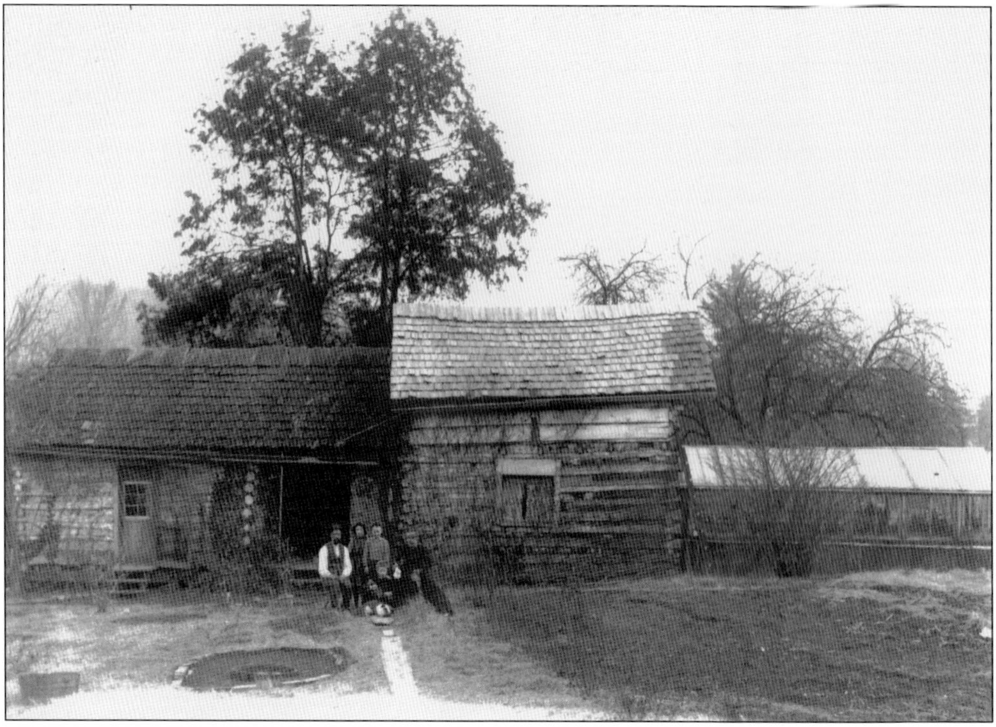

E.J. Bridge's cabin and greenhouse was located on Pansy Hill, just across the Emory River from downtown. This photograph was taken around 1900.

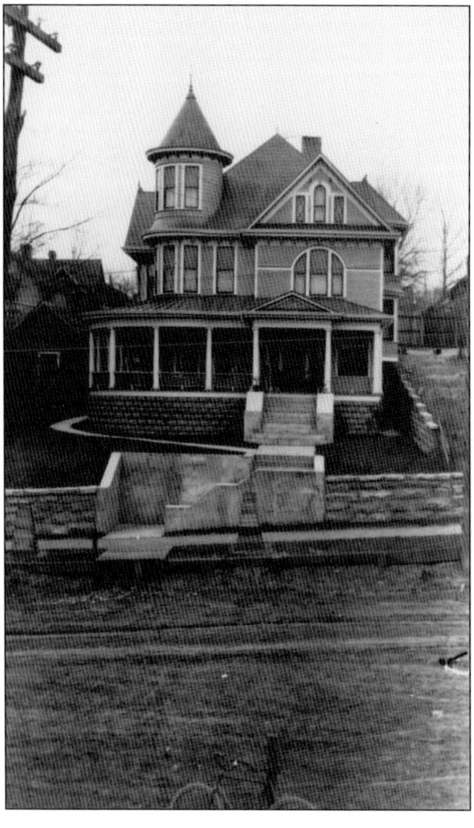

Charles P. Flanders's home was located at 424 Walden Street. Flanders, along with his brother, was an early Harriman pioneer, establishing Flanders Manufacturing Company in 1891. C.P. Flanders also served as an alderman for the city during the 1910s. The house still stands and is listed in the National Register of Historic Places.

This photograph of the interior of the Charles P. Flanders home was taken in March 1909.

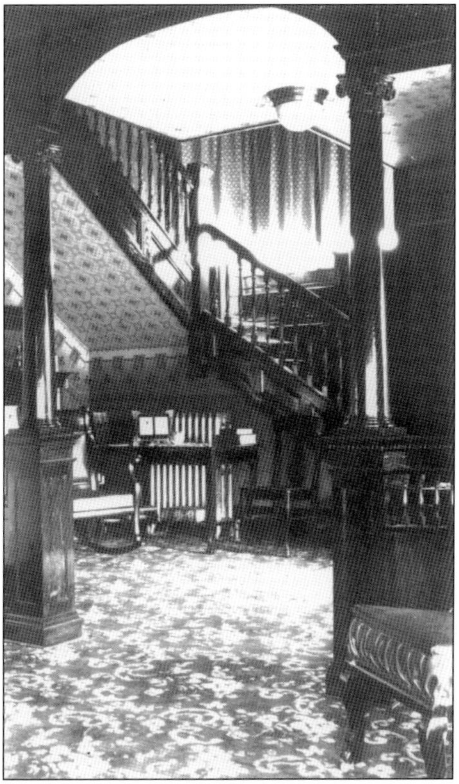

The 400 block of Walden Street is seen here in 1900. The house on the far left belonged to David Gibson.

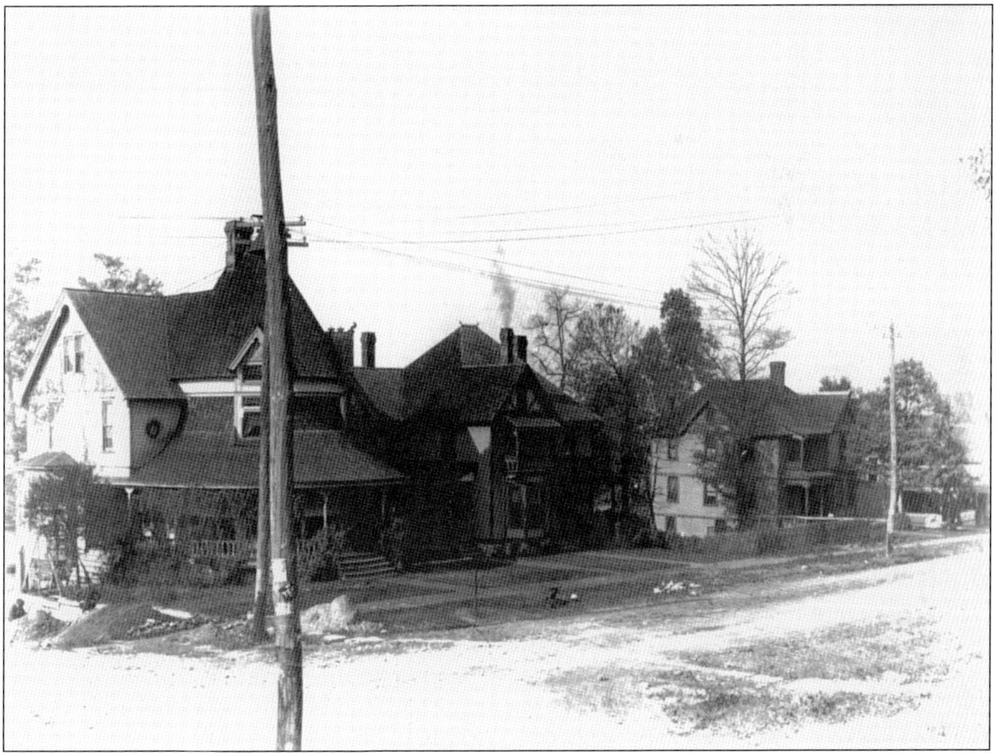

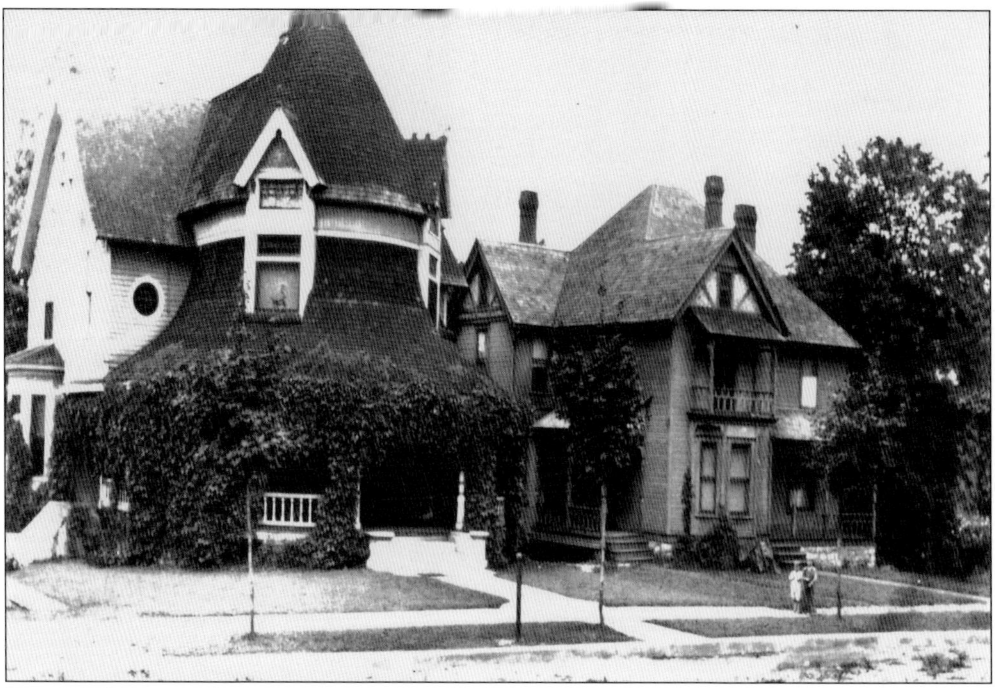

David Gibson's residence was on Walden Street at the corner of Cumberland Street, pictured here around 1900. Gibson, who moved to Harriman from Chattanooga, served as president of Gibson Agricultural Works, a farming implement manufacturer. An early promotional booklet described his home as being "of general design—very pleasing."

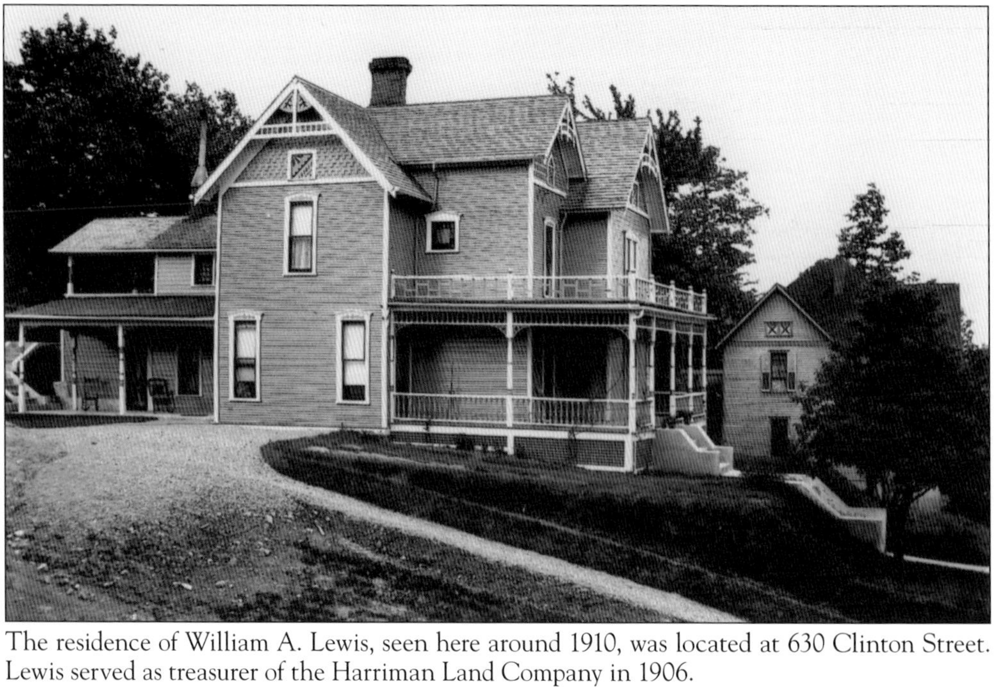

The residence of William A. Lewis, seen here around 1910, was located at 630 Clinton Street. Lewis served as treasurer of the Harriman Land Company in 1906.

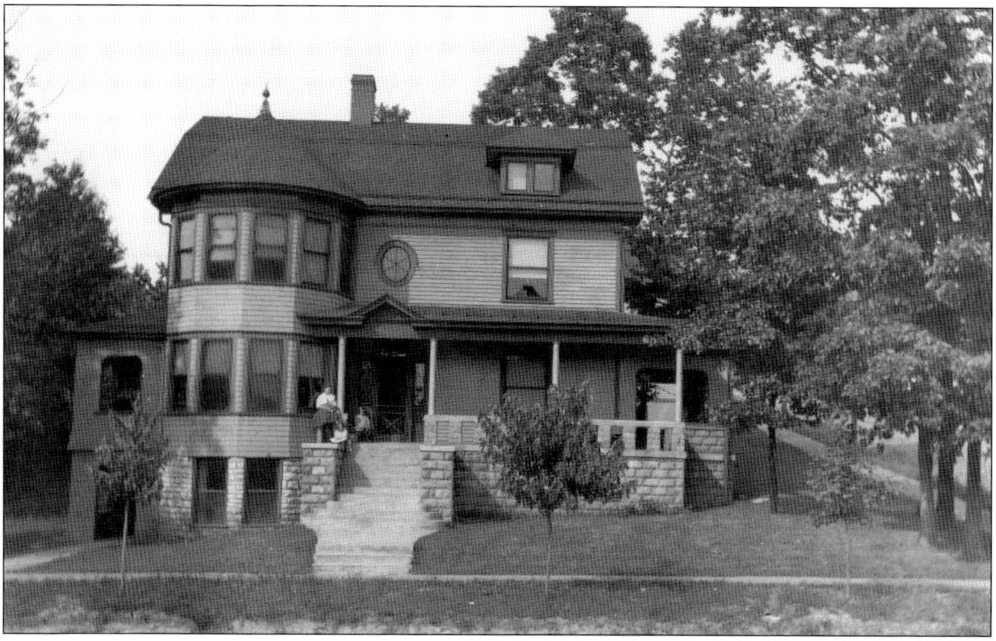

Pictured here around 1910 is the residence of Moses W. Emery at 402 Walden Street. Emery served as alderman during the 1890s. The home was later known as Yeargan Apartments.

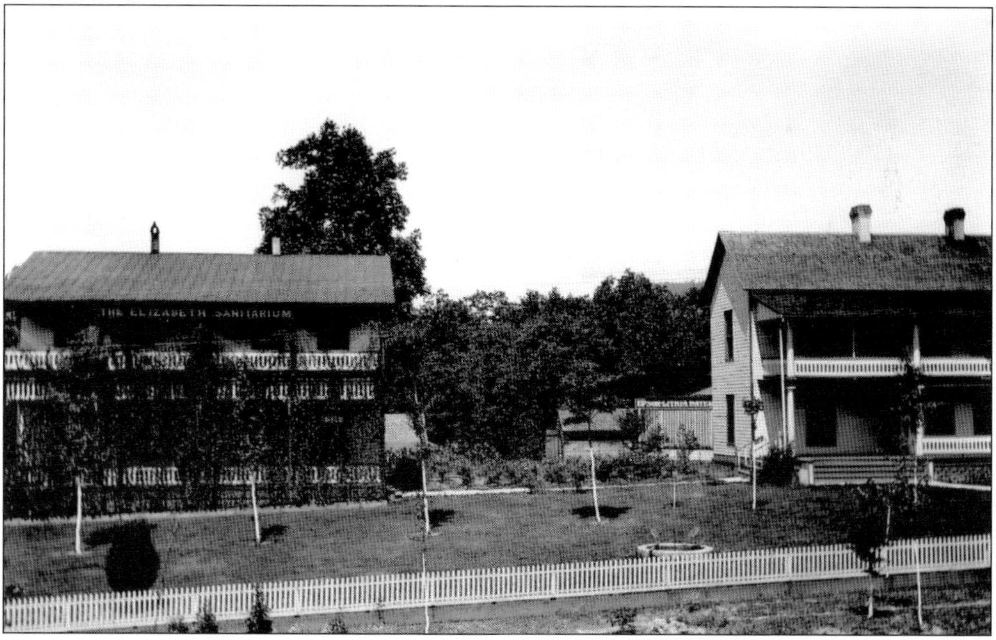

The residence of Dr. J.B. Goodwin is on the right, and the Elizabeth Sanitarium (operated by Dr. Goodwin) is on the left. They are located at the corner of present-day Ruritan Road and Carlock Avenue in South Harriman. This photograph was likely taken around 1920.

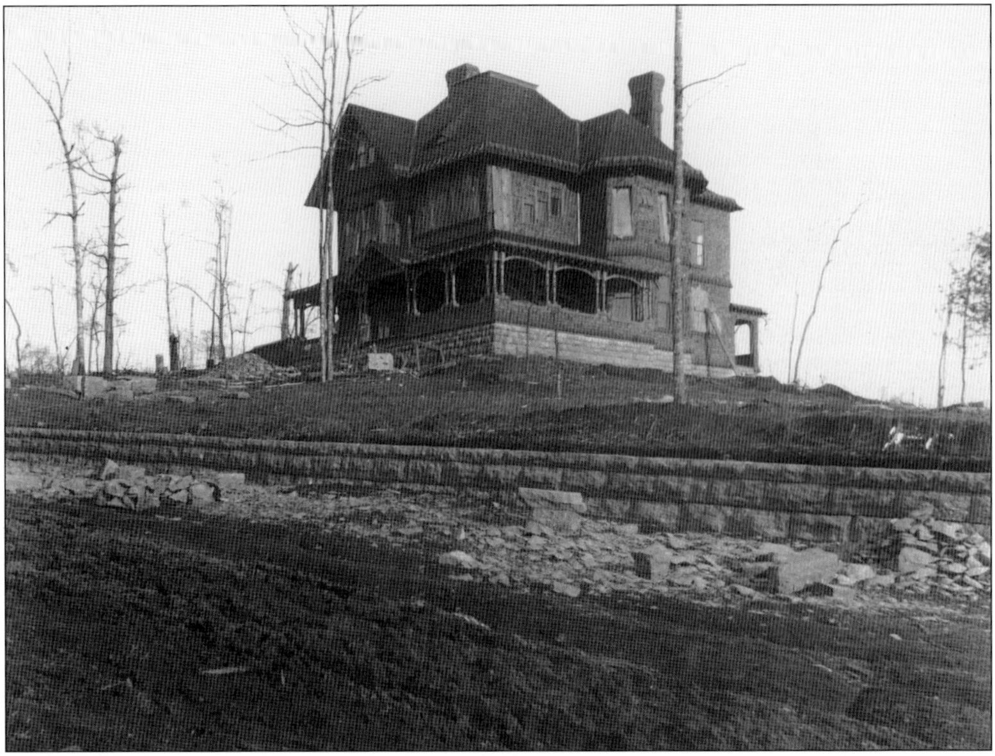

The S.K. Paige House was located at 414 Cumberland Avenue in 1891. In this photograph, the windows are not yet finished. The home was said to rival the Gates residence in refinement and cost. Paige, an early leader of Harriman, managed the S.K. Paige Lumber and Manufacturing Company, which provided much of the materials for early Harriman's construction.

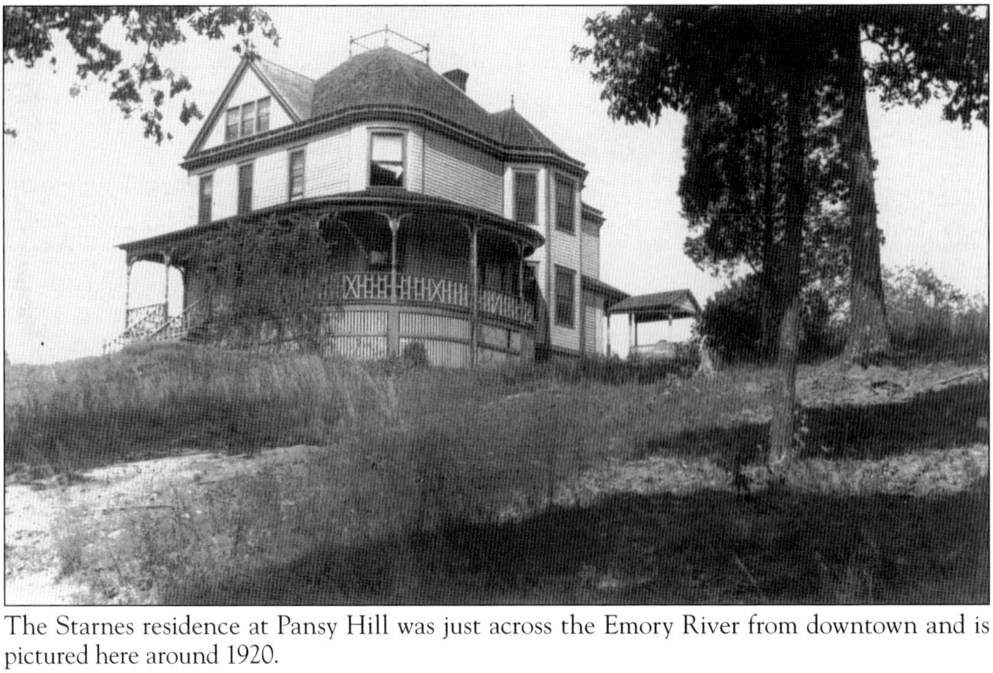

The Starnes residence at Pansy Hill was just across the Emory River from downtown and is pictured here around 1920.

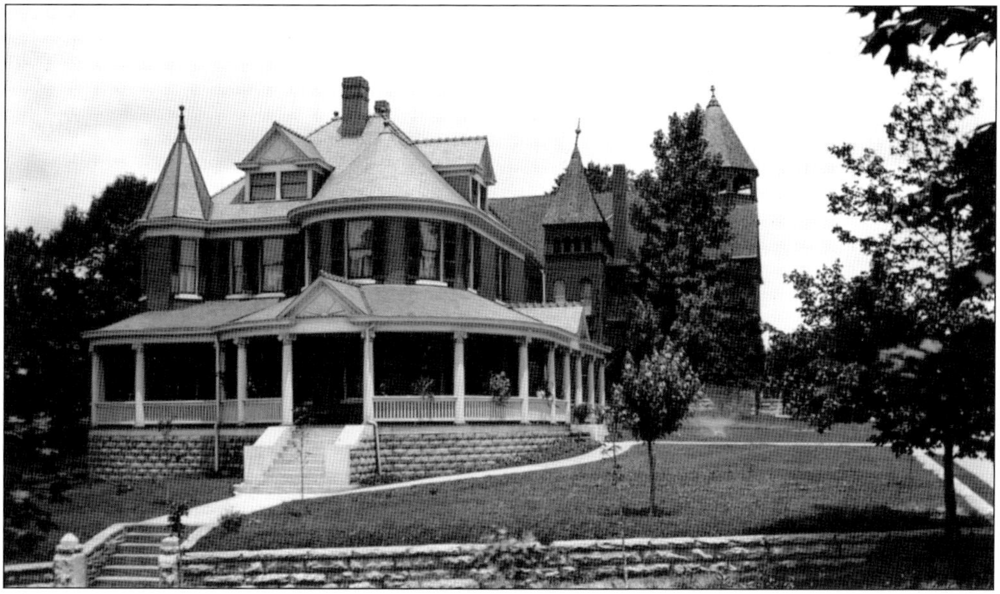

The home of Sam P. Sparks, on the hill on Cumberland Street, is pictured here around 1920. Sparks served as treasurer of the East Tennessee Land Company and on the board of trustees of American University.

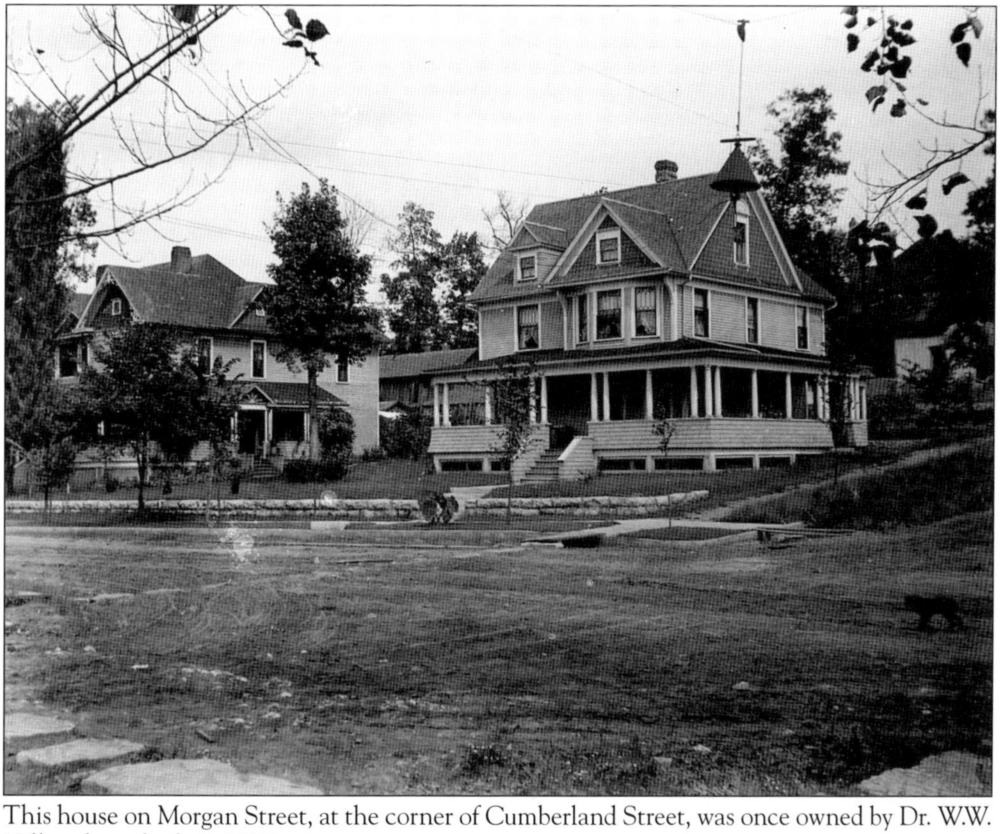

This house on Morgan Street, at the corner of Cumberland Street, was once owned by Dr. W.W. Hill and was built in 1908.

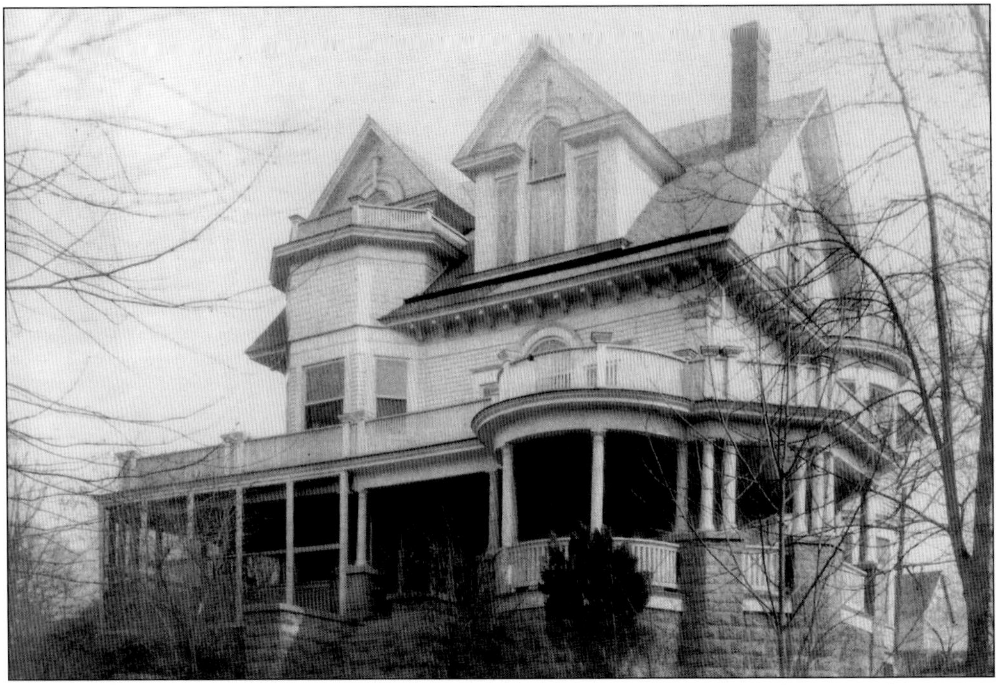

The old Dr. Rockwell home was located on the 500 block of Cumberland Street. This winter photograph was probably taken around 1920.

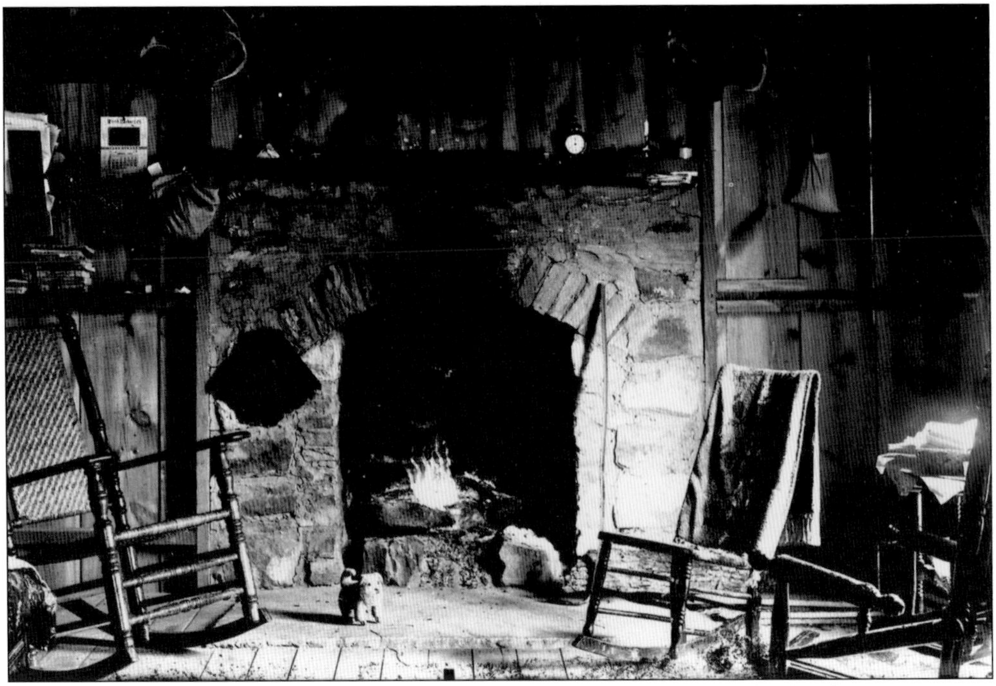

A fire warms an unidentified home in Harriman. Note the puppy near the fireplace.

Nine

Sports

Sports have been a part of Harriman's cultural fabric since the earliest days. Early settlers of Harriman, educated at Ivy League institutions, brought a new and dangerous sport known as football to the city. In 1891, a team representing Harriman participated in one of the first football games in East Tennessee, defeating a Knoxville team on Thanksgiving Day.

The American Temperance University also had a football squad, but its results would not be quite so impressive. In 1905, the team played the University of Tennessee in Knoxville and suffered a humiliating 104–0 loss, which still stands as UT's most lopsided win ever.

The following year, American would play UT twice, with the second meeting in Harriman, the only time UT has ever played in the city. UT won the first contest 10–0, but the second game ended in a forfeit by American when the players walked off the field after a fight broke out between the two teams.

By 1909, Harriman Central High had a football team, which played Rhea County and Mooney's second team, but discontinued the sport in 1911. Harriman High School would begin play in 1921 with two games against Rockwood, losing both by scores of 77–0 and 12–7 but beginning one of the most enduring rivalries in Tennessee high school football.

In addition to football, baseball and basketball have long histories in Harriman. The city even briefly had a professional baseball team, when Harriman's team joined the Appalachian League for one year, competing against Knoxville, Bristol, Johnson City, Chattanooga, and Asheville.

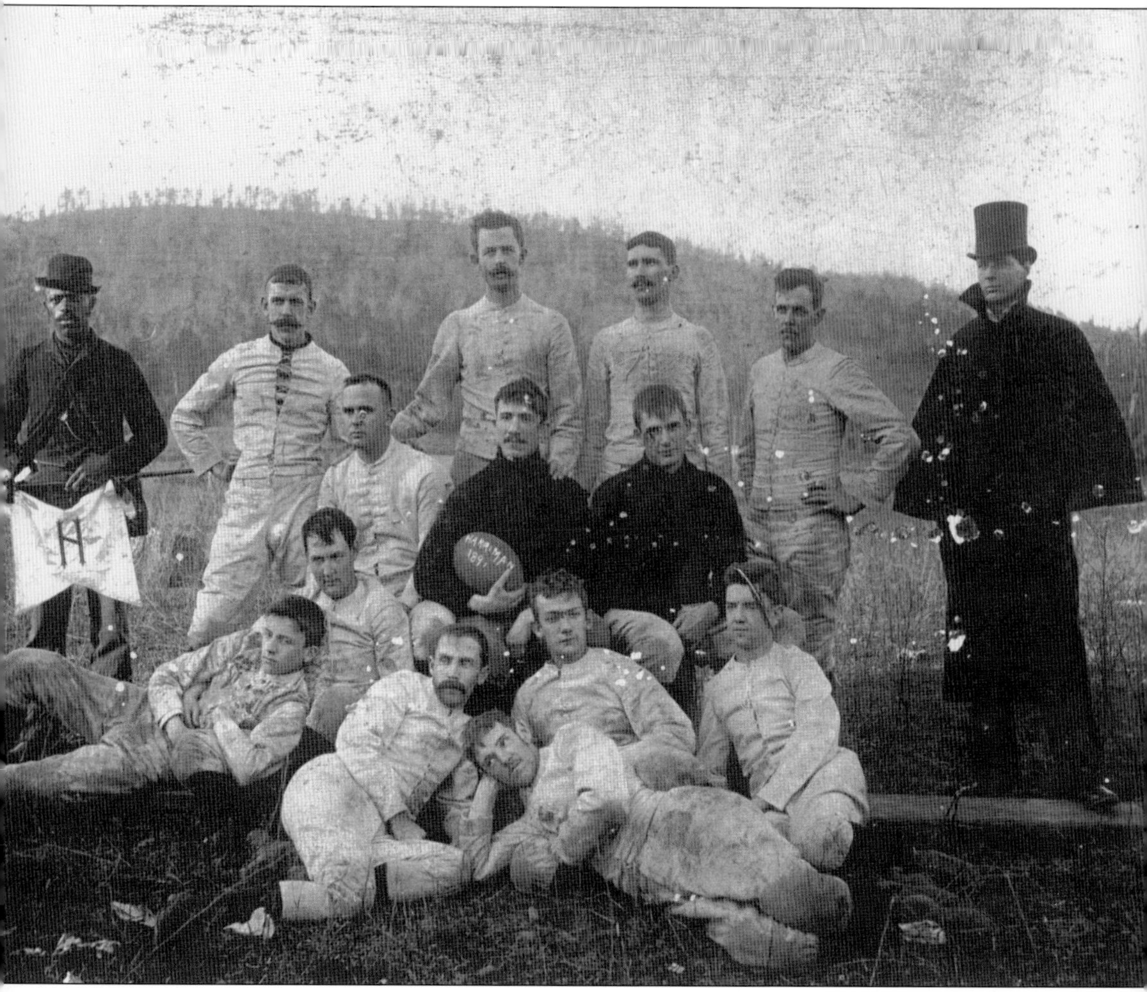

Harriman's first football team formed in 1891. This team played a game in Knoxville against a team representing that city on Thanksgiving Day 1891 and returned home with a 14–4 victory. It was the first football game played in Knoxville. Two Harriman settlers, Harry Durrell and W.C. Spicer, had played football on the 1890 Princeton squad and brought the sport to Harriman. Spicer, who served as team captain, is the player holding the ball. Harry Durrell is to the right of him. The identities of the other players are not known.

An unidentified Mooney athlete is pictured around 1909. American University was succeeded by the Mooney School, a preparatory institution administered by William Dromgoole Mooney. Mooney, who already had a school established in Murfreesboro, moved his institution to Harriman in 1908. The school would also be short-lived, however, folding in 1912.

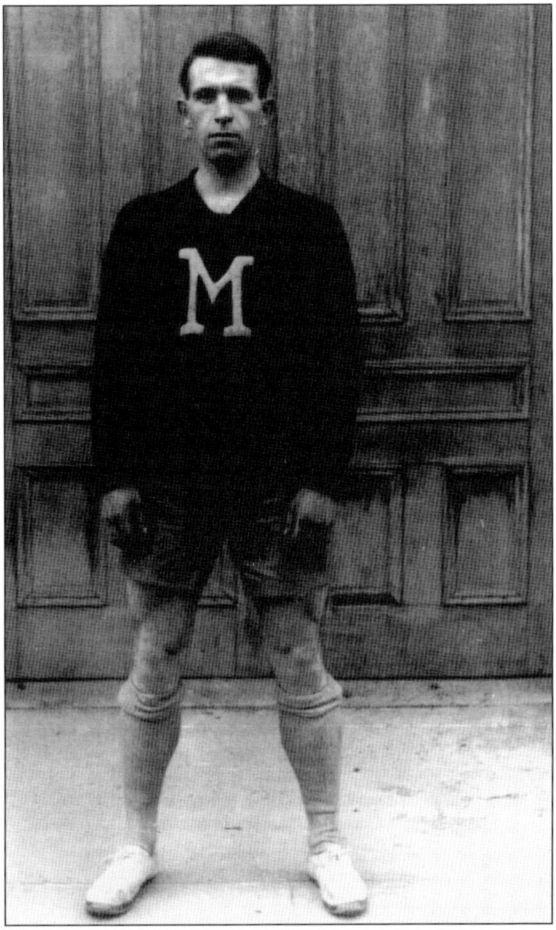

This 1908 photograph shows an early Harriman baseball team, probably representing the Central High School. The names of the players are not known.

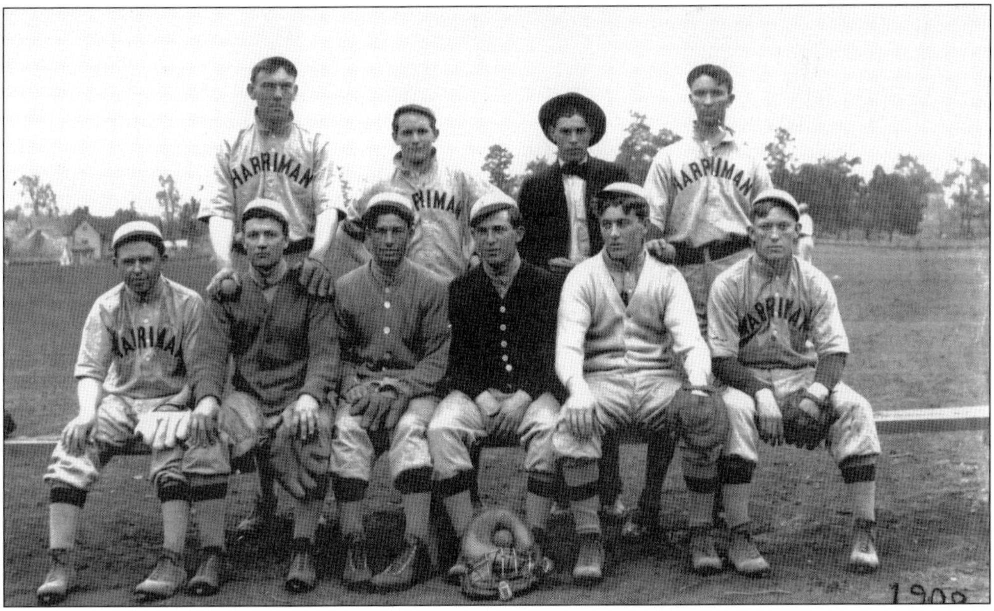

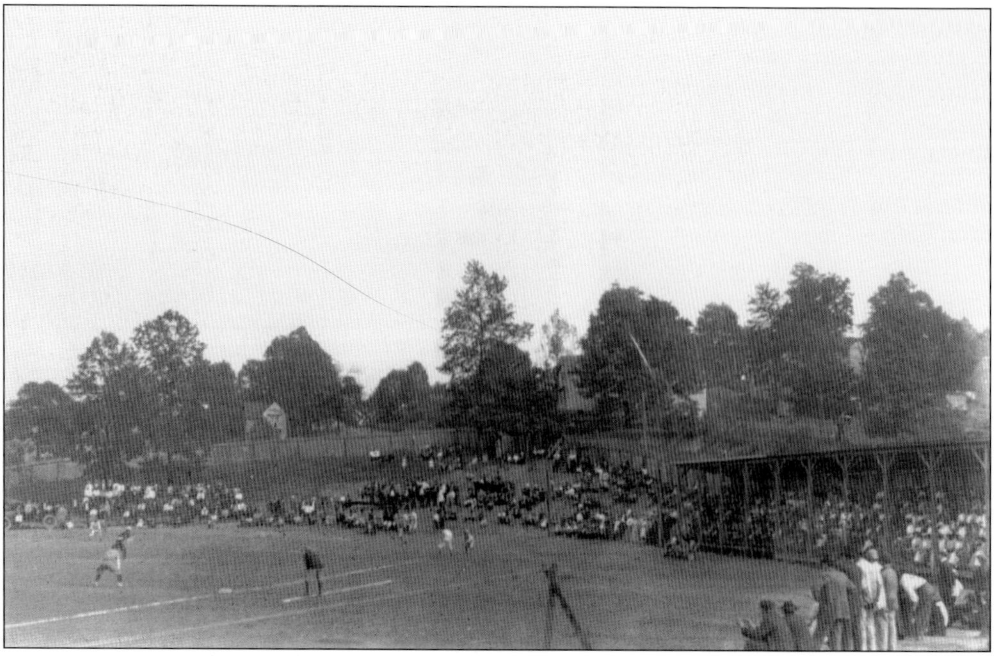

The first professional baseball game in Harriman occurred on May 18, 1914. Beginning in 1912, Harriman had a city baseball team, which went semi-professional in 1914, joining the Appalachian League for part of the season.

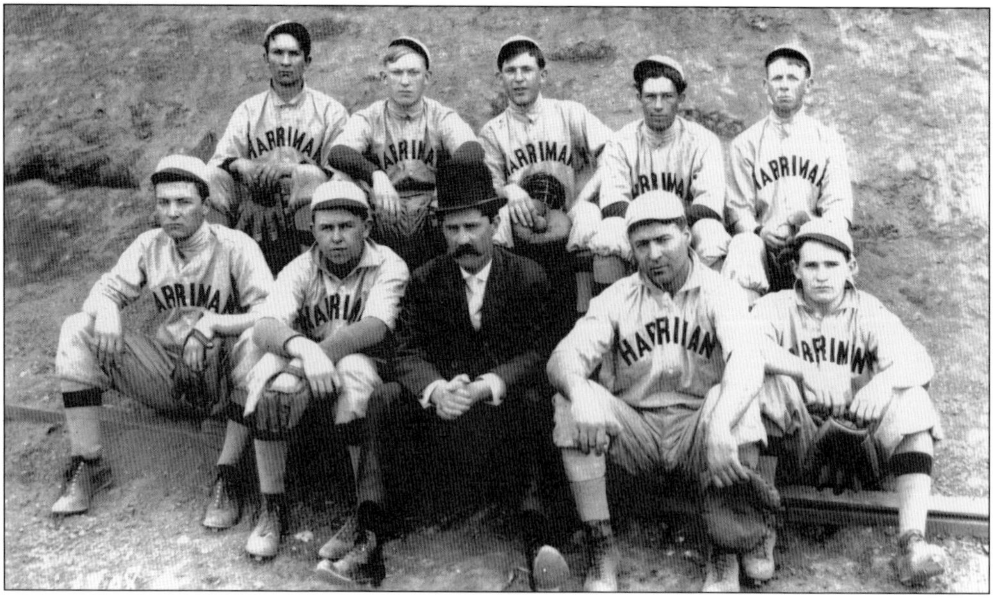

This photograph shows an early Harriman baseball team.

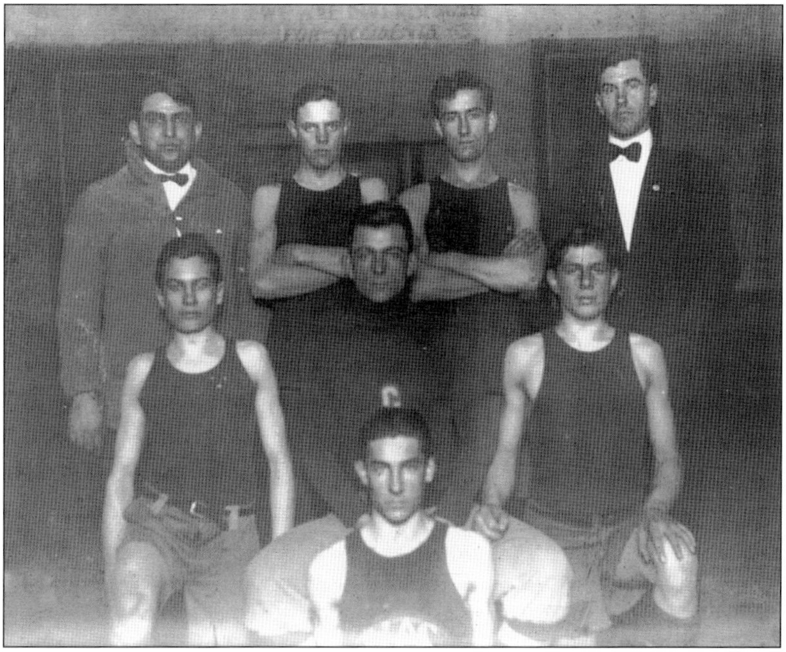

The basketball team for Central High School is seen here around 1908. The identities of the players are unknown.

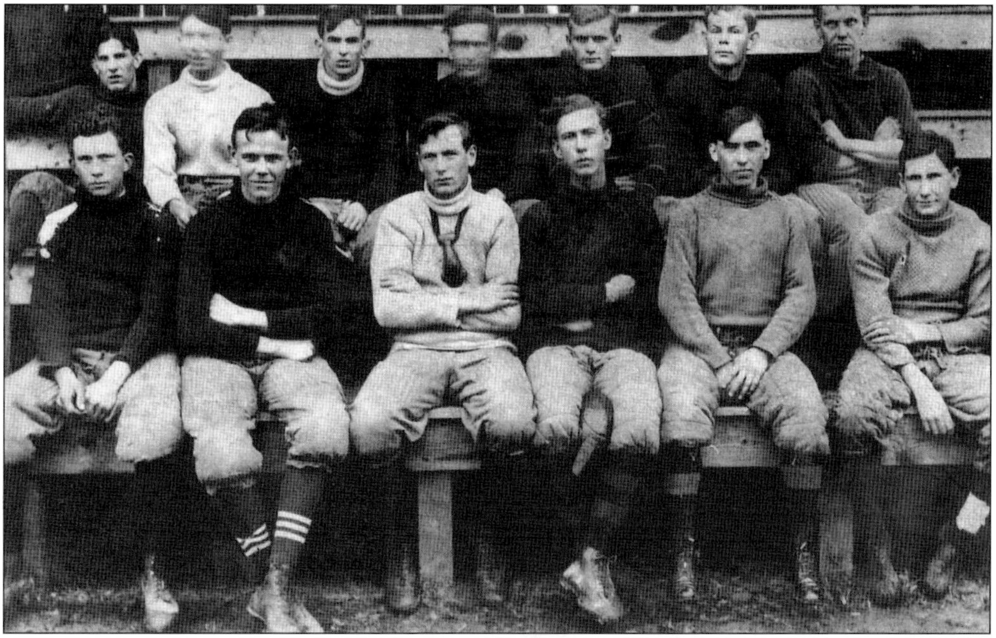

Harriman Central High School's 1909 football team played at least two games during the season: Rhea County on October 8, and the Mooney School's second team the next day. At the time, it was not uncommon for high schools and colleges to use "ringers," or non-students. The players shown here are (first row) unidentified, Gary Renfro, Paul Darnell, Harry Green, unidentified, and Rueben Hurst; (second row) ? Ingram, ? Pelham, ? Sheflett, ? Roster, unidentified, Ed Sander, and Earl Parrish.

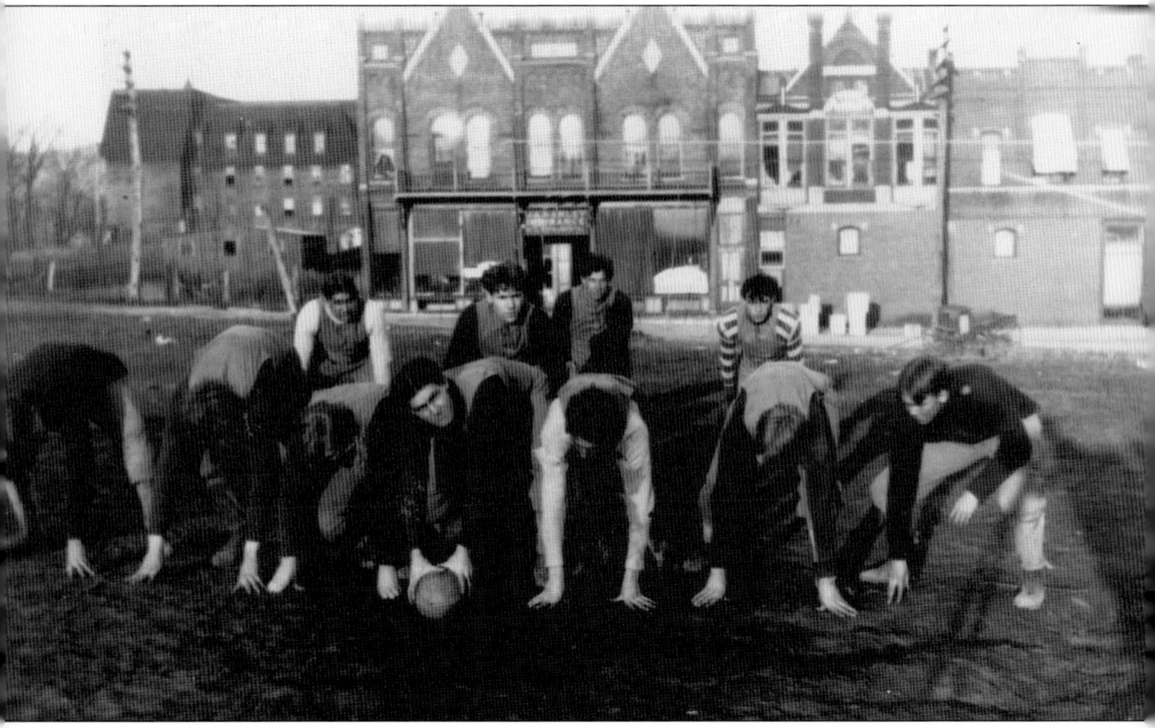

This 1920s team represented Harriman High School. The photograph was taken on Walden Street on the present site of the parking lot for the former Harriman Hospital. The Cumberland Hotel is in the background, and was located on the corner of Devonia and Queen Streets.

Harriman High's 1928 football team is pictured in this team photograph. From left to right are (first row) Ted Newman, Clayton Breashears, Charles Delaney, Bob DeLaneym, Rusty Berry, Chester Harvey, and Sanders "Red" Bowman; (second row) Rip Cox, James Iddins, Foster Lane, and John R. Cate.

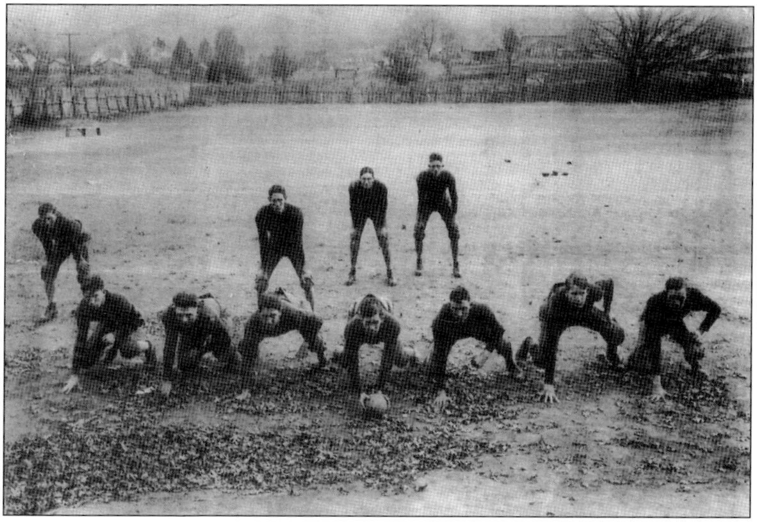

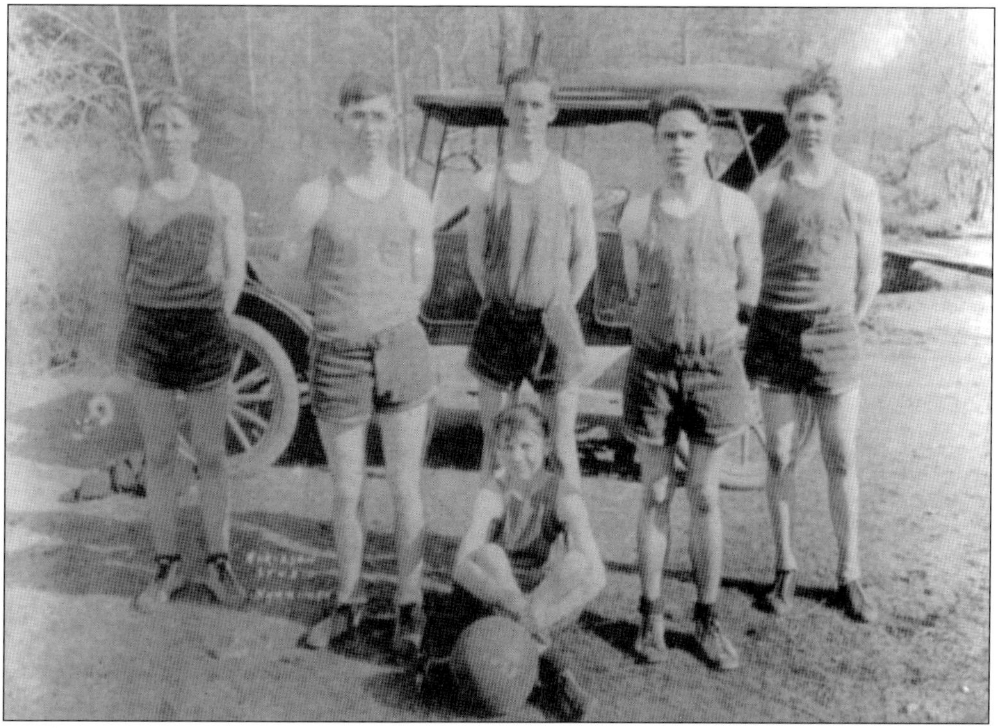

South Harriman High School's 1928 basketball team was photographed with what appears to be a Model T Ford in the background.

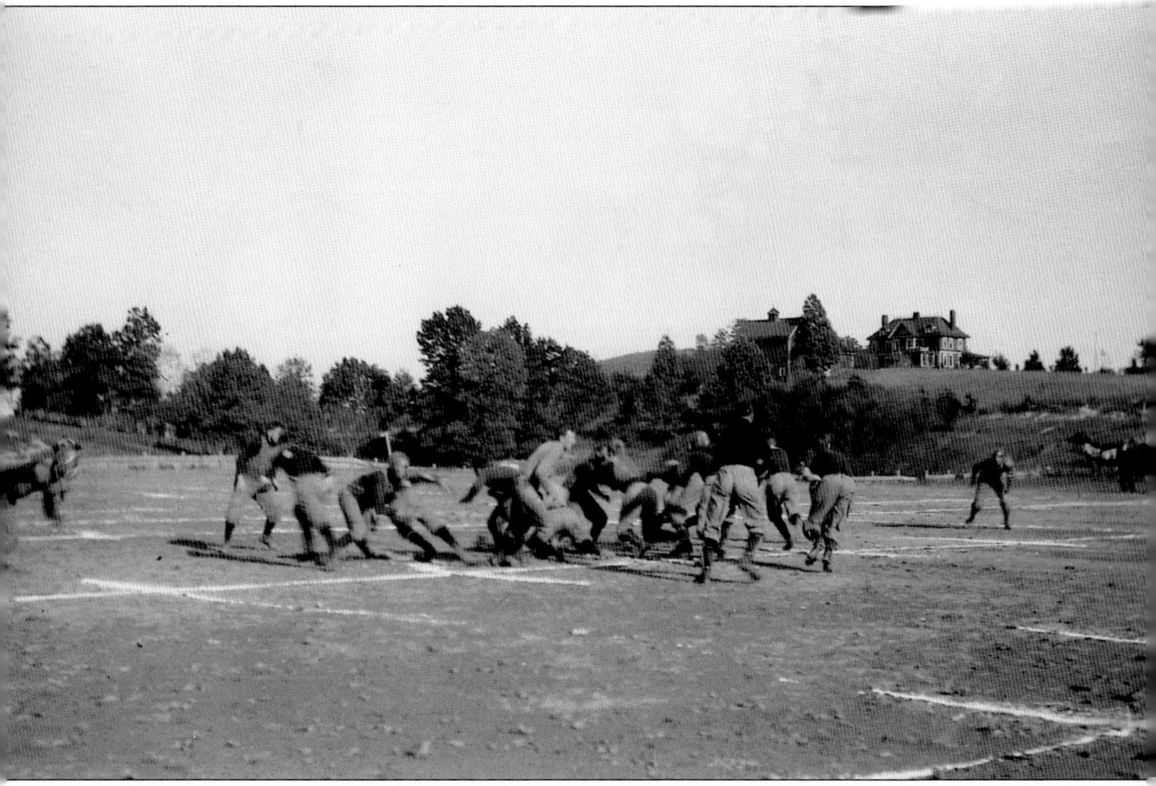

This early Harriman football game probably took place in the 1920s. The field was located at the corner of Roane and Georgia Streets. The Gates Mansion is in the background.

Ten

People

Though it may sound cliché, it is Harriman's people who truly make the city special. The founders of Harriman were prominent, highly educated men who excelled in business (though their business went bankrupt). Early residents were drawn by the appeal of temperance, which attracted well-meaning folks who sincerely wanted to make the world a better place by creating a model city.

Among the earliest leaders was Gen. Clinton Fisk, who ran for president on the Prohibition Party ticket in 1888. Due to his prominence, he was featured heavily in Harriman's promotional material, though he sadly died in July 1890 before his vision could be fulfilled.

Alphonso A. Hopkins was a longtime friend of General Fisk and was a prominent author and lecturer. A devout advocate of temperance, he had been a candidate for governor of New York on the Prohibitionist Party ticket. In Harriman, he served as editor of an early newspaper.

Ferdinand Schumacher of Quaker Oats, nicknamed "the Oatmeal King," was also an early leader. Schumacher served for a time as director of the East Tennessee Land Company and later as director of the Harriman Manufacturing Company.

Walter C. Harriman, after whose father the city was named, was a former member of Congress from New Hampshire, a Civil War veteran (serving as a boy), and journalist.

Though the city experienced turbulence in the early years, it continued to grow thanks to the efforts of the civic-minded. The Tarwater family helped establish two hosiery mills that would employ generations of Harriman residents. Citizens would lobby for, and eventually secure, a library from Andrew Carnegie and a hospital for the city.

Of course, for every great man (or woman) there are numerous other unidentified people who simply labored to support themselves and their families. They work in the mills, they serve us our food, they enforce our laws, and they teach our children. Though less recognized, they are no less important and without them no city could survive for a year, let alone over a century.

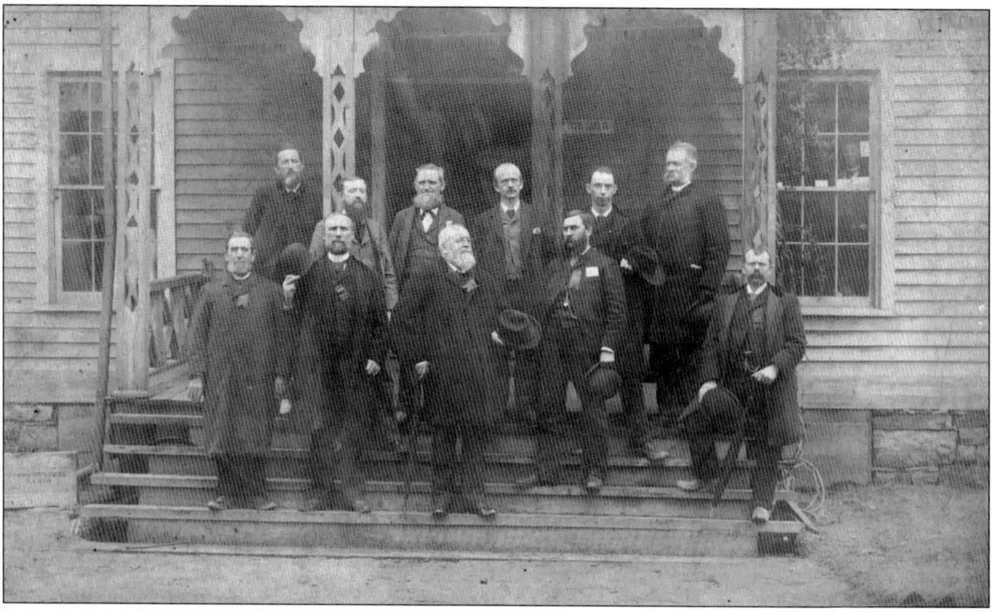

Seen here is the board of directors of the East Tennessee Land Company in 1890. From left to right are (first row) William Silverwood, A.W. Wagnalls, Gen. Clinton B. Fisk, A.A. Hopkins, and H.A. Buttrick; (second row) P.S. Mason, Frederick Gates, Ferdinand Schumacher, Walter C. Harriman, W.H. Russell, and Dr. I.K. Funk. At its height, the East Tennessee Land Company owned or controlled 300,000 acres in Roane and neighboring counties.

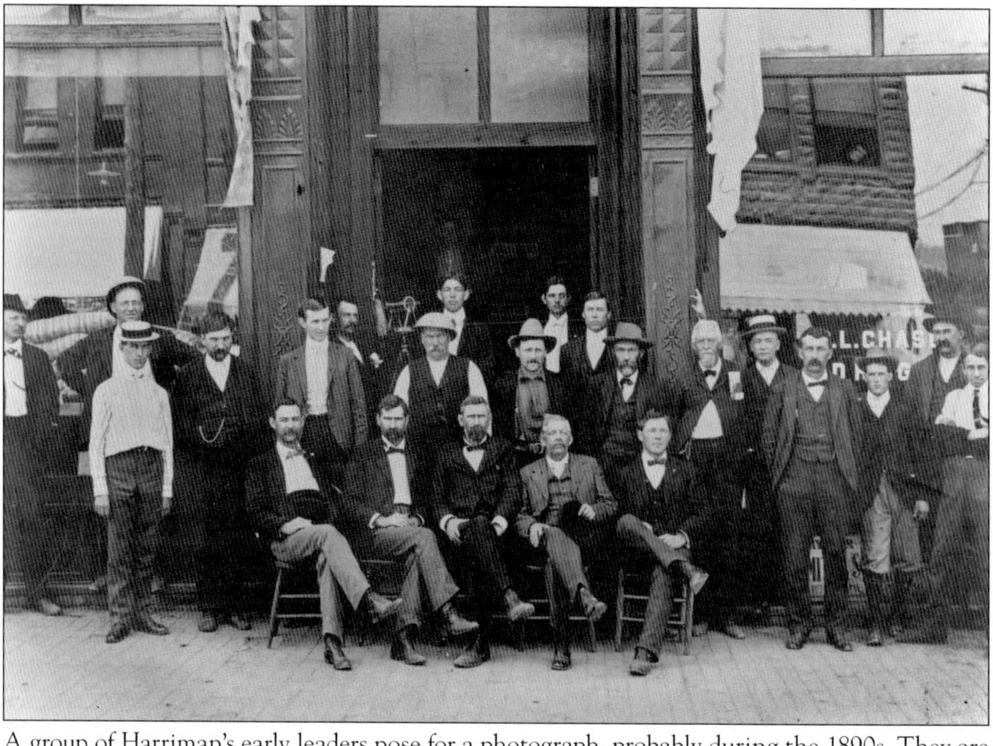

A group of Harriman's early leaders pose for a photograph, probably during the 1890s. They are in front of the O.L. Chase Drug Store.

The Victorian virtues of piety and hard work are on display in this photograph, taken around 1896. An unidentified lady churns while reading the Bible. The kitten is just underneath the churn—no doubt waiting for drops of milk to fall.

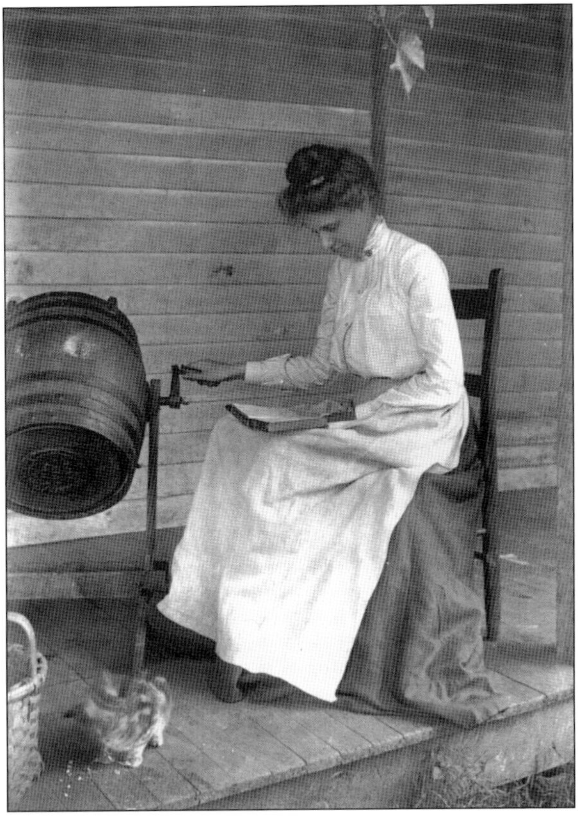

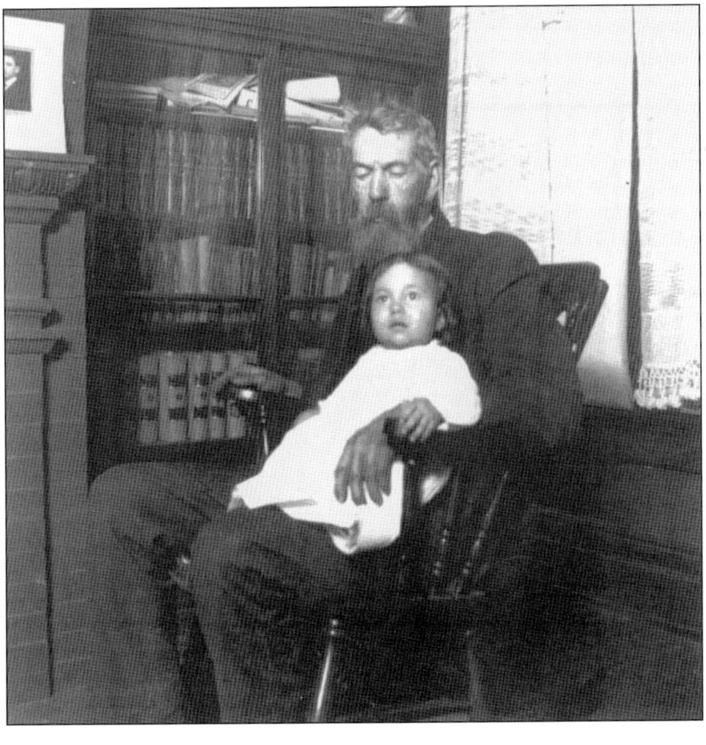

Capt. Isaac A. Hill (1844–1906) is pictured with his granddaughter Margaret Cassell Overton. Captain Hill, a veteran of the Union Army who participated in the Battles of Shiloh, Stones River, and others, was a native of Roane County and early leader in Harriman. He served as a city supervisor, was on the board of controls of American University, and worked as Harriman's third postmaster. This photograph was taken in 1906, shortly before the death of Hill.

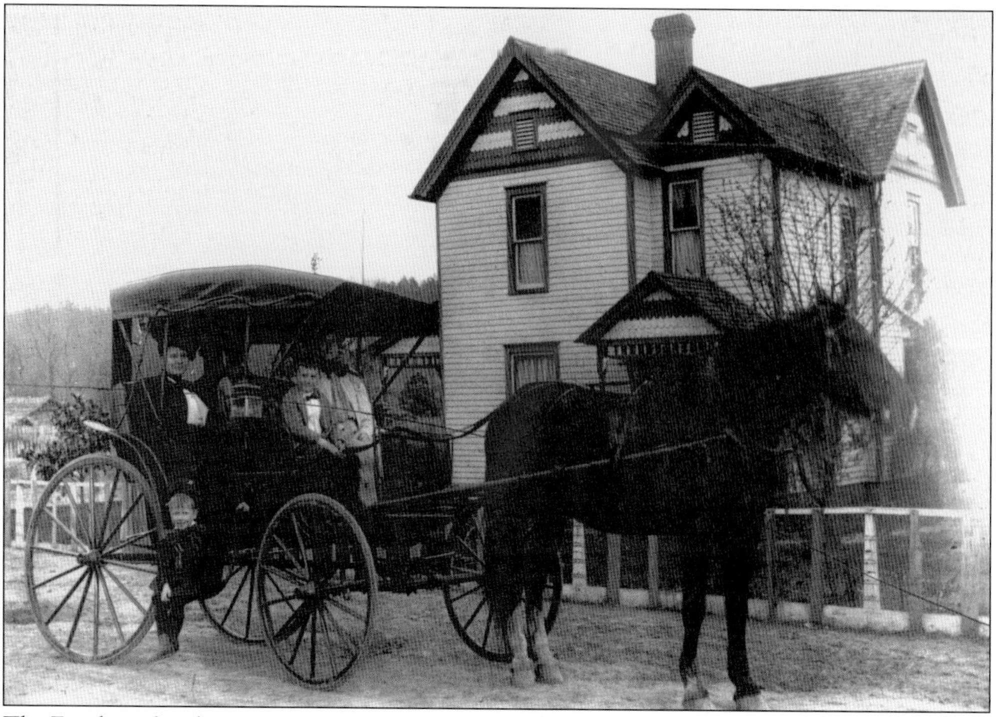

The Farnham family is on a buggy ride. Theodore Clyde Farnham was a prominent figure in early Harriman, arriving from Wisconsin in 1892. He owned a store at 505 Roane Street specializing in photography, typewriters, and bicycle supplies, and was the first Kodak agency in Tennessee in the late 1890s.

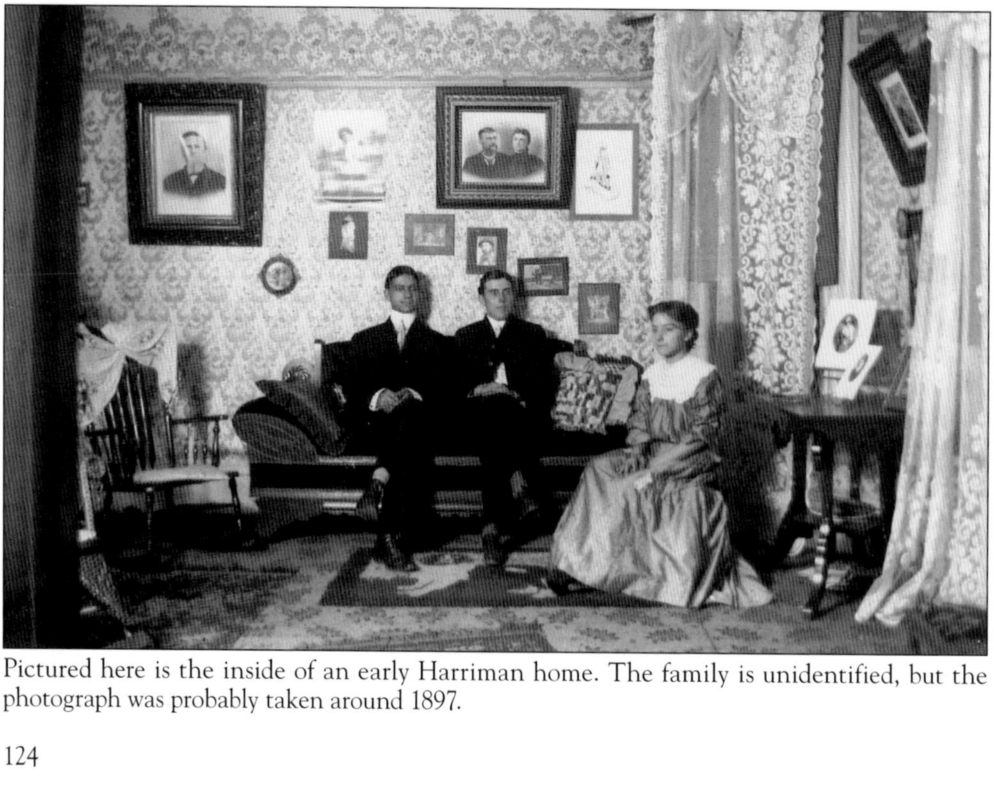

Pictured here is the inside of an early Harriman home. The family is unidentified, but the photograph was probably taken around 1897.

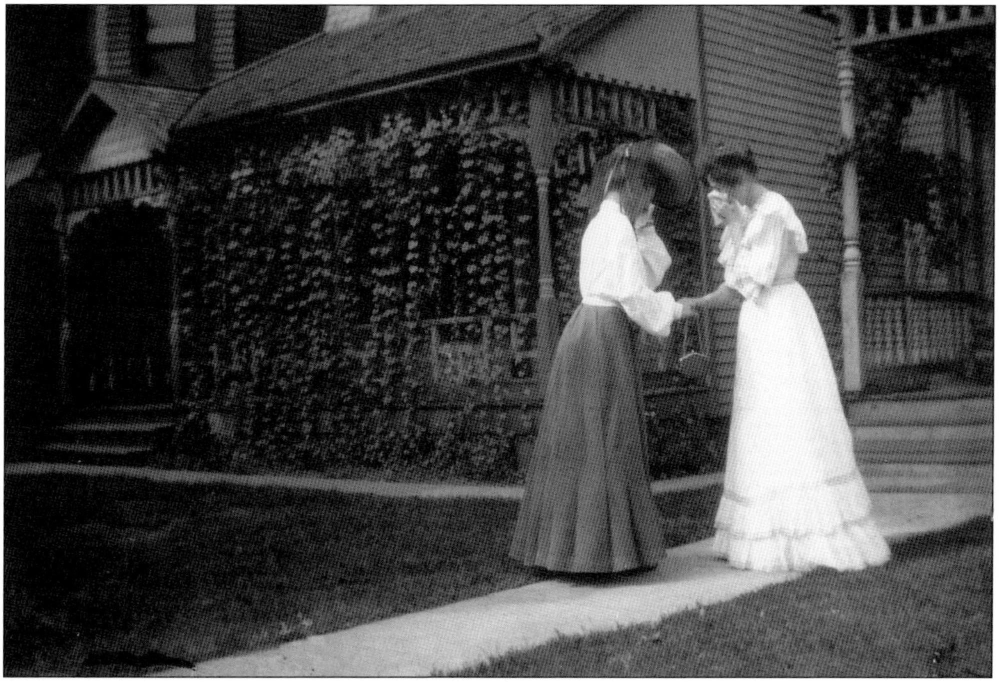

In this haunting photograph, probably taken around the turn of the 20th century, two Harriman ladies appear to be crying. It will likely never be known what news they had just received—though it is also possible they are just posing for the camera.

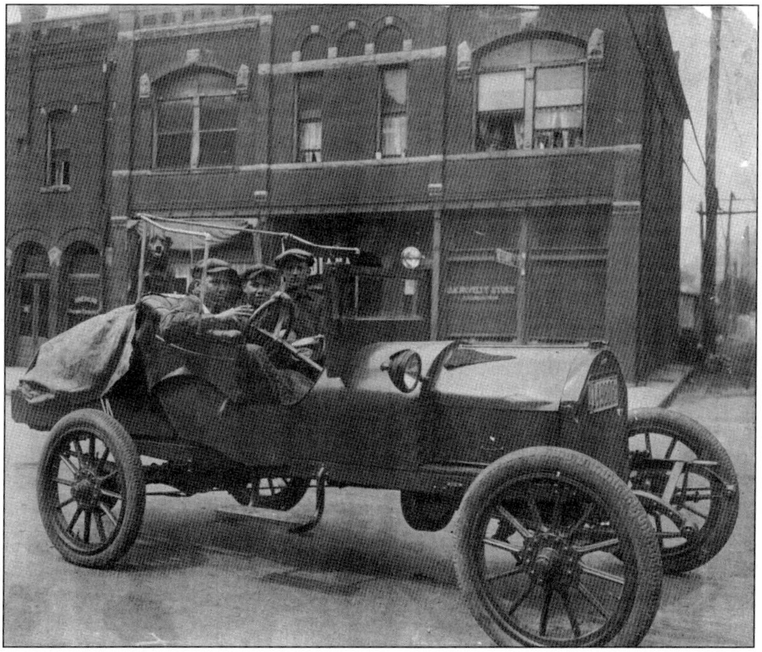

From left to right are brothers Briggs and Pete Keach with Grady Adkisson, probably around 1925, on their way to California. They may have built this vehicle themselves.

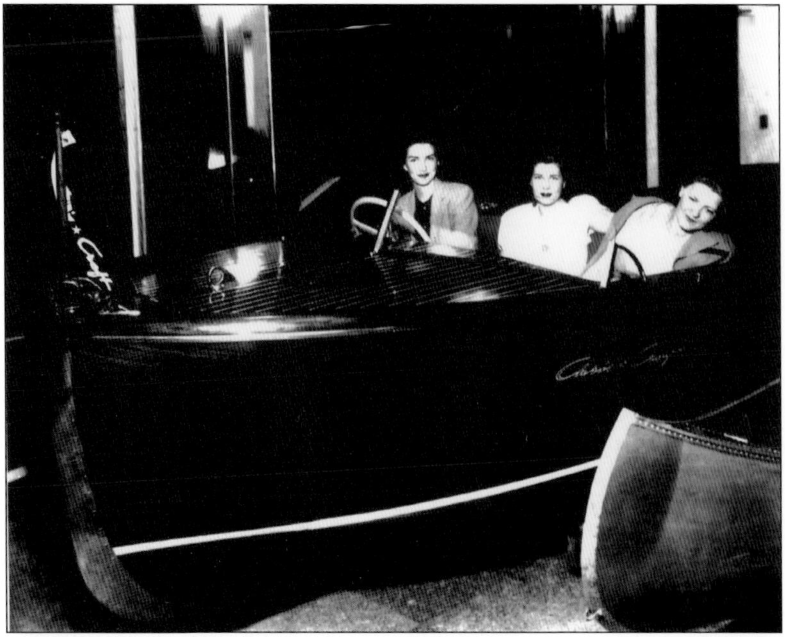

Bea Sigmon, Ruth Evans, and Sarah Arnold Hembree are having some fun in a display boat. This probably was taken inside a building around 530 Roane Street in the late 1940s. Sigmon, the daughter of Bob Irwin, was a longtime teacher in the Harriman school system.

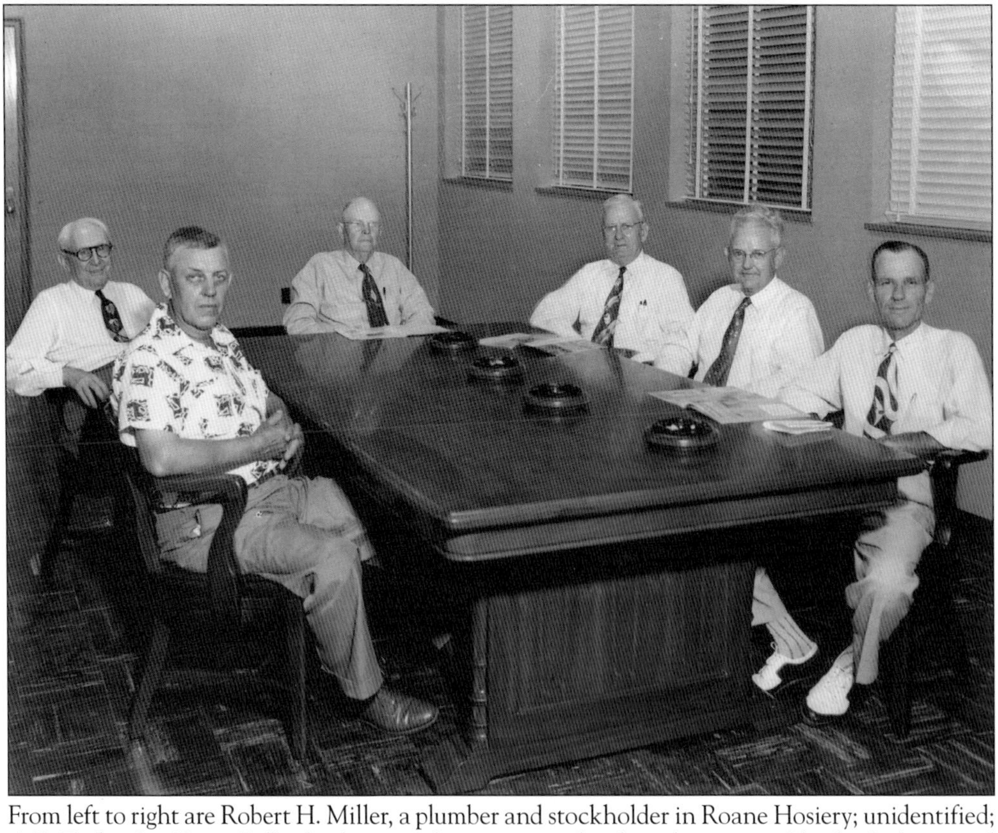

From left to right are Robert H. Miller, a plumber and stockholder in Roane Hosiery; unidentified; A.E. Taylor Sr.; Harry Dillard, who served as mayor; utility board manager Charlie Perkins; and Raymond Shipwash.

Bibliography

Abramson, Rudy and Jean Haskell, eds. *The Encyclopedia of Appalachia*. Knoxville: The University of Tennessee Press, 2006.

East Tennessee Land Company. *Two Years of Harriman, Tennessee*. New York: South Publishing Company, 1892.

Pulliam, Walter T. *Harriman: The Town That Temperance Built*. Maryville: Marion R. Mangrum Brazos Press, 1978.

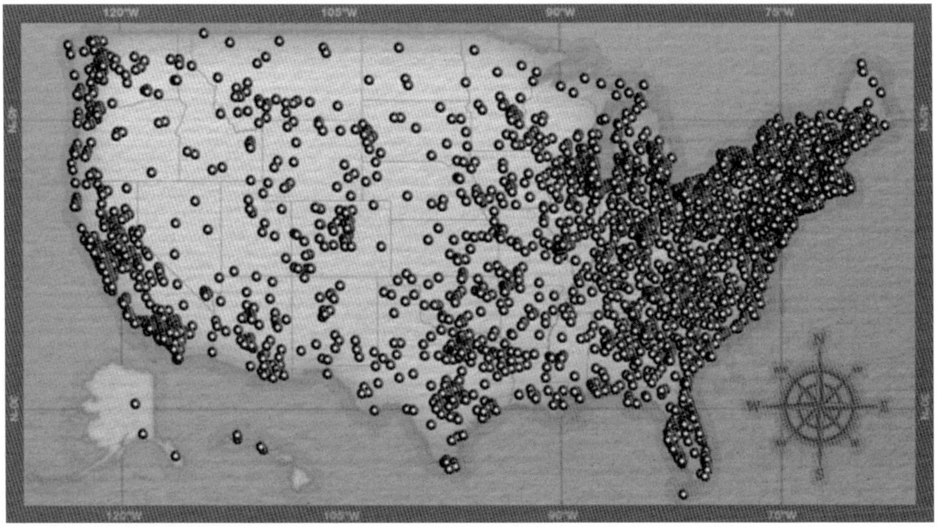